SECOND EDITION

VOLUME 2

SECURING THE FUTURE

IMPLEMENTING YOUR FIRM'S SUCCESSION PLAN

D1474449

15231V2-349

AICPA® PCPS

Bill Reeb, CPA/CITP, CGMA
Dom Cingoranelli, CPA, CGMA

Notice to Readers

Securing the Future, Volume 2: Implementing Your Firm's Succession Plan does not represent an official position of the American Institute of Certified Public Accountants, and it is distributed with the understanding that the author and publisher are not rendering legal, accounting, or other professional services in the publication. This book is intended to be an overview of the topics discussed within, and the author has made every attempt to verify the completeness and accuracy of the information herein. However, neither the author nor publisher can guarantee the applicability of the information found herein. If legal advice or other expert assistance is required, the services of a competent professional should be sought.

ISBN: 978-1-94023-560-8

Publisher: Linda Prentice Cohen
Acquisitions Editor: Erin Valentine
Developmental Editor: Katie Hurst
Project Manager: Amy Sykes

Acknowledgments

First, we want to thank the PCPS Executive Committee for engaging us to do this project. George Willie (chair of the PCPS Executive Committee) provided strong leadership in the level of information covered in this manuscript as well insight into overall content, which will prove to meet the needs of the profession.

We also want to thank the many firms that participated in the 2012 PCPS Succession Survey (our survey update).

Finally, we would like to thank Erin Valentine, our editor, for putting up with us, riding hard on us, and making sure this product was the best it could be. She was easy to work with and did a great job of balancing being flexible and forceful in organizing, simplifying, and improving our work.

The following AICPA/PCPS staff are people that we specifically want to name who supported us in this project:

PCPS Staff Members

Mark Koziel   Natasha Schamberger

AICPA Editorial and Production

Erin Valentine, Acquisitions Editor   Annmarie Piacentino, Copy Editor

Kathleen Hurst, Developmental Editor   Amy Sykes, Production Manager

The following are members of the PCPS Executive Committee who provided direction for and supported this book.

Cheryl Burke   Jason Deshayes, CPA
DiCicco, Gulman & Company, LLP   Butler & Company, CPAs
Woburn, Massachusetts   Albuquerque, New Mexico

Loretta Doon, CPA   Joseph Falbo, CPA, CGMA
California Society of CPAs   Trconi Segarra & Associates, LLP
San Mateo, California   Williamsville, New York

Chris Farmand, CPA, CITP   Melody Feniks, CPA, CGMA
Chris Farmand + Company   Feniks & Company, LLC
Jacksonville, Florida   Fairbanks, Alaska

Charles Fredrick, CPA
FredrickZink & Associates, CPAs
Durgano, Colorado

Carter Heim, CPA, CFF, CGMA, MST
HeimLantz
Annapolis, Maryland

Alexandra Kessler, CPA, CGMA
Aronson LLC
Rockville, Maryland

Scot Phillips, CPA
Eide Bailly, LLP
Boise, Idaho

James Walker, CPA
Cherry Bekaert LLP
Richmond, Virginia

Robert Goldfarb, CPA, CFP, CGMA, PFS,
CFE, DABFE, DABFA
Janover LLC
Garden City, New York

Karen Kerber, CPA, CITP, CGMA
Kerber, Rose & Associates, S.C.
Shawano, Wisconsin

Joel Olbricht, CPA
Olbricht Storniolo Group LLC
Hampstead, New Hampshire

Jacquelyn Tracy, CPA, CGMA
Mandel & Tracy, LLC
Providence, Rhode Island

George Willie, CPA, PFF, CGFM, CGMA
Bert Smith & Co.
Washington, District of Columbia

About the Authors

Bill Reeb

Bill has been consulting for over three decades to all sizes of businesses, from mom and pop operations to Fortune 100 companies. Prior to his life as a CPA, he worked for IBM in sales back in the late '70s. As an entrepreneur, Bill has founded seven small businesses, from retail to software development to advisory work.

An award-winning public speaker, Bill lectures throughout the U.S. and Canada to thousands of executives and CPAs each year. As an award-winning author, Bill is internationally published, with numerous magazines, journals, newspapers, and books to his credit. Besides *Securing the Future*, Bill and his partner Dom Cingoranelli have also authored *Becoming a Trusted Business Advisor: How to Add Value, Improve Client Loyalty, and Increase Profits*. In addition, Bill has a new book out on managing your life titled *The Overachiever's Guide to Getting Unstuck: Replan, Reprioritize, Reaffirm*.

Bill is an active volunteer within his profession, having served in many leadership roles in both the state and national organizations. He is an avid golfer and skier, but spends the majority of his free time learning and teaching martial arts.

Dom Cingoranelli

Dom's consulting experience over the last three decades includes organizational development work for CPA firms and associations, as well as on construction projects for the Big Three auto makers; for regional, national, and international contractors; and for organizations in a variety of other industries. He has performed strategy consulting and planning; process improvement studies; management consulting, training, and development; team building; coaching; and group process facilitation for a variety of groups.

He co-authored *Securing the Future* and *Becoming a Trusted Business Advisor: How to Add Value, Improve Client Loyalty, and Increase Profits*, as well as the AICPA PCPS Succession Resource Center and Trusted Business Advisor Resource Center. Dom has also written numerous articles and CPE offerings on executive recruiting, performance management, leadership, planning, and organizational culture. He speaks frequently on management and consulting topics throughout the country.

When he is not working, you may find Dom doing volunteer work at his church, tying flies, fly fishing, or touring on his Gold Wing.

CONTENTS

Chapter	Page

Chapter 1: Getting Started

How to Use This Workbook

This text is a companion to *Securing the Future, Volume 1: Building Your Firm's Succession Plan*. In that book, we provide a high-level review of the what, why, how, and when of succession management. Although these volumes are focused on CPA firms, they apply to any personal service businesses, and indeed, to other businesses and industries, as well. After reading volume 1 to gain an understanding of the principles behind succession management and the various choices you face, you can use the tools and resources included in this volume to create and implement your organization's step-by-step succession management plan. Or, another way of exploring the complementarity of these two volumes might be as follows:

- Get all your partners and key leaders in your firm to read volume 1 so they can have a high-level understanding of what it takes to move your firm to the next level of best practices.
- Use *Securing the Future, Volume 2: Implementing Your Firm's Succession Plan* as a field guide to help the management team actually make the changes your group decides to make.

Organization of This Workbook

For each chapter in volume 1, there is a corresponding chapter in this book. For example, if after reading volume 1, chapter 4, you wish to begin cleaning up operations at your business, you can refer to this volume's chapter 4 for some tools, tips, and techniques for making your organization better, faster, and stronger. What we've found in working with clients throughout North America is that the real barriers to effective succession management arise when partners begin to develop and implement a plan for their own firm. Regardless of how robust a concept is, the devil is always in the details. Reviewing and adapting a particular concept to fit the circumstances in your organization is the piece of the puzzle most often left out of discussions like this. Together, these companion books supply a detailed roadmap to help you more easily overcome the more common barriers to success when implementing your firm's succession management plan. In future chapters, we will open by summarizing a number of key themes from the corresponding chapter in volume 1. The themes from chapter 1 follow.

Key Themes from *Securing the Future, Volume 1: Building Your Firm's Succession Plan*, Chapter 1

- No one is getting any younger
- Personal service businesses create additional problems with respect to transitioning and succession
- What worked yesterday won't necessarily work for tomorrow (or, what got you here won't likely get you there)
- Dealing with the scary issues—retirement, health, mortality, and identity
- The need for sustainability
- The need for a plan
- Why CPAs don't effectively manage succession processes
- Crisis succession planning
- Orderly succession planning
- A step-by-step look at how to develop your own customized robust succession plan

Dealing With the Barriers

The following checklist is a tool we devised to help you determine your readiness to begin succession planning for your firm.

Succession Institute's The Barrier Scale™: Barriers to Overcome for Succession Planning

Use this checklist to perform an initial diagnosis of readiness for succession planning at your firm. Read each of the common excuses and then score your firm based on your personal opinion of the applicability of the excuse to you or any of your partners. Using a five-point scale, rate where your firm now stands.

1. I strongly <u>agree</u> that this describes me or some of our partners at this time.
2. I somewhat <u>agree</u> that this describes me or some of our partners at this time.
3. I neither agree nor disagree.
4. I somewhat <u>disagree</u> that this describes me or some of our partners at this time.
5. I strongly <u>disagree</u> that this describes me or some of our partners at this time.

No.	Common Excuses	Score
1	We don't have time, or other business demands preclude it at this time.	
2	We have plenty of people here who might be candidates, but there are no legitimate candidates now—we will watch to see who develops, if anyone develops.	
3	We have a number of partners in our organization, but they are technicians and not suitable for leading this firm.	
4	None of our partners are planning on retiring for another 5–10 years, so there is no reason to pursue this just yet.	

No.	Common Excuses	Score
5	Some of the senior partners plan on selling the firm to another CPA firm because they don't believe we have the leadership talent in-house necessary to pay us off.	
6	Some of the senior partners plan on selling the firm to another CPA firm because they believe the remaining partners will run this business into the ground once they leave and, therefore, feel they have no assurance that they will ever see their retirement paid in full.	
7	Some of our partners plan on working until they don't want to do this anymore, and at that time, we will see what our options are.	
8	Some of our partners expect a son or daughter to come to work here for a while and step into the position, so we don't need to worry about it now.	
9	Some of our partners may be having trouble dealing with their own mortality.	
10	Some of our senior partners have not developed any significant outside interests and don't have a clear idea of what they will do with their time if they retire. We don't want to create any additional pressure for them to move on.	
11	Key partners do not want to give up the authority required to develop decision-making skills in their people.	
12	Some of our partners are laboring under the view that it takes money out of their pocket to develop overlapping talent. Besides, the current owners have the skills needed for now, and when the time comes to retire, we will see who is out there that can take over the firm.	
13	Some of our partners don't want to develop a younger partner to take over because the younger partner may get tired of waiting and try to force a senior owner out before he or she wants to leave.	
14	Some of our partners enjoy being the go-to person and running the firm his or her way, so those partners surround themselves with people that make his or her life easier instead of developing successors.	

If your score is

Higher than 60: Great! You should be able to pull this off without a lot of trouble.

From 43 to 59: Caution. You will need to take a little more time and effort to achieve readiness.

Lower than 42: Danger! Much preparation may need to be done to achieve readiness.

What you do with your score on the Barrier Scale depends on your current facts and circumstances. We can illustrate this by describing two example firms that fall on nearly opposite ends of the spectrum. We will call the first example the Short Fuse Firm and the second example the Long Fuse Firm.

At the Short Fuse Firm, there are three partners, two of whom are in their early 60s and one of whom is in his late 50s. The two older partners expect to be retiring in the next 3–4 years. The third partner expects to work another 10–12 years or so. All three partners have decent books of business and are making moderately good incomes. None of them have developed any direct successors (at least that have stayed with the firm). Their staff consists mostly of some associates and a couple seniors. The partners do most of the work themselves, except for what they feel that they can safely pass on to their staff because it is so rudimentary in nature. Although all the partners perform tax work and some compilations and reviews, they each have their own industry niches—one works a lot with small contractors, another with professionals such as doctors and dentists, and the third mostly with individuals and a few very small nonprofits. Because each partner is already pretty fully utilized, they really have no significant capacity to devote to serving a retiring partner's clients, even if they wanted to perform work in the niche practice of the retiring partner.

The partners, particularly the older two, are on a short fuse relative to their retirement—they hope to exit the practice in the next three to four years. However, both have built practices that are not adequately leveraged, and they have ignored development of the next tier of leaders who would be a logical first choice to buy them out. Most likely, their billing rates also haven't kept pace with the market, but that's a story for another time. Time flies when you are having fun, and it flies even more quickly when you have too much to do, and these owners have a lot to do if they hope to create any viable options for their retirement and exit. In a scant three years, unless they can (1) hire quality, experienced people to act as buyers or (2) develop existing staff to be able to buy them out, they will probably have to sell or merge upstream, which will likely create havoc by and animosity from the third partner. Although strange things do happen from time to time, unless this firm is extremely lucky (the lottery-winning type of lucky), finding *any* experienced people to come to work for them in the near term who can be ready to take over is improbable at best. It will approach the "impossible" end of the spectrum if they're located in a smaller, rural, remote, or stagnant market.

But what about developing the existing people to get them ready for buying out the older partners? Although this is not impossible, there are a number of hurdles to clear in order for this to work:

- The existing staff may or may not actually have the horsepower, regardless of training and coaching, to take over the firm. If the firm has operated this way for many years, the most entrepreneurially inclined staff have probably turned over multiple times, leaving those who are comfortable working for someone and who are not very inclined to step up and take over the business.

- Even if members of the staff have some entrepreneurial spark, depending on the competency gaps that have to be closed, three years may not be a sufficient amount of time to close those gaps.

- Taking time to train, coach, and develop staff is a major shift of mindset, and it will create some inefficiency, at least in the short run, which translates to potential decreases in the bottom line for the retiring partners. Besides having to get in the mode of training and coaching, they could be faced with earning a little less than before in the critical years heading into retirement.

- Another significant factor involves the effort required by a partner nearing retirement age to develop less experienced, younger people. This can be done, but the older, experienced owner is so far away in terms of recent experiences that it's difficult for him or her to really empathize with and relate to the younger, less experienced staff person—to understand what can and cannot be expected at that level. In other words, it's been so long since the partners were at this basic level of knowledge that they simply can't recall what it was like for them and, therefore, have difficulty teaching and coaching at the proper level.

- Even if an owner wants to do a better job of training and developing people to better secure his or her retirement, the owner simply may not have the skills to do so and may not be willing, at this stage of their career, to try to develop those skills.

- Finally, even if the retiring owner is ready to train, has the capability of training, and is committed to training, it is possible that the staff members at the firm don't have an interest in the specialty area of work currently being performed by the retiring partner.

All in all, the Short Fuse Firm, with only a few years left before the key owners retire, has a narrow range of alternatives available to it for all practical purposes.

1. Get on a very fast track for developing its people and make development the firm's number one focus, which means that the partners need to be willing to change what they do, how they work, and how much time they will spend developing their people.
2. Because the effort required in number one is overly burdensome, extend the retirement horizon of one or more owners to allow the firm a little more time to create the leverage and develop the people it needs for internal succession. (This option runs into the hurdles mentioned previously—see chapter 5 for some tips on how to make this happen.)
3. Sell the business, or sell the retiring partners' books of business to outsiders or possibly a combination of outside and inside sales, with some amount of the client book being sold inside to the remaining partner, and the remainder being sold to outsiders. (See chapter 14 of this book for a treatment of sales and mergers.)
4. Merge the business upstream to create a retirement option for the retiring owners.

The Long Fuse Firm has a significantly different set of facts and circumstances facing it than does the Short Fuse Firm. These factors could include the following:

- A generally younger set of partners.
- More leveraged work—there is more of a pyramid in the firm, and partners generally are more effectively leveraging their time through others.

Either of the preceding factors normally leads to the increased ability of the partners to create multiple attractive options for their future retirement. The more time partners have to prepare for their exit, the more they can accomplish. The better you've leveraged your practice, the more easily you can transition it. For example, many of the firms we work with don't have a "number of partners" problem, but a book size per partner problem. If there are three partners at the Long Fuse Firm in this scenario, with two of them retiring and each owner managing, on average, a $600,000 book, and they're doing similar work, this is very doable. The firm simply needs to build the capacity and leverage for one partner to run a $2 million book. This can easily happen if the partners have the luxury of time to make it happen, but even if a firm has the right people on hand, it still might need a minimum of three to five years to make the various changes needed to facilitate seamless transitions when partners retire. Most importantly, you need a serious commitment from the partners to make it all happen properly.

Getting Buy-In

If, like so many firms, your business has at least some Eat What You Kill (EWYK) (see chapter 4 regarding business models) elements to it, or partner accountability is not as robust as you'd like it to be, what can you do to get everyone on board and begin making the changes you know in your heart of hearts need to be made? Although some firms may want to force the recalcitrant individuals into submission, that normally doesn't work. Even if a tough-minded approach seems to work initially, once the bruises fade away, employees forget about the change and go back to doing what they want, so we really can't approve of that method. What you need to do is to appeal to their hearts and minds in your discussions with them. What is it that they have at stake? What do they most want? What do they most fear? Take some time to think through what each key partner's concerns are and plan to address them in a way that creates some sense of urgency about doing things at least a little differently going forward.

For example, you might have a senior partner who refuses to change, and although he or she is extremely influential (some might go so far as to say bullying), that senior partner doesn't own a majority of equity in the firm. Once the rest of the partners decide that they wish to pursue a change, a vote will be the signal for change for the senior partner. This means that the majority of the partners (by equity voting) have now put themselves in a position to negotiate with the bullying or passive-aggressive partner in a way that allows the firm to address key needs and concerns within the context of the change. We see this all the time. When it is clear that change is going to happen, previously immovable partners change their tune quickly as their rational self-interest takes over to mitigate damage and maximize their new situation. The good news is that there are many levers to pull, including retirement amount, retirement age, current compensation, post-retirement employment, and so much more, that can be leveraged to create an equitable situation for both the firm and the senior partner.

Another common barrier to change is when some partners claim that they ultimately don't want to make changes that would have them being held more accountable to anyone. For example, they'll claim they left a larger firm to "practice accounting" and not have someone telling them what to do. At first blush, their rational self-interest seems to be autonomy, but what they commonly have is a somewhat disordered view of life in a group practice. What they omit in their statement about not having someone tell them what to do is directly in opposition to the idea that they expect the firm to guarantee a retirement benefit for them when they decide to leave. The real trigger for change will likely come down to economics once again. Often, without making some necessary changes, it becomes clear to both the senior and junior partners that the firm is not positioned to be able to "make good" on paying those expected benefits.

In most cases, when a partner is close to retirement, the last thing he or she wants to hear is that you're planning on making major changes in the firm or the way it operates. Rocking the boat could make the retiring owner think that his or her retirement benefits could greatly diminish, or even disappear, in a worst case scenario. How can you structure the discussion and the plans to help this partner see that his or her retirement is going to be protected, with even greater security than before? It takes some time to think through these issues and create the communication approach each person requires to see that there is a better future waiting on the other side of the change. Many times, we have heard, "We know what we have is broken, but it is a 'broken' that we can manage and suffer through. What if the changes we create make our situation even worse? What will we do then?" So, when you consider all the anxiety, politics, risks, and natural resistance to change that exists in the partner group of a typical firm, consider a three-pronged approach:

1. Have each partner and firm leader read *Securing the Future, Volume 1: Building Your Firm's Succession Plan*. It's written in a way that's easy to understand and that provides the reader with a high-level view of what might happen in their firm and how firms are commonly addressing succession management challenges and opportunities. This should help all the partners get closer to being on the same page.

2. Direct each partner and firm leader to other outside sources, such as the Private Company Practice Section (PCPS)/SI Succession Management Survey[1] to understand current best practices in succession management.

---

[1] The PCPS/Succession Institute Succession Management Surveys are available in the following locations online: www.aicpa.org/InterestAreas/PrivateCompaniesPracticeSection/StrategyPlanning/center/ DownloadableDocuments/SuccessionSurveySoloComm.pdf
www.aicpa.org/InterestAreas/PrivateCompaniesPracticeSection/StrategyPlanning/center/ DownloadableDocuments/SuccessionSurveyMultiComm.pdf

3. If appropriate, bring in someone from the outside to update your leadership group about succession best practices in order to help your group understand where your firm sits relative to the best practices. This also allows questions about proposed changes to be discussed with an objective third party, rather than pitting one partner against another to resolve the dispute.

Consider that any time you are negotiating, you need to negotiate on a principled basis, using objective standards. By looking outside the firm at what others are doing and what experts are suggesting, you can refer to objective standards in negotiating agreements. Don't dig in over positions. Look behind the positions to find out what each person's interests are. Often, seemingly contrary positions have fairly common interests behind them that can lead to working out a deal that makes sense for all concerned. For example, a partner's *position* might be that he or she won't accept a dollar less than $XXX,XXX in retirement benefits. However, the underlying *interest* might be that he or she feels that what he or she is getting in terms of pay, benefits, and retirement are not equitable given what other, lower performing partners are getting. Once you know this, you can open up multiple options for addressing his or her concerns and those of the firm.

Wrap-Up

In each chapter of this book, we will have a narrative in the beginning identifying relevant concepts, including implementation and organizational issues, approaches to take, obstacles to avoid, areas to leverage, and so on. After the conclusion of each chapter, we will have a "Tools and Resources" section that will house various forms, checklists, action plans, and other material we believe can help you implement the various ideas outlined in the same numbered chapter in volume 1 or the ideas expanded upon in this chapter in this book. Let's take a look at the brief aid for this chapter, which will help you think through who your go-to people might be in a crisis succession management situation.

Tools and Resources

Crisis Succession Planning Aid

For your firm's key positions, take a look at who is available to fill in—at least temporarily—for the incumbent in the case of an unplanned vacancy. Consider the competency gaps you must close for the potential successor, even if he or she fills the role only on a temporary basis, and what it will take to develop these potential replacements for all key positions. Examples follow.

Position/Incumbent	Potential Successor in a Crisis	Competency Gaps
CEO/MP	Andrew C.	Leading change
COO/Firm Admin	Tina G.	Vision and strategy
Partner A	Todd C.	Execution, coaching, and mentoring
Partner B	John P.	Most trusted business adviser
Partner C	Steve A.	Business savvy
Partner D	Pam D.	Developing a following
Senior Manager A	Eric B.	Communication
Senior Manager B	Bob Z.	Judgment and decision making
Senior Manager C	Jill R.	Marketing focus
Senior Manager D	Dan D.	Building teams

This list should be expanded as necessary to include all key positions in your organization.

In addition to identifying potential candidates to fill key positions, you should ensure that job descriptions and competency definitions for the key positions are updated periodically. And what about documenting the incumbent's key clients and other external contacts, both of which are critical information for anyone stepping in to carry out this person's duties? Is that information updated periodically? Does anyone else in the firm know where to find this documentation if it is needed? Who has his or her passwords and can get access to files? Does anyone else in the firm actually know the clients, referral sources, and other key parties with whom he or she has been dealing?

Additional Learning Resources

Now that you are done reading through the materials in this chapter, if you're not sure you are ready to tackle the final section (Building Your Firm's Robust Succession Plan) and you want to do a little more research, this section contains some additional support materials for your consideration. We have developed a learning management system (LMS) with many self-study continuing professional education (CPE) courses available for your review. Many of them are all-video courses developed from our streaming video webcasts, and others were created from the various books we have written. These courses can be found at www.successioninstitute.com/PMRC.

Once you arrive at our LMS, the Succession Institute Practice Management Resource Center, you can take a quick look at all of our available courses by clicking the "Search All Programs" link in the left-hand bar under the log-in areas. This will list every program available.

Next, if you decide you want to take one of the courses, just click the Register button. During your course registration process, a coupon code field will be displayed. At that time, you can enter the discount code that came in this book. If you type in the word in the code field, generally speaking, you will receive a 15-percent discount for each course (at the time of publishing of this book, the only course that was excluded from this full discount is our "SOP Partner Agreement" course due to its downloadable materials). It is possible that there will be others that fall into this same category, and although you will get a discount on all the courses listed, and you will get the full 15 percent on the majority of courses listed, a few courses will be reserved for only a partial discount. To get the discount, type "succession" into the coupon code field.

For this introductory chapter, here are several all-video courses you might want to review to provide you with some additional valuable insight into building a robust succession plan for your firm.

To cover some of the highlights of the PCPS/Succession Institute 2012 Succession Survey, we have two all-video courses available. The first is a one-hour CPE course for small firms with one to three owners. The second includes highlights of the survey for firms of all sizes:

- Succession Management and the Small Firm (all-video)
- The Succession Management Landscape (all-video)

To watch an overview of important elements required to build your plan, we have a two-part all-video series available:

- Building Your Firm's Succession Plan—Part 1 (all-video)
- Building Your Firm's Succession Plan—Part 2 (all-video)

Building Your Firm's Robust Succession Plan

As a final step in each relevant chapter, we will ask you to jot down your thoughts based on the materials we covered. Once you complete this last section of the chapter, by the time you finish this book, you will have written down all the ideas that resonated the most with you or that you felt were important to include in your firm's succession plan.

When you pull the last section of the chapter together, you will have developed a draft framework of the fundamental issues that you believe need to be included in your succession planning document; your recommendations about how to handle each issue (or, at a minimum, questions the partner group needs to answer); and a document that can be presented for discussion, modification, and eventual approval that will guide the changes in policy, agreements, governance, and culture your firm will undertake over the next few years.

Although we don't have as specific a set of issues for you to address as we will in the remaining chapters because this is the introductory chapter, we are posing one question based on what you have read or courses you have reviewed thus far.

What are the issues that you have taken note of thus far that will be the biggest hurdles your firm will face when making the transition to a firm poised for succession to the next generation of leaders? (This is a free-form section for you to come back and address when you finish the book to make sure you have tied up all the loose ends).

_____

_____

_____

_____

_____

_____

_____

_____

_____

_____

Chapter 2: Developing and Implementing Your Strategy

Key Themes from *Securing the Future, Volume 1: Building Your Firm's Succession Plan*, Chapter 2

- Thinking strategically should drive all your business decisions
- Strategic planning overview
- Mission, vision, and values
- Strategies, action plans, and metrics
- Some typical strategic initiatives for CPA firms

Developing Your Plan

During our last three-plus decades of providing consulting assistance to CPA firms, we've seen the power of strategic planning drive change and greater profitability for our clients. Successful businesses in every industry are built on sound planning for the future. Although entrepreneurs typically have a good idea of what they want their organizations to achieve, without a clear focus and direction that can be documented and communicated throughout the organization, it is difficult to turn that good idea into a reality. Robust, ongoing success does not occur by accident—it requires deliberate and consistently applied planning and implementation to sustain it.

One of the common best practices our most successful CPA firm clients embrace is regular planning followed by the creation of action plans to ensure that the strategy is fully implemented. We believe that every significant change in a firm's operation needs to originate from the planning process. It is through this process that an individual idea can grow into a firm vision. Unless the owners or partners can get together to form a shared direction for the future and articulate it so that everyone can understand and commit to it, change will likely fall victim to inertia and only be incremental at best. Inertia rarely produces a new level of better, faster, and stronger.

Rather than electing to drift along with one of their largest, if not the largest and most valuable, assets they own, small-firm practitioners can now easily implement a structured, step-by-step process to create a robust strategy for their organizations.

In the "Tools and Resources" section, we have provided the highlights of our approach to strategic planning, including planning to plan; dealing with strengths, weaknesses, opportunities, and challenges; creating performance metrics; and action plans. For more detail and depth, especially for smaller firms that want to adopt a do-it-yourself approach, our Strategic Planning Virtual Facilitator™ program will allow them to take our video process with them to wherever the partners want to meet and conduct their strategic planning session. Partners can view each video segment of the process, follow the step-by-step directions contained therein, and individually fill out the forms and use the tools provided. That would be followed by an open discussion about what each person wrote down, partners coming to a consensus, and everyone moving on to the next segment. Now, for the first time ever, partners from small CPA firms can easily and affordably walk through a proven approach developed by Succession Institute (SI) to create their own strategic plan.

Monitoring and Accountability

Unless someone in the firm is tasked with overseeing implementation of action plans and monitoring results from the implementation of the plans, you probably aren't going to realize many, if any, significant changes at your firm. Visions without accountable actions are simply wishful thinking. This brings up a couple of key questions:

- Who is going to hold whom accountable for carrying out implementation projects, tasks, and activities?
- What sort of accountability will the overseer be able to exercise over the rest of the partners and staff?

As we have covered in chapters 6 and 15 of volume 1 and will address with more specificity in chapters 6 and 15 of this volume, the managing partner or CEO should be tasked with implementation of the strategy that the partners have agreed upon. In turn, the managing partner then needs to be able to hold other owners and staff accountable for doing their share of the implementation. The accountability your firm can achieve under a one-firm concept will differ from what you can expect under an EWYK business model, so be reasonable in setting your expectations.

Tools and Resources

Succession Institute's Planning to Plan™ Worksheet

No.	Planning to Plan Activity	In Charge	Due By
A	**Planning the Logistics**		
1	Determine who will be involved in providing or generating front-end information for use in planning (who will be surveyed or interviewed—owners, principals, managers, staff, and so on).		
2	Determine who will be involved in the first meeting for planning.		
3	Schedule the meeting(s) and related dates for other activities: *a.* First planning meeting *b.* Diagnostic data gathering		
4	Identify the venue for the first meeting.		
5	Make arrangements to reserve the venue for the first meeting, including meals, refreshments, and so on.		
B	**Diagnostic Phase**		
1	Determine what information you want to generate internally regarding: *a.* Ideas and opinions from owners or staff *b.* Financial and nonfinancial practice management trend data		
2	Identify methods to be used in gathering ideas and opinions from owners and staff: *a.* Internally generated online survey *b.* Externally generated and administered online survey or interviews, focus groups, and so on		
3	Conduct front-end data gathering—obtain ideas and opinions from different levels of individuals as desired and as applicable (owners, principals, managers, staff, and so on).		
4	Conduct front-end data gathering. Pull together key financial and nonfinancial trend data for use in planning. This is typically the last two to three years of the following: *a.* Overall firm financial results—balance sheets, P&Ls, and so on *b.* Production summary—total hours, charge hours, nominal rate, production, write-ups and write-downs, billings, realization percentage, effective rate by person and in total for firm by year for last two to three years *c.* Summary of work by function—A&A, tax, business write-up work, consulting, and so on by year, showing gross production, net realization by year for the last two to three years *d.* Other _____		

(continued)

No.	Planning to Plan Activity	In Charge	Due By

5	Determine what information you want to generate about external trends and best practices, such as the following:
	
	  a. AICPA/Texas MAP statistics for your firm size and location
	  b. AICPA Top Technology survey report
	  c. AICPA Top Issues survey report
	  d. PCPS—Succession Institute Succession Survey report
	  e. State and local economic forecasts
	  f. Industries served—using trade association publications and forecasts, if applicable, or be able to discuss
	  g. The competition—be able to discuss major competitors in your market, what they seem to be doing, and their strengths and weaknesses compared to your firm
	  h. Managing Client Satisfaction—SI online course
	  i. Managing for Accountability—SI online course
	  j. Managing Your Business Development Efforts—SI online course
	  k. Managing Your Firm by the Numbers—SI online course
	  l. Managing Your Workload—SI online course
	  m. Other _____		

6	Gather external trend data identified previously:
	
	  a. AICPA/Texas MAP statistics for your firm size and location
	  b. AICPA Top Technology survey report
	  c. AICPA Top Issues survey report
	  d. PCPS—Succession Institute Succession Survey report
	  e. State and local economic forecasts
	  f. Industries served—using their trade association publications and forecasts, if applicable, or be able to discuss
	  g. The competition—be able to discuss major competitors in your market, what they seemingly are doing, and their strengths and weaknesses compared to your firm
	  h. Managing Client Satisfaction—SI online course
	  i. Managing for Accountability—SI online course
	  j. Managing Your Business Development Efforts—SI online course
	  k. Managing Your Firm by the Numbers—SI online course
	  l. Managing Your Workload—SI online course
	  m. Other _____		

7	Other firm-specific considerations with regard to your planning:		

Top (Internal) Strengths and Top Weaknesses (Up to 10 Each) of the Firm

In the following space, list what you believe to be the top strengths of your firm, based on your review of internal trends and the status of your firm at this time, and then indicate the order of priority, with "1" being highest in priority:

_____

_____

_____

_____

_____

_____

_____

_____

_____

_____

_____

_____

_____

_____

_____

In the following space, list what you believe to be the top areas for improvement, or weaknesses, to address at your firm based on your review of internal trends and the status of your firm at this time, and then indicate the order of priority, with "1" being highest in priority:

_____

_____

_____

_____

_____

_____

_____

_____

_____

_____

_____

_____

_____

_____

Top (External) Challenges and Opportunities (Up to 10 Each) Facing the Firm

In the following space, list what you believe to be the top external opportunities in the marketplace available for your firm to pursue, based on your review of external trends at this time, and then indicate the order of priority, with "1" being highest in priority:

_____

_____

_____

_____

_____

_____

_____

_____

_____

_____

_____

_____

In the following space, list what you believe to be the top external challenges facing your firm that you need to be aware of and address, based on your review of external trends at this time, and then indicate the order of priority, with "1" being highest in priority:

_____

_____

_____

_____

_____

_____

_____

_____

_____

_____

_____

_____

_____

Mission Statement or Statement of Core Purpose

The mission statement provides the overarching, high-level reason for your firm's existence—why it is in business. It should be succinct and easy to remember, repeat, and explain if you want it to be effective. Keep it short and sweet.

If you need to develop a mission statement or want to review your existing mission statement, use the following questions to provoke your thinking:

1. Why do clients come to our firm?

   _____

   _____

   _____

   _____

   a. Review your previous answer. Why is that important to clients?

   _____

   _____

   _____

   _____

   b. Review your answer to letter (a). Why is *that* factor important to clients?

   _____

   _____

   _____

   _____

Core Values Statement

Core values define what is important at your firm in terms of how you do business. There are no right or wrong core values, but a core value should be authentic to your firm, and it should be something that shows up in people's daily behaviors at the firm. If you would like to see more emphasis on a *potential* core value that presently isn't all that predominant in your firm, you can always build it into the vision statement for your firm (which we will cover in the next exercise), but if it is not a value in action that shows up consistently in your approach to doing business, you shouldn't consider it an existing core value.

As with your mission statement, brevity and focus are key factors, so you should try to limit the list of core values to those that are the most significant, important, and prevalent at your firm. The following can help you identify your firm's core values:

What are the top four or five core values in action at our firm—those that we not only give lip service to, but that we also faithfully live out in our day-to-day actions?

_____

_____

_____

_____

_____

_____

_____

_____

_____

_____

_____

_____

_____

_____

_____

_____

_____

_____

_____

_____

_____

_____

_____

_____

Personal Vision

Assume that, as of today, you are going to focus your efforts so that you can live your life exactly the way you want to live it. Now, imagine that you are watching a videotape of your life three years from now and you are seeing the results of your focused efforts.

What did you see regarding your personal life?

What did you see regarding your business life?

How did you feel about what you saw?

How has your life changed from where you are now?

What should you stop doing?

What should you start doing?

Your Firm's Three-Year Vision

Imagine you are sitting here three years from now looking back on your planning and implementation processes and successes.

1. What do you want the firm to be like in three years?

   _____

   _____

   _____

2. If, at the end of three years from now, your firm were to be featured as the cover story of a major professional journal, what would the article say about your firm regarding the following?

   a. What your firm has achieved.

   _____

   _____

   _____

   b. What your firm is like for clients; for staff; for the owners.

   _____

   _____

   _____

   c. What is unique about your firm.

   _____

   _____

   _____

3. Based on what you'd like to see, what might your firm look like in each of the following areas?

   a. Size of firm—revenue and number of full-time employees

   _____

   _____

   _____

   b. Offerings

   _____

   _____

   _____

   c. Types of clients

   _____

   _____

   _____

d. Technology

_____

_____

_____

e. Staff development

_____

_____

_____

f. Other elements you believe are important

_____

_____

_____

Resource: "Introduction to the Eat What You Kill and Building a Village Models of Operations" SI course.

Identifying Your Top Strategic Objectives or Key Initiatives

Once you have performed your internal and external trend analysis, looked at your mission and core values, and developed a vision statement or overall strategic direction for your firm, it's time to determine where you need to focus your efforts to achieve the vision you've laid out for your business.

Based on the firm's key strengths and weaknesses, together with the most significant challenges and opportunities facing your business, what are the top issues (up to five) that must be addressed to operationalize your vision? You may find as you go through your top ten categories of strengths, weaknesses, opportunities, and challenges that some of them represent subsets or portions of others—that is, they are related to a higher-level initiative that must be addressed, and they may actually represent some tactics or actions required to achieve the higher-level initiative.

List them in the space provided, and after some consideration, indicate what you believe the relative order of priority might be for each—which should be approached first, second, third, and so on? (Based on the work you've done already, you probably have a pretty good idea of the top three or four.)

Performance Metrics or Vision Targets: How Will We Know If It Is Working?

For each key strategic initiative or objective, it is important *before* you craft action plans to identify what success will look like, both at the end of the three-year period covered by your strategic plan and at interim points along the way. Unless you know what you are looking for, you will have no objective way of measuring whether your action plans are working for you.

For example, if you hope to increase your annual billed or collected revenues from $1 million to $1.5 million over three years, you might identify vision targets similar to the following (keep in mind that this is simply an illustration, and you need to use what makes sense for your practice):

Initiative or Objective: Increase revenue to $1.5 million over three years

Vision Target or Performance Metric	End of Yr. 1	End of Yr. 2	End of Yr. 3
Meetings with referral sources	8	12	16
Meetings with key clients as their trusted advisers	20	28	40
Billed revenue increase over prior year	$100K	$150K	$250K

Initiative or Objective:

Vision Target or Performance Metric	End of Yr. 1	End of Yr. 2	End of Yr. 3

Initiative or Objective:

Vision Target or Performance Metric	End of Yr. 1	End of Yr. 2	End of Yr. 3

Initiative or Objective:

Vision Target or Performance Metric	End of Yr. 1	End of Yr. 2	End of Yr. 3

High-Level Action Planning

Action planning simply consists of identifying who will perform which task or activity and by when it will be performed. Following is an example of one format that can be used, together with some blank forms that can be used for your planning.

Initiative: Technology		
Objective: Upgrade corporate phone system		
Identify and notify the person who will be responsible for carrying out this project *(T.M., in this example)*	Nov. 30, 2013	R.S.
Investigate options; compare and prepare summary for evaluation	Dec. 31, 2013	T.M.
Identify system of choice	Dec. 31, 2013	R.S.
Purchase and install system	Jan. 31, 2014	T.M.
Conduct user training on system	1st week in Feb., 2014	T.M.

Initiative:		
Objective:		
Identify and notify the person who will be responsible for carrying out this project		

Initiative:		
Objective:		
Identify and notify the person who will be responsible for carrying out this project		

Additional Learning Resources

As you know from the materials at the end of the first chapter, additional self-study CPE courses are available for your review. Many of them are all-video courses developed from our streaming video webcasts, and others were created from the various books we have written. These courses can be found at www.successioninstitute.com/PMRC.

Remember to take advantage of your discount by entering the word "succession" into the coupon code field.

Dynamic Leadership, part 3 of 3, is an all-video course you might want to review to provide you with some additional valuable insight into planning for your firm. This course gives you a quick overview of the planning process for your firm.

As well, Dom has created a video called the Strategic Planning Virtual Facilitator™ that is available for purchase and walks small firms step-by-step through all the steps outlined previously. Visit our website at www.successioninstitute.com for more information on this offering or for instructions on how to order it.

Chapter 3: Monitoring Your Practice With Metrics

Key Themes from *Securing the Future, Volume 1: Building Your Firm's Succession Plan*, Chapter 3

- Cleaning up operations—information systems and performance metrics
- Strategies for improvement that will yield high return on investment:
  - Creating capacity at the top
  - Improving your overall profit stream
  - Charging clients a fair fee
- Managing through the trough

Benchmarks to Consider

In volume 1, chapter 3, "Clean Up Your Operations," we provided a list of some key metrics you should be monitoring regularly to help you better manage your firm and position it for succession. These metrics will provide valuable information for you and anyone who is interested in getting a thumbnail sketch of what's going on at your practice. Note that there are two benchmarks, and in some cases, three, that you should consider when reviewing your performance metrics. The first is *actual performance to budgeted performance*, which, of course, requires that you proactively budget your operations and then compare your actual outcomes to what you budgeted. The second is a trend line: *actual performance compared to the last three years*, which, although it is looking back, will actually alert you to trends before they develop to the point that they are not reversible. The third benchmark that may apply is that of *comparable firms*. In other words, if you have access to operating statistics from other firms, know and trust the source, know that the firms are reasonably comparable to yours, *and* you are confident that the numbers are being generated using a consistent set of rules, then consider using benchmark comparisons to other firms.

Notice that we list using benchmark statistics as the last option. This is because managing your business is about connecting the dots between your strategy, your improvement efforts, and your progress against your plan or the past. These comparisons are far more important than just comparing your numbers to those from organizations you don't know. As well, there are many reasons why some firms achieve the metrics they do, and regardless of whether those numbers look good or bad, they may not be telling you the real story at all. For example, average partner income of the firm you compare to may be exceptional, but that might be because each partner is expected to work 3,000 hours per year (which sets a false metric for what a reasonable work expectation should be). On the other extreme, average partner income could be low compared to yours, but that might be because the firm just added several new junior partners to prepare for some near term succession; this is also providing you a false metric for comparison.

It all comes down to knowing the firms against which you are comparing your firm. You need to be able to ask who, what, where, when, and how those results were accomplished. Consider this example: Firm A has a 4-percent technology/revenues percentage, whereas the average is 2 percent. This would imply that Firm A is making a bigger commitment to technology than the average. However, Firm A could just be a laggard in this area because the average firm has been keeping up with, or ahead of, technology, while Firm A is performing some deferred maintenance in this area. Or, Firm A included its technology consulting company fees and direct technology training costs in its numerator, whereas the other firms only included the technology hard costs like hardware and software in their numerator. The point is that putting a lot of stock in a comparison when you don't know why something is occurring doesn't have nearly as much value as managing to your strategy and your trend lines. So, although we want you to consider benchmarking data to look for trends and common statistics among a number of firms, we believe your internal progress and accomplishment against your past and budget is far more revealing about your management and change management efforts than any other effort.

In the "Tools and Resources" section of this chapter, we lay out a shorthand version of how we assess a company and what we glean from these statistics using the metrics we presented in volume 1, chapter 3. Then, we provide you with a tool for setting your billing rates at your firm for the owners and for all your professional and paraprofessional staff.

Tools and Resources

Comments on Key Performance Metrics for CPA Firms

Total Hours Worked

This is a helpful number to have, broken down by staff level. Your partners' total hours versus managers' total hours versus other professional staff total hours will provide insight into which group is working the hardest and how much capacity you have. Obviously, capacity is a key component when mapping out your growth strategy.

The appropriate range for total hours worked depends on short-term and long-term circumstances and firm objectives. For decades, our profession has stated to employees that they work for a 50- hour-per-week employer, with many weeks during tax season requiring 60 hours or more. Historically, many firms have had significant variances in their business cycles, with tax season being crunch time, followed by a much more relaxed, slower time period. Today, although many firms still have an intense tax season, it is backed up by 3 more quarters of intense work, as well. A final common variation that affects the appropriate range of work hours is situational. Employees will rally around a firm's short-term situation and do whatever it takes to complete several unusual, large projects or dig in to overcome because they are short-staffed as a show of support for the firm.

However, some firms take these techniques to the maximum, continue pushing, and then wonder why there is fallout. For example, if a firm has been short-staffed for five years, this can no longer be sold as a short-term problem and will be widely recognized as a management commitment problem. The same is true if the seasonality is virtually gone from the firm's workload, and every month is crunch time. Back when staff labor was in greater supply (or if you were one of the largest firms, for which people plan to work for a couple years just to associate themselves with the brand name and leave), this "grin and bear it" approach was easier to get away with. However, today, in order to attract and retain staff, more and more firms are selling themselves as work/life balance organizations with more overtime flexibility. In addition, a growing number of firms are starting to do away with overtime requirements altogether. If you are running a CPA firm that is doing well, but your profitability and success are based on everyone working a ton of hours, then you are swimming upstream. This will not be easy to maintain. If this is your firm's approach, make sure you are paying your people a lot of money (top of the market), or you may soon find yourself losing your top people to competitors because the market is currently paying top wages for 40-hour work weeks. Even if you and some of your people are nuts about public accounting and this is what everyone wants to do all day and night, recognize that this approach always burns people out. Make sure you properly manage your total work hours for the sake of the long-term health of your people and your organization.

Total Chargeable and Non-Chargeable Hours

Again, broken down by staff level of employee, this number will be used in other calculations and, when compared to total hours, indicates how they are being utilized. Comparing the chargeable and non-chargeable hours of partners to managers and other professional staff will provide some interesting insights, as well. Do your owners and managers have as much chargeable time as your staff? If yes, this normally means that you're not pushing tasks down to the lowest possible level, and you're not developing your staff as fully as you should. To this comment some CPA firm owners might respond that they don't have the time to train the staff in some of this work because of its complexity and the staff's lack of experience. However, this is one of the most common traps that catch CPA firms. If you persist in this type of thinking and action, your staff will never have the experience they need to do more complex work, and you will still be doing work you shouldn't be doing from now until the end of time. Owners and managers will likely find themselves having to work even more hours to find new staff to replace those people who left to work for organizations that are committed to taking the time to develop them.

So, what's a good number here? Again, it depends. We typically see the real ranges of chargeability within CPA firms depicted in table 3-1.

Table 3-1: Typical CPA Firm Ranges of Chargeability

Partner	1,000–1,200
Manager	1,300–1,500
Senior	1,400–1,600
Staff	1,500–1,700
Bookkeeping	1,600–1,800

What if your total firm-wide charge hours are not as high as they should be? The reasons are usually one of the following six: poor training, improper delegation, poor training, improper delegation, poor training, or improper delegation. Each higher-level worker should have an obligation to constantly pass work down and train. As non-chargeable hours increase with each higher level, although the training hours are still the same, other activities, such as client management and internal firm management, consume the unencumbered time.

On the other hand, we often find situations in which people are not charging for all the time they spend on clients' work. This may be true because some people make an assessment at that moment about whether time will be billable. If this is the case, set a policy to record it all, with the freedom to make that judgment later. For example, everyone may agree that a 10-minute phone call should not be billed. But, what if the client made twenty 10-minute phone calls asking for help during that month? Let's make sure we are making that decision with all the information available by recording all charge time.

Another common reason people don't record all the time they spend on client work is because of punitive management practices. For example, if the owners have recently brow-beaten someone about not making budget on his or her jobs, don't be surprised if the employee starts to "eat" some of his or her time to avoid this kind of interaction with you in the future. What makes this really unfair is that many owners brow-beat their staff for the *owners'* failings—setting budgets that were unattainable in the first place due to the owners' giving away the work by proposing unrealistic fees or succumbing to clients' unreasonable demands or expectations.

If people are writing their time down and the owners are selling the service at a reasonable price, then constantly coming in over budget could be as simple as work inefficiency. This can be the case when the firm has not developed concentrations or specialties that allow people to really get good at what they're doing. If your firm has a lot of one-off engagements or won't allow personnel to pick a specialty area to concentrate on (audit, tax, and so on), it's probable that the learning curve or start-up time between jobs is out of line. Similarly, if the people doing the work haven't been properly trained, they could be spinning their wheels or performing unnecessary procedures that drive up the time without adding value. In any event, there are systemic approaches that can help you begin to fix this problem.

Gross Production, Net Revenue, and Realization Percentage

Obviously, gross production is important, and it's particularly important when you look at it compared to net revenues. Net revenues represent gross production, net of write-downs and write-ups, and the comparison of the two creates realization percentage. A large gap between gross production and net revenues (large write-downs) could be the result of one or two higher-level causes: (1) the firm simply isn't billing enough for the work it performs, or (2) the firm is experiencing unusual inefficiencies due to inadequate supervision and training of its people or its pursuit of one-off engagements.

Net Revenues by Department or Service Group, Net Revenues Per Full-Time Employee, Net Revenues Per Owner (Average Book Size), and Net Payroll to Revenues

Net revenues by department or service group is very straightforward. The real focus of this number is for trend-line analysis as well as percentage of total revenues to mark shifts in workload. *Net revenues per full-time employee* (FTE) is a key indicator of the relative financial condition of your firm. The higher the net revenues per FTE, the more attractive your firm will generally be to both insiders wishing to buy into ownership and outsiders looking at the firm.

A high revenue per FTE is certainly no panacea because this number can also be very misleading. For example, this ratio can be very high because the partners work all the time, and their personal billings make up a significant portion of the firm's income or because the firm operates in a very affluent marketplace (which means that although they are most likely charging a great deal for the time, they also are likely to be paying a great deal to the people who are doing the work). In both of these cases, although this ratio would lead you to believe that the firm has a very profitable operation, that is really not the case.

One of the key things to understand about using performance metrics is that they are meant to help uncover important questions to ask, not be the answer in themselves. In day-to-day management, as you focus on improving one metric, you may find that a counterbalancing metric deteriorates, resulting in a negative outcome. In some cases, you may improve several metrics without realizing the rewards you anticipated, so your focus may need to shift to uncovering or creating new measures that will more readily help you monitor the changes you are trying to manage. For example, you might focus your attention on improving realization and find that your firm moves from an overall 76 percent to 85 percent. Clearly, this is a significant improvement; however, if the cause of this improvement was due to a drop in charge time recorded because people started shifting more charge time to non-chargeable time or working more hours and not recording them, then you have just traded one problem for another (which, over the long term, might have a greater negative impact). So, the key is to constantly refine the metrics you manage to give you the balance you are looking for.

Now that we have covered how this metric can be misleading, let's focus on its positive side. What's a good range for this number? The first answer is: trending upward from your previous years' results. A firm under $125,000 per FTE is usually throwing away some serious income that should have gone to the owners. When revenue per FTE is that low, it is common for the partners to not be making much more than some of the senior employees. This creates a bad operating model. These firms will find it harder and harder to attract new owners because there clearly is, as we would say in Colorado, no gold in them thar hills. If you want people to want to become owners and take on the additional risk and headaches, there needs to be a pot of gold in clear sight. So, you want a distinctive, meaningful gap between *any* owner and *all* non-owners, or you will be motivating people to remain employees or, worse, move on to other firms that have figured this out.

On the other hand, when you examine the results of various PCPS surveys, you will find firms operating in excess of $400,000 per person. Clearly, if you have one partner (solo practitioner) who operates in a specialty area, this kind of number is easier to achieve. But when firms of 25 people or more are doing this, they are doing some creative things to leverage their earnings.

We typically find that when firms outside of the large market areas (because of the skewing that occurs due to much higher than average billing rates) are able to generate between about $130,000 to $200,000 per FTE annually, they have plenty of profit to build a sustainable operating model.

Net revenues per owner is just a quick indication of the book size that the owners typically manage. The specific breakdown per owner is often referred to as *owner book* or *owner run*, which is simply a list by owner, including each client assigned to that owner and total fees billed during that period. The larger the firm, the more you'll see principals, directors, and managers carrying books of business, too. Although this is just an indicator, if a firm has $3 million in revenues and six partners, that tells you that the average partner manages $500,000 worth of business. As we will discuss in more detail later, this average book size indicates a number of problems the business will likely encounter, which will be exacerbated as partners retire.

The final ratio in this grouping was net payroll to revenues. This is just a handy cost-of-goods-sold number. As we stated in the definition, this number can exclude all owner compensation, or it might include the guaranteed salaries of owners. The number is for your internal use to track your inventory (your people) cost relative to revenues (the impact it is having on your profit margin). Often, when guaranteed salaries are included, it is because a couple of partners have so little equity in the firm. When the compensation system is really directed to the heavy-equity players (and junior partners are making just a little more money than they did as senior managers), adding those owner-income guarantees to the numerator is more reflective of the firm's cost-of-goods performance. If you wanted, it would make sense to include employee benefit costs, as well. Metrics are for you to use in whatever way they help you make better management decisions. But as you can see, because they are so easily customized, many of these ratios are difficult to use when comparing your firm to others.

Leverage and Net Book Managed

Leverage is a quick ratio to determine whether owners are utilizing staff in the work they manage. This is why the numerator includes owners' personal billings against their book divided by the book they manage. This is not meant to be exact because some charges will be misapplied or inappropriately coded, but to get it close enough, you can run a report from your time and billing system that shows a partner's personal billings against his or her clients, then add any other partner's personal billings against that same book to get the denominator. For example, if an owner has an $800,000 book, and his or her personal billings are $300,000, and no other owners billed time against that client work, the leverage ratio would be 2.66. If another owner billed $100,000 of time against that book, then the ratio would be 2 ($300 + $100 = $400 / $800,000). The reason is that it takes zero management skill or development for an owner to turn a project over to another owner. Firm-wide leverage is created by breaking projects down, involving managers and staff, and training and coaching them through the work. This is what creates leverage in a firm.

You can develop this into a much more sophisticated metric by regularly obtaining runs of all owners' time by client and then rolling up from there. This extra effort can be especially important when a number of partners serve in support roles to those partners managing client relationships.

Net book revenues is a simple number that shows the margin available to the firm after the partner is compensated. If a partner has a $350,000 book, and that partner takes home $300,000, then total revenues available to pay support staff, overhead, and so on are only $50,000. Remember, each of these metrics tells a story, but none of them tell the full story. On one hand, if the owner of the preceding book doesn't support a number of other partners, then he or she doesn't contribute much to the firm's long-term success. As you can see, he or she probably takes out more than he or she contributes. As the firm grows, it will likely continue to manage its small book, and the success of the firm rests on the backs of the other partners. We have seen cases in which a partner, because of the success of the firm (not that partner's personal efforts), manages a book of business and takes home more than he or she grosses in revenues. Not only are these partners not contributing to the overhead and working capital of the firm, they are taking working capital away because of their minimal contribution.

On the other hand, if the partner in the preceding example does a great deal of work on other partners' clients, then it might be one of the other owners who is not pulling his or her weight rather than this one. Performance metrics can help you identify which of these scenarios are true.

Multiplier

This is another measure that reveals what kind of contribution each employee is making to the firm. It compares the net revenues of each employee to the compensation you pay them to generate that revenue. Besides using the metric on a person-by-person basis, it can be also be used to look at staff levels of employees. This ratio can be especially telling for part-time workers because too many of them are tied up in too many hours of non-chargeable duties. Although you might have a situation in which both full- and part-time workers at the staff level put in about the same number of non-chargeable hours, the part-time workers' profitability tanks because their work hours are so limited.

What should the multiplier ratio be? That is a good question. We did a little research on this with a group of our clients several years ago; the range of firms included some exceptionally profitable ones as well as firms with average profitability. In our work with firms since performing that original analysis, these metrics have proven to be a good starting place for analysis. These metrics, once again, are just a guide. They are not set in stone. We address this further in the discussion on our billing worksheet, but to shed some light on this here, you can use the following as a general guide:

3.25 – 3.50 for paraprofessionals

3.00 – 3.25 for staff

2.75 – 3.00 for seniors

2.50 – 2.75 for technical managers

2.25 – 2.50 for supervisory managers

0.75 – 2.00 for partners and principals

These should be base ratios, not what you aspire to. They are a starting place for a minimum return on investment (ROI) for each level of personnel. There are plenty of reasons why someone would fall short of his or her targets. The most common answers, and you have seen them before, are as follows:

- Partners giving away projects and then blaming their write-offs on staff.
- One-off engagements requiring too much start-up time.

- Too many non-chargeable hour duties assigned to a particular worker.
- A staff member who handles several "firm exception" clients. These are situations in which the work is billed way below standard because the client provides value to the firm in other ways. For example, that client refers a lot of business, or we make up for the low fees on this work because of the other projects we do for that client, and so on.
- A staff member handling the most unprofitable work. For example, many firms might perform a number of nonprofit audits for local organizations as part of community involvement efforts or because the firm wants those organizations on their client list.

Situations like the ones discussed previously, and many others, will lower the multiplier ratio, and that's okay. However, the firm owners should be making conscious decisions about why they expect less profit from one employee versus another. Looking at each employee's multiplier, as well as multiplier by staff level, is also a great starting place for putting together an employee performance compensation plan. At the end of the day, if there are no easily identifiable reasons for someone's ratio being too low, then it most likely means that you are simply not charging nearly enough for your people's time relative to what you're paying them. If this is the case, then raise the employees' billing rates to an acceptable level and then raise your project fees to accommodate those rates, and everything will start coming into line.

Growth in Net Revenues, Net Profits, and Percentage of Net Profits

The value of growth in net revenues is obvious, and both uses are for a trend-line perspective. It is a historical benchmark worth watching to see how fast your firm is evolving as well as a good factor to consider as a predictive index to plan for where you will likely be in the next few years. Although last year's growth isn't an actual predictor of next year's growth, it is a metric that helps you see, over a period of time, what a low, high, and average growth expectation has been so that you can staff accurately and prepare for likely changes.

Also, comparing your growth in net revenues to growth in net payroll can give you an indication of whether or not you're keeping up with your increased costs of production resulting from annual pay increases, bonuses and overtime payments, and so on.

Net profits and net profit percentage are very straightforward. The blurred part of this calculation comes from whether or not to include guaranteed salaries of owners. For internal use, it doesn't matter; however, when you compare your net profit percentage to other firms, this inconsistency makes it hard to interpret how you are doing against the benchmark. If you are a solo practitioner, your net profit percentage is likely to be 80 percent or even more. The bigger the firm, the more this percentage shrinks. Because net profit can vary dramatically from year to year due to a turn in the market, long-term investing in the firm (technology, training, and so on), tax planning, transaction timing, employee turnover, retirement, and so much more, a good net profit percentage is one that is consistent with your strategic plan and strategic budget. But, from a general perspective, if your net profit percentage is in the low 30s, you have some cleaning up to do. If that percentage is in the high 40s, you might be relying too much on your partner group for your income or not investing in the firm at the level you should (see ratios below on technology, CPE, and marketing). For net profit percentages in the high 30s to low 40s, your focus can shift to other metrics because that range is a good general average.

Average Owner Compensation

Average owner compensation tells us how the owners are faring against the likely senior manager employees. When we see an owner salary around $150,000, then we know the owners are not making much more than some of the top people in the firm. As we stated previously, we like to see a meaningful gap in order to motivate non-partners to become partners. Why would someone want to be a partner if he or she can make $120,000 as an employee versus $150,000 as a partner (and he or she might even be paying his or her own social security as a partner, which unfortunately makes the salary even more comparable)? Who would want to take on the risk of the business, the working capital needs, debt owed, and the future retirement obligations for such a pittance of additional money? So, if you are a very small firm, and your partners make a living that you are very happy with, you still need to think about building your business to a level that others will be happy with. It doesn't matter that you can live comfortably on $150,000. That is probably not enough to motivate someone to want to buy you out. And, if you are planning to try to merge, the firm you merge into is likely to be paying a senior manager about that much, so where are the extra profits for the partners to skim off to justify the effort of buying you out?

One of the most significant problems a lot of firms have is signaled by average owner compensation. Most of the time, although there are definitely problems to address when running a profitable organization, the main problem is that the firm has too many partners for the amount of business being managed.

Staff Turnover and Staff Additions

These two are the most commonly overlooked metrics we find when discussing firm strategy. They are the foundation data to understanding the hiring practices a firm needs to manage their growth. Some of you may be thinking, "This doesn't apply to me—I've got a small firm, and this is only relevant for big firms." The fact is, unless you truly work as a one-person shop, this does, indeed, apply to you. In fact, it's more critical for smaller firms than for larger firms. To illustrate this concept, consider a firm with 20 employees. If 1 employee leaves, that's 5 percent turnover for that year, and although it may be a little uncomfortable, spreading the person's work around to the remaining 19 people should not be too difficult. Next, take a firm with 5 employees. If just 1 of them leaves, that creates a gaping hole in capacity due to 20 percent turnover, with less people to whom you can spread the excess work left by the departing staff person.

Now, let's compound the problem for both the larger firm and the small firm mentioned previously. If the partners are looking to train their people and push more work down while growing the practices, they need more capacity than they probably have right now. So, it's a double-whammy in human resources availability that occurs in the context of demographic trends that leave the firm with fewer candidates for entry-level jobs than it needs.

For example, let's say we are working with a firm that has $2 million in net revenues, 16 FTEs (an average of $125,000 per FTE), and 2 partners (an average owner book of $1 million), and it has been growing at a minimum of 20 percent for the last 3 years. If you assume, for planning purposes, that their growth will continue at 20 percent, then the firm would be looking at net revenues of almost $3.5 million over a 3-year period. If average revenue per FTE holds (and during rapid growth, it usually goes down, not up), this firm will need to have 28 employees by the end of the second year to do the work, an increase of 12 employees. When you consider the additional information—(1) that this firm has been experiencing a loss of 2 people per year (either due to termination or staff quitting), (2) that the firm believes 2 of their current people are very marginal (they can't let them go because of the current overload of work), and (3) that they are at least 1 person short right now—an entirely different hiring plan starts to come into focus.

Based on this information, in order to be staffed to produce $3.5 million in revenue, the firm suddenly needs to hire 12 new employees to manage the growth, 6 new employees to reflect the 2 per year they have been losing, at least 1 staffer to compensate for the marginal employees being replaced, and 1 more person because the firm is currently short-staffed. That puts the firm at a total of 20 people that need to be hired by the end of the second year, or 10 people per year. Although a reasonable amount of the $1.5 million in growth will come from increased fees (so we could factor that into our equation), we did not factor into this example the idea that a reasonable amount of the new people hired will be terminated or quit because the new job did not work out.

So, here is a 16-person firm, growing like a weed with full expectation of continuing that growth, that needs to start hiring at a rate of 10 people per year for the next 2 years to be in a position to do the work that will likely come in. Usually, firms like this have a plan to hire 2 or 3 people at the most, which is why so many firms keep pushing their people so hard and running them off so quickly.

Remember this: People are our inventory. When you run out of time to sell, your business will flatten. Yes, when you hire more people than you can keep busy, you run the risk of having excess inventory and not enough buyers, but we believe that this overcapacity is a short-term response. In the worst case, just let go of that marginal employee or two you have been threatening to fire for the past five years. In almost every case—and we see a lot of them—when firms hire good people, the work comes in because the partners are motivated to use their freed-up time to take better care of their top clients, which instantly converts into more opportunity (to learn more, read our book on how to expand your advisory skills, *Becoming a Trusted Business Advisor: How to Add Value, Improve Client Loyalty, and Increase Profits*).

On the opposite side of this spectrum, we have also seen what happens when firms try to live with a labor shortage for too long:

- First, growth flattens, except for price increases because there is not more labor to sell.
- Second, clients get frustrated with late work and leave.
- Third, because of the stress of keeping up with in-house project demand, good people quit, thereby reducing inventory.

Then, the firm struggles to find people to replace those who left, only to find the capacity of the new people is less than the capacity of the people that are gone because the people who left already knew how to do the work and were familiar with the firm's processes and procedures. Ask any retailer: Learning to manage inventory is the key to success and profitability. We, as CPA firms, need to do a better job managing our inventory (building the right level of time capacity and developing the competencies available with that time).

Days' Revenues in Work in Progress and Receivables

Most CPAs probably have counseled their clients about the importance of these ratios and the importance of keeping them as low as practical. Yet, we find that many practitioners are sloppy about their billing and collection practices. We run across firms all the time in which one or more owners have more than 60 days' revenues in work in progress (WIP) and were just "too busy" to get their billing done on time. Similarly, it's unfortunately not uncommon to find receivables on a CPA firm's books that amount to more than 120 days of revenues. Now, if that same partner who was slow to bill is also slow to collect, then you're looking at up to 180 days (half a year) of cycle time to get the cash for the work done. You have two cycles to be attacking. The first is how long time stays in WIP, and the second is how long until collection. The first one isn't that hard to manage. Sometimes, your billing practices are part of the problem. Rather than bill once a month, bill all the time. As soon as a presentation is made on project status, as soon as a certain time period elapses, as soon as a project is finished, bill it! Don't wait for some arbitrary cycle. Look at it this way: If you finish a project on the third of the month and don't bill it until the end of the month, you have thrown away 27 days on average of unnecessary interest against your line (or interest you could have collected).

Keep in mind that the longer you wait to bill a client, the less likely they are to recall the warm glow of success that you helped them create, and the more likely you'll be having fee discussions with them and facing adjustments or write-offs. Ultimately, the more you can collect of what you charged, the better your net revenues per FTE will be, the larger your bottom line will be, and the more valuable your CPA firm, not to mention the quicker you can take that money home.

Marketing / Net Revenues

In order to convert your business model from an EWYK or Superstar model to a Building a Village (BAV) or Operator model, you'll need to make a switch from relying on business development by an individual superstar to creating and implementing a firm-wide marketing strategy. By marketing, we mean more than just advertising budgets—it includes all forms of business development, including promotional content on your website, handout pieces, meals with referral sources, seminars, advertising, and more. This will take resources to carry off. It will require conscious decisions about types of clients served and service offerings. Most CPA firms devote entirely too little funding to marketing. How much marketing is enough?

Yes, we get it. Why spend this kind of money when you have an owner that is great at it? We hear it all the time. You would just be spending money that you don't need to because he or she can bring in all the work you can do. Well, the longer you go under that Superstar strategy without backfilling with supportive operating processes, the more likely that superstar will eventually start holding the firm hostage. The superstar will likely demand a premium in salary, require special perks, an unreasonable retirement benefit, more ownership or control, and on and on. Leverage your superstars' skills, but don't rely on them solely, or the price you will eventually pay will easily be 10 times what it would have cost you to operationalize the same growth engine.

What should your marketing percentage be? Interestingly enough, this metric has fallen off the critical radar list in the last two years because most firms currently have all the business they need and are focusing on getting their people trained to do the work in-house. But, looking at the data over the past 10 years, this has commonly averaged less than 1.5 percent of net revenues for the average firm. But, many firms are catching on to the importance of institutionalizing marketing, and they are spending in excess of 5 percent on those processes. Generally speaking, your marketing budget should probably average around 3 percent, with every couple of years hitting 4 percent to 5 percent just to keep your messages in front of your clients and referral sources.

By the way, this is not a fully allocated number. So, if a partner is responsible for marketing, then we would not allocate part of his or her salary to this category. Also, you would not charge the marketing budget with partners' time managing their clients (which is how a lot of new business is generated). You would, however, include the expenses for lunches and so on. If you have someone whose full-time job is to manage marketing activities, this person would be included in the numerator.

As far as marketing expenses, some firms buy a luxury box at a stadium, sponsor a local golf outing, buy seats at local theaters, and so on, as part of their marketing plan. There is nothing wrong with this, and it can be quite effective, but you are basically using the marketing funds to support a personal interest of the partners, so at least be realistic about the expected return on these funds. Partners commit to using these types of perks to generate business all the time to convince the other partners that this is a valuable use of funds. However, after the first game or two, these perks often go unutilized, or they are used by the same clients, family, and staff. We are not saying this isn't valuable; but it may be more of a perk than a marketing strategy if it isn't part of an ongoing monitored marketing effort that the partners and managers are held accountable to leverage. This type of perk might be part of staff retention, too, or something else just as worthwhile. The point is to make sure that you use your marketing funds so that they support the firm's marketing efforts. If you don't, then at least for management purposes, fund your marketing program with a reasonable budget and then roll those disguised perks back in on top.

Technology / Revenues

Firms have three basic ways to crank work out. They can use people to do the work and bill for their time, they can highly leverage technology to make their people more efficient in order to increase throughput through their limited human resources, or they can leverage people outside of the country through the use of technology and outsourcing. Given the difficulty of finding, hiring, and retaining staff, we believe firms should be looking for every possible way to incorporate technology into their firms. Technology is a plentiful resource, but people are not.

Successful CPA firms are not only looking at technology to help assist with labor-intensive administrative work, but they are also looking for ways to utilize it for strategic advantage as well. Technology has become integral to the practice of accountancy, so your firm should have a technology plan with specific strategies (and budgets) to make sure you are utilizing everything your hardware and software have to offer.

Although general ledger accounting and electronic spreadsheet software applications have become more or less ubiquitous, we find that there are still CPAs not making use of them as they could. In this day and age, it's hard to imagine an accountant not being at least a beginner in using spreadsheet software, but we've run across some who still prefer green columnar pads and pencils to Excel. At the next level of technological sophistication, there are numerous potential benefits to electronic working papers—the "paperless" audit and tax return. At this time, most firms have at least begun to embrace this technology, with many of them being four or five years into this process. And, what about digital phone systems that allow multi-office firms to call between offices essentially on an intercom, saving long-distance costs as well as simplifying the process for the clients when they need access to the firm's talent? We believe that every dollar spent on technology that helps leverage the staff's time is the best money you can spend.

For those firms fighting technology, this is a battle we don't believe you can win. Your costs are going to rise (people cost too much), and finding additional capacity will be your albatross to carry; at the same time, the software application market is changing. Key providers of accounting, tax, and audit software are going to Enterprise systems—everything integrated, everything connected. This evolution is forcing firms to select one vendor for all their accounting software, rather than have a potpourri of best-of-breed applications running. If you can't beat 'em, join 'em.

For succession purposes, the more your firm uses technology, the more valuable you will be to a buyer or a merger. Most larger CPA firms have embraced technology. If you and your people are accustomed to working with up-to-date enterprise (integrated) software performing your specialty functions, then the acquiring firm knows that the learning curve to get your people up to speed with their processes will be quick. If your people follow processes of their choice, with each of them deciding what technology to use, this retraining to bring your people into the 21st century will come right out of the bottom-line offer you will receive.

When we hire people, we have no problem charging for their time to create a profit. When technology played a lesser role in our profession, many firms at least tried to recoup some of their technology costs by showing the service bureau fees in their bills. Today, we are using technology to find every way possible to leverage our people's time. And our technology budgets are significantly higher than they have ever been before because of it. No, we are not suggesting putting a technology charge on your bill again, but we are suggesting that technology be considered a cost component of each hour of work performed. Therefore, you need to be writing up the WIP to reflect the real cost of operations. And once you write up WIP, you need to work with the owners to make sure the new fee pricing reflects an adequate amount to cover this. We work with firms that will write up WIP almost 20 percent to reflect the profit recovery they expect from their technology investment. When you substitute technology for people, you also have to find a way to make money on that technology. Otherwise, you should revert back to all manual processes—at least that way, you will allow yourself to bill an appropriate amount for the work being performed.

What is a reasonable budget for technology? Past surveys we did showed this coming in around 2 percent, which is a little low. As with marketing, a suitable technology budget allocation should probably average 3 percent, with that number spiking to 5 percent or more every three years or so. We know that technology spending has been up in recent years, so for it to be down for the PCPS Succession Management Survey wasn't surprising. Just as with marketing, the cost of people or consultants hired exclusively to support your technology would be included in the numerator, but not as an allocation of an owner's cost that might have management responsibility for this area. As we said, technology spending often has a spike effect, with significant dollars spent to upgrade the hardware and software in year one, but less money required during the next few years in order to implement all the functionality just acquired.

Training (CPE) / Revenues

We've saved the best for last regarding operating expense line items as a percent of annual net revenues. Training (CPE) is huge in the CPA profession, evidenced by the various annual CPE events that most CPAs attend to maintain their licenses. Yet, when you calculate the percentage of yearly net revenues that this comprises, it has been running less than 1 percent for at least the last five years. That's pretty interesting when you consider that our "inventory" and capacity to earn revenue is all based on people—our most critical and scarce resource. To be able to make the changes required for effective succession for CPA firms now and in the future, there is no metric more important to monitor than this one. Everyone in the firm will be required to learn new skills and behaviors, from the owners on down through the ranks. They are not going to learn the skills necessary with just on-the-job training because emulating their current boss may be the worst behavior they can adopt.

To fill the missing talent gaps with competent staff, more time needs to be devoted to training and education on a routine, ongoing basis. CPAs will need to learn how to better manage larger books of business and how to better manage and develop their people. Much of what this will entail is learning some of the qualitative, nontechnical skills (often referred to in somewhat of a misnomer as *soft skills*).

We believe that the successful firm of the future will be spending even more on training than we are suggesting for either marketing or technology. Most firms will need to consistently spend 3 percent to 5 percent for at least the next 5 years, or maybe forever. Training has become a best practice issue as many firms are setting their minimum training standard operating procedure at 80–120 hours per person per year or more. In today's market, this not only helps the firm advance the skills of its personnel faster (thereby reversing the upside-down pyramid more quickly), but it also becomes a competitive edge in recruiting and retention. For those that feel like no one spent this kind of money on them and, therefore, they shouldn't have to commit this level of resources to their employees either, suffice to say that someday the labor market will shift from a shortage to a surplus. When this happens, because many people will be fighting for few jobs, firms can go back to the old way of "survival of the fittest" and quickly cull those who don't build the skills they need on their own. But if you think the marketplace will shift back to a survival of the fittest model in your lifetime, we hope you aren't holding your breath. You got this luxury for a few years between 2008 and 2010, and we think that will be it for a while.

Staff hired exclusively to support the training function would be part of the numerator. The good news is although we have a gap in talent between partner and staff, because most firms have not focused on training at the proper level for a long time (or maybe never), we can close this gap fast with a concerted effort. It should only take about two years to build what we refer to as a five-year-skilled CPA now. In today's model, we leave these people alone except for on-the-job training and CPE. It takes them about five years to get two good years of training. So, although there is a steep road to climb, firms that make this a priority will get there much faster than they think. Remember, they're not called "human expenses," they're "human *resources*." Consider also that employees are demanding more training and development from their employers. If you want to attract and retain quality staff, you need to sell them on your development processes. We will have much more on developing competencies in chapter 9.

The Succession Institute's Billing Worksheet

Manager Example

Billing Rate Analysis

	Actual Charge Hours—2010	Current Billing Rate	2010 Actual Realization	Salary	Estimated Multiplier	Expected Revenues Based on Actual	Estimated Revenues Based on Est. Multiplier
Manager	1,500.00	$125	90%	$90,000	2.5	$168,750	$225,000

Estimated Billing Shortage (Overage)
$56,250

Calculated Targeted Hours
2,000

Current Earned Multiplier
1.88

Calculated Billing Rates
$167

Multiple Position Example

Overhead Analysis and Billing Worksheet **Billing Rate Analysis**

Accountants	Budgeted Charge Hours	Billing Rate	Realization	Salary	Suggested Multiplier	Budgeted Revenues	Suggested Revenues	Billing Shortage (Overage)	Calculated Target Hours (1)	Current Expected Multiplier (2)	Automated Suggested Billing Rates (3)	Rate Variance, Current to Suggested (4)
Managing Partner	800	225	90.00%	300,000	0.85	162,000	255,000	93,000	1,259	0.54	354	129
Partner	1,000	210	90.00%	275,000	1.25	189,000	343,750	154,750	1,819	0.69	382	172
Principle	1,200	185	90.00%	175,000	2.00	199,800	350,000	150,200	2,102	1.14	324	139
Supervisory Manager	1,300	150	90.00%	95,000	2.25	175,500	213,750	38,250	1,583	1.85	183	33
Technical Manager	1,500	125	90.00%	90,000	2.50	168,750	225,000	56,250	2,000	1.88	167	42
Senior Staff	1,550	105	90.00%	70,000	3.00	146,475	210,000	63,525	2,222	2.09	151	46
Staff	1,650	90	90.00%	55,000	3.25	133,650	178,750	45,100	2,207	2.43	120	30

(1) Calculated Targeted Hours is the number of hours that would meet the suggested multiplier without changing rates or hours.
(2) Current Expected Multiplier is the multiplier that is currently calculated considering current hours, billing rate, and realization.
(3) Automated Suggested Billing Rates is the billing rate that would allow the current hours and realization to achieve the suggested multiplier.
(4) Rate Variance is the increase (decrease) between the suggested billing rate and the current billing rate.

Using the Billing Worksheet

The billing worksheet is one of many tools we use to get a feel for our clients' performance and compensation issues. As you read through this explanation, please keep in mind that this is simply a way to begin looking at the ROI provided by each of your people, especially at the lower levels where the main focus is on their production, compared to managers and partners, where, for example, the focus should be on client management, people management, and the like. What you're trying to do here is to see if charge rates, pay rates, hours utilized, and realization all make sense in a bottom line context. We're going to use some assumed numbers to illustrate how we process the billing worksheet. The numbers in the preceding illustration simply are sample numbers used to illustrate concepts, so don't get hung up on them if they are out of line with your marketplace or expectations.

The billing worksheet focuses on four variables:

1. Charge hours
2. Billing rates
3. Realization
4. Annual salary

In both examples, you can see that we've chosen a manager with 1,500 actual charge hours from the prior year, whose billing rate is $125 an hour with 90-percent realization. He or she is being paid $90,000 a year in our example. This pay figure typically is the base pay plus overtime pay. It does not include bonuses or benefits such as health insurance, life insurance, retirement plan, profit-sharing, and the like.

In this illustration, we use 2.5 (two and a half times) as a multiplier. This is the multiplier we used times the compensation paid to determine what the expected revenues from this person should be. In this sample case, 1,500 actual hours times the hourly rate of $125 an hour, reduced to 90-percent realization, comes up to $168,750 actual net production generated by this $90,000 a year (before bonus and benefits) person. So far, so good, but what happens when we apply the multiplier of 2.5 to his or her salary and compare this number to the previous performance? In this case, a salary of $90,000 and a 2.5 multiplier indicates that to get a reasonable ROI the firm makes for the manager's compensation, net production should be a total of $225,000. This means that when you compare our expected ROI against the actual performance of this manager, we're looking at a $56,250 shortfall in billings for this person. That's $56,250 of profit that could have gone to the partners lost forever. (In other words, with a salary of $90,000, a 2.5 multiplier indicates net production that should be a total of $225,000 versus $168,750. That's how we got to the $56,250 shortfall.)

Now, let's take a look at what we could do about this. Could you make up this difference by making that person more chargeable at his or her current billing rate and realization? Theoretically, you could, but based on the spreadsheet, you'd need to get 2,000 charge hours out of him or her, and that is not very realistic unless you want the manager to pad his or her hours. The problem is that if the manager pads hours, then the 90-percent realization rate wouldn't be attainable, so he or she will still be underperforming. If we back into it, this model points out that your actual multiplier for this manager is current at 1.88 times salary, quite a bit lower than the 2.5 times salary for estimated revenues that we used earlier. If you decided to stay with the lower multiplier here, then you would be saying that given the work this person is doing (because of its other value to the firm, like taking care of great referral sources, and so on), you would be willing to accept a lower ROI on their work. Think about it. Using $90,000 for base pay, you'll still need to cover payroll taxes, insurance, other fringes, plus some share of overhead, and then what's left, if anything, goes to the partners. So, think about what an extremely low multiplier will actually be doing to the bottom line with respect to this employee and the contribution to the partners. It will be taking money away from the partners, but there are circumstances when this could make sense for a specific employee doing a specific job. (One of the likely fixes to situations like this, unless the employee is known for being a poor and slow performer, would be to also put pressure on the partners to sell the jobs this employee is doing at a more reasonable price.)

As an alternative to status quo or increasing charge hours in this illustration, you could get back to the appropriate ROI on this manager by bumping their billing rate up to $167 an hour. This would provide a reasonable ROI for the partners. You may be thinking, though, that the market won't bear that rate. If the market won't bear that rate for this person, does it really require you to pay the level of pay you've committed to this position? It's one thing to try to pay market, but unless you're charging appropriately in the market, it's doing nothing for your firm. We have not seen a situation in which a firm had to pay high dollars for staff, but their market would only pay low dollars for the work. If that is the scenario you believe you are operating under, to us, that doesn't make sense. In rural markets, people cost less, and fees are less. In large cities, people get paid more, but the market also allows for those fees to be passed on.

The next questions to ask yourself are how efficient are your work processes, and how well trained are your people, if your overall efficiency is off? And of course, whose fault is it if the people aren't adequately trained? It all goes back to what you value as a firm and for what you're willing to pay.

You have four variables to consider:

1. Are you paying this person the right amount? This is the least flexible value, but it could affect how you offer future raises and bonuses.
2. Are you using a billing rate that makes sense with what you are paying this person? Often, this is part of the problem.
3. Is this employee efficient in his or her work? Often, this is a combination of training opportunities and partners giving away work.
4. Are you getting a reasonable amount of charge hours? Often, this is a combination of performance expectation, poor delegation from partners, managing the pipeline and scheduling, and so on.

Many times, this billing worksheet points out a number of problems the firm needs to address simultaneously in order for you to create a pay-for-performance system. In other words, most firms have trouble implementing a pay-for-performance system because they want to put all the blame on poorly performing people, when, in fact, much of the problem lies with poorly performing partners and managers.

On another note, we'd like to address a common objection we hear when we suggest the need to raise staff and manager rates: "Our partners only charge (fill in the blank here, say, $225 an hour, for example), so how can we charge that manager out at $167 an hour?" The answer is far simpler than it first appears. If that's the case, your partners aren't charging high enough rates. If the rates for partners were where they should be, it would be easier not only to bill appropriately for managers, but also to move some of the work off your plate over to them because the clients would see a true price differential between your rates and that manager's rates. Whenever you raise rates, you rarely see enough client attrition to offset dollars earned from the new, increased billing rates. In fact, you usually end up net ahead, even with client attrition. If you do lose a client or two, it just means that you have more time to devote to managing the business, working with the remaining good clients, and developing your people, all of which will pay far greater dividends to you in the long run.

In summary, the odds are that by completing this worksheet, you're going to find out that there are several people whose billing rates don't make sense because billing rates should be a function of pay, not position. Several of your people whom you considered to be billing stars are actually not outperforming some of your average people when you take into account pay differences. And finally, it is not uncommon for our firms to find, based on the way they are utilizing some of their part-timers, that part-timers are killing them profitability-wise.

Multipliers

One of the most common questions we get is, What multiplier should I use? There are no set-in-stone rates or range of multipliers that you need to use, but a starting place might be with the list that follows. Remember what we covered earlier—this is about improving your performance and trends.

3.25 – 3.50 for paraprofessionals

3.00 – 3.25 for staff

2.75 – 3.00 for seniors

2.50 – 2.75 for technical managers

2.25 – 2.50 for supervisory managers

0.75 – 2.00 for partners and principals

You can see that multipliers range all the way from less than 1.0 for a partner on up to 3.5 or so for a bookkeeper or paraprofessional staff. These ranges are based on our surveys of client firms. Certainly, some firms use higher (and a few may use lower) multiples, but these ranges are a good starting place for anyone interested in doing the analysis we just reviewed with you.

If this is your first time going through this analysis, consider starting at or near the lower end of the range, or perhaps even a tad under the low end, and then easing into the changes over a year or two as you go forward. In other words, if you find that you need to raise your rates, you should not feel compelled to do it all in one year. Try to start moving them up so that over the course of two to three years, they're up to the right place. Don't try to make up for five to eight years of previous bad practices by trying to fix it all at once.

Another point that's worth mentioning with regard to the use of this billing worksheet tool is that it should generate some questions that need to be asked. When you find out somebody's not performing based on his or her numbers and a reasonable multiplier, it's time to then ask why. Is it just them? Is it how we're interacting with them? Is it how we're assigning them business? Is it the fact that we've got them tied up in a bunch of administrative duties? Don't jump to conclusions. Remember, the fish stinks at the head, so once you uncover a problem, know that the partner group is very likely playing a large role in perpetuating it, especially when a problem recurs across numerous people.

You can go to our website (www.successioninstitute.com) and download the spreadsheet we introduced in this chapter for free. Just register and ask for access to the CPA firm folder.

Additional Learning Resources

As you know from the materials at the end of the first chapter, additional self-study CPE courses are available for your review. Many of them are all-video courses developed from our streaming video webcasts, and others were created from the various books we have written. These courses can be found at www.successioninstitute.com/PMRC.

Remember to take advantage of your discount by entering the word "succession" into the coupon code field.

Following are three courses that may be beneficial in the consideration of performance metrics for the small CPA firm.

- Managing Your Firm by the Numbers (all-video)
- Managing Your Workload (all-video)
- Managing Client Satisfaction (all-video)

Chapter 4: Determining Which Business Model Your Practice (Mostly) Follows

Key Themes from *Securing the Future, Volume 1: Building Your Firm's Succession Plan*, Chapter 4

- The difference between the Eat What You Kill (EWYK) and Building a Village (BAV) business models
- The problem with replacing the superstar
- Modes of operation within the EWYK and BAV models
- The most commonly found disconnects between the Success and Continuation Modes

As we covered in volume 1, chapter 4, you need to have a clear understanding of which business model you are using for your firm and why. Your choice of business model has far-ranging ramifications for other decisions related to practice management and succession management. In this chapter, we provide a quick diagnostic checklist you can complete to get a better sense of which model you're likely operating under.

Tools and Resources

The Succession Institute's Determining Your Present Business Model Worksheet

Instructions: Take a moment to read and react to each of the 10 statements in the left-hand column. For each statement, indicate your level of agreement or disagreement opposite the statement by placing an "X" under the column that best matches your agreement or disagreement based on your firm's practices.

	My Firm's Practices	Strongly Disagree	Disagree	Somewhat Disagree	Somewhat Agree	Agree	Strongly Agree
1	The firm's identity in the market is very tightly tied to a partner or partners.						
2	Generated book is a major source of power, influence, and compensation in the firm.						
3	Many partners have their own style and approach for working with their clients. Staff need to change how they do the work depending on which partner they are working for.						
4	Partners and managers are financially motivated to get client work done themselves, rather than always trying to pass it down to lower level staff.						
5	I feel that the skill gap between the partner group and the managers, or even the senior partners and the youngest partners, is larger than ideal.						
6	The firm places a high premium on a few rainmaking partners and managers, rather than forcing everyone to play a role in marketing.						
7	The firm has a number of partners who manage small books of business ($800K or less) and who do most of the work on those clients themselves.						

	My Firm's Practices	Strongly Disagree	Disagree	Somewhat Disagree	Somewhat Agree	Agree	Strongly Agree
8	Making myself better, faster, and stronger is a higher and better use of time (and is supported by the pay system) than making those around me better, faster, and stronger, which is not supported by the pay system.						
9	Partners make the decision about whether a new client is accepted, rather than going through a formal client acceptance process.						
10	Partners and managers are not really held accountable to the strategic plan of the firm.						

Total Xs per column (A)							
Times (B)		1	2	3	4	5	6
Total scores = A × B							
Grand total, all columns							

Scoring

Multiply the totals in each column by the number shown below the total line, then cross-foot all of those products. The result is your total score on this snapshot tool. The higher the score, the more likely you are operating as an EWYK (silos) firm. The lower the score, the more likely you are operating, at least in some respects, under a BAV (one-firm) business model.

Your Results

10–25:   BAV

26–35:   Hybrid

36–60:   EWYK

Note that most firms are operating either as an EWYK firm or a hybrid model. Firms that score in the hybrid range likely look to an outsider and any insiders like a BAV firm, but foundationally, the firm typically still has some very strong elements of EWYK that permeate the organization. Even a firm with a score of 50–55 may have functional areas within the firm that operate from a BAV perspective; but in this range, rarely does the firm manage the partners and hold them accountable to anything other than their silo.

Additional Learning Resources

As you know from the materials at the end of the first chapter, additional self-study CPE courses are available for your review. Many of them are all-video courses developed from our streaming video webcasts, and others were created from the various books we have written. These courses can be found at www.successioninstitute.com/PMRC.

Remember to take advantage of your discount by entering the word "succession" into the coupon code field.

Here are two all-video courses we recommend that could provide you some valuable insight into writing this section of your succession plan.

- Introduction to the Eat What You Kill and Building a Village Models of Operations (all-video)
- Moving From Eat What You Kill to the Building a Village Model (all-video)

Building Your Firm's Robust Succession Plan

We are now back to the succession planning development phase. As we have covered before, once you complete this last section of each chapter, by the time you finish the book, you will have written down foundational ideas to review with your partners. Once you pull together these final sections, you will have identified your recommendations about how to handle each succession planning area (or, at a minimum, questions the partner group needs to answer), and you will have a document that can be presented for discussion, modification, and eventual approval that will guide the changes in policy, agreements, governance, and culture your firm will undertake to implement this succession plan over the next few years.

Now that you have completed and scored the quick diagnostic checklist, consider the following:

1. The checklist is meant to be a shorthand reminder of some of the basic issues found between the two models.
2. Your firm is likely a hybrid of the two models but will lean more toward one model or the other.

Having given some thought to how your firm operates and which model or hybrid best describes your firm, write down your thoughts to these questions.

Eat What You Kill Tendencies

Describe the various ways, if any, that your firm operates under the EWYK model.

_____

_____

_____

_____

_____

_____

_____

_____

Building a Village or One-Firm Concept Tendencies

Describe the various ways, if any, that your firm operates under the BAV model.

_____

_____

_____

_____

_____

_____

_____

_____

Strengths and Values of Our Current Operating Environment

Describe what you truly enjoy about your firm or working at your firm that you would always want to retain, regardless of the growth and changes your firm might undergo in the next 5–10 years.

_____

_____

_____

_____

_____

_____

_____

_____

Conflicts and Weaknesses of Our Current Operating Environment

Describe those areas that are in conflict for the partner group because of those different operating models. In other words, what are those things you know that you need to fix regarding the way you operate in your firm but on which you never get any traction?

_____

_____

_____

_____

_____

_____

_____

_____

Chapter 5: Exploring Valuation and Related Considerations

Key Themes from *Securing the Future, Volume 1: Building Your Firm's Succession Plan*, Chapter 5

- Determining the value
- Other retirement benefit issues to consider
- Mandatory sale of ownership
- Vesting
- Actions that should negatively affect value

In volume 1, chapter 5, we covered the general considerations for valuation of a partner's interest in a firm and the fact that three methods are commonly used to value an owner's interest in a CPA firm:

- Book of business
- Multiple of salary
- Percentage of ownership times firm annual revenues

In this chapter, we'll delve a little deeper into this issue of valuation and related considerations. In addition, even though we've written this book and its companion volume to help professionals plan for internal succession management, we cover mergers and sales in this chapter because we know some of you are interested in these external transfer options, as well.

Using Book of Business as a Valuation Method

A major challenge facing many smaller CPA firms is that of using the appropriate buy-sell or retirement agreement for the firm based on the firm's business model.

Use the Correct Type of Buy-Sell Agreement for Your Business Model

Some firms try to use retirement agreements that simply do not and cannot work properly because of the firm's business model. Although every firm's retirement policy and related buy-sell agreements are likely to have some unique qualities, there are some practices that are more commonly associated with different business models in use throughout the profession. In chapter 4, we categorized the two predominant business models in use among CPA firms: the EWYK (silo) model, in which the model focuses on the partner's production—book, charge hours, realization, write-downs—as if the partner was running his or her own profit center or practice within a practice, and the BAV (one-firm concept) model, in which the focus is on the firm's strategy and aligning all the partners to not only achieve the strategy but also to develop and leverage their people, follow firm processes and policy, and incentivize individual performance to align with what is best for the firm.

Because of the differences in these business models, retirement policies should be radically different for each.

Buyout, Retirement, and Business Model

So, why does all of this matter? Quite simply, it makes a big difference in what a retiring partner is selling as well as what the remaining partners are buying. If your firm is functioning as an EWYK firm, using the book of business method to set a partner's retirement, in most instances, would be appropriate for you. For firms operating under the BAV model, the partner's share of equity times revenues and multiple of salary would likely be the most appropriate methods for valuation.

We see the greatest conflicts and disconnects in situations in which a partner wants the privilege of using a retirement benefit formula inconsistent with the business model actually in place. For example, it is common to see a partner operating in an EWYK environment who wants to be paid retirement as if he or she were working under a one-firm or BAV model.

Yet, at the same time, these same partners often feel entitled to fixed, agreed-upon retirement benefits payable to them, even though all of the following are true:

- They are leaving a book of work that perhaps no one else wants to do, knows how to do, or has the time and capacity to devote to it.
- They have not built any bench strength in the people below them (in their opinion, it's the firm's fault for not having hired "experienced" people).
- They've not adequately leveraged their book through the use of effective delegation to others.
- Many of their clients will be up for grabs when they depart, leaving the firm without a significant amount of annuity relationships from which to pay the retirement benefit.

It should be obvious that a common fixed buy-sell or deferred compensation arrangement makes no sense for situations like this. What these firms should have in place is not a BAV buy-sell and deferred compensation arrangement, but rather, a right of first refusal. Under this type of arrangement, the firm and its remaining owners are not required to buy out the retiring partner. The partner is free to sell his or her book under whatever terms can be negotiated with the other owners within the firm. We would recommend that this kind of purchase be based on client retention, not a fixed price paid up front. Should the departing partner not find the offers of his or her partners to be sufficient, he or she can look outside the firm for buyers, and the firm and remaining partners will have a first right of refusal after the partner obtains a bona fide offer from an outsider.

This represents the best option for both the buyers and the seller when operating under the EWYK business model. The buyers get to negotiate which clients they wish to take on and at what price, and the seller has the freedom to manage his or her practice in any reasonable manner, toward whatever consequences come with those business decisions when it's time to pull the trigger on an exit strategy. In other words, because the other owners had little say about the services the retired partner offered, what clients were in his or her book, what pricing and other arrangements the partner worked out, how he or she did the work (through developing people and leverage), and had no mechanism to require the appropriate transition of clients, then why would the remaining owners feel any responsibility to take on the departing partner's book and carry the debt burden for it?

Using Multiple of Salary as a Valuation Method

To us, only the "purchased book option based on retention" covered previously makes much sense for the smaller firms that are still very heavily EWYK-oriented. If your firm is operating under a true BAV model, then coming up with a fixed formula, often based on either the partner's share of equity times revenues or on some multiple of salary, makes sense because the investments and infrastructure have been put in place to force the partners to build and manage books consistent with the firm's strategy as well as to build the capacity to work the book.

Multiple of salary is a method that we find commonly used in larger firms, and it makes sense that larger firms would use something like this for a variety of reasons. For one thing, the larger the firm, the more diffused the ownership will be. So, although ownership is still important for voting purposes, in larger firms, the difference in percentage owned may not be all that great from partner to partner. Larger firms typically operate under a more corporate style of structure in which partners are highly compensated executives. Compensation is based on perceived value to the firm, with higher contributing partners earning more than other partners.

For those firms large enough to warrant using the multiple of salary method for calculating retirement benefits, safeguards need to be implemented to avoid encouraging the wrong behavior in the partner's last few years of work. For example, if your retirement package is based on an average of your salary for the last three to five years, and your compensation plan rewards you for working with clients, producing high charge hours, and dollars of revenue, the firm could be in for trouble. In the last two to three years with the firm, the partner should be focused on transitioning client relationships and referral sources to others within the firm according to a plan crafted by the managing partner. If a partner's current compensation (which leads to future retirement benefits) is not driven by transitioning activities, but instead by production, critical transitioning may suffer. A word to the wise: In addition to crafting retirement policies that require transitioning, place partners who are on the way out on a transition pay plan as well. Provide them with current incentives to do the right thing (transition relationships) in a way that won't diminish their retirement pay.

One of the biggest problems with multiple of salary valuation is the potential overvaluation of the firm. In other words, the total of the retirement benefits that could be owed exceeds the market value of the firm. We will provide two different scenarios regarding how this can occur.

Under the first scenario, upon 100-percent vesting of all partners, the retirement obligation exceeds market value. For example, assume the following average earnings for each of the partners, with a multiple of three times salary being used for retirement valuation as shown in table 5-1.

Table 5-1: Example of Average Partner Earnings Retirement Valuation

Partner	Average Comp	Retirement at Three Times Average Comp
A	$ 400,000	$1,200,000
B	350,000	1,050,000
C	200,000	600,000
D	250,000	750,000
E	300,000	900,000
F	200,000	600,000
G	300,000	900,000
Totals	$2,000,000	$6,000,000

Within this scenario, there are a number of issues. First, one factor that contributes to creating an overvaluation gap is that most of these formulas consider an average of the highest salaries during a period, like an average of the three highest salaries over the last five years or an average of the three highest salaries over the last five years starting from the date of your two-year declaration of retirement. The fact that this benefit is calculated based on the highest salaries of everyone gives it an excellent chance of being overstated.

Next is the idea that compensation may not reflect market value. For example, if this was a $6 million firm, then the $2 million in partner compensation would at least fall into an acceptable range of about one-third of total revenues available for partner compensation. But, what if this was a $5 million firm and partner compensation was about 40 percent of revenues? On the face of it, some might say, "Well, if that is the case, it means the firm is performing at a rate better than best practices and, therefore, should be worth more." They would almost always be wrong when it comes to professional service businesses, however. Of course, there are rare occasions when this level of performance is indicative of excellent firm practices, but for the most part, when compensation is much higher than best practices would suggest, it is usually for one of two reasons. Either the partners are (1) working a ridiculous number of hours, maybe averaging 2,800 or more or (2) they are milking their cash cow, taking everything out each year because they don't invest nearly at the appropriate levels in people, technology, marketing, and development. So, in this case, just considering all the partners' salaries could easily overvalue the firm as compared to market.

Finally, under this scenario, if you assume that a firm has revenues of $6 million, with one-third of that available for partner compensation, you still are overvaluing the firm because the market doesn't pay one dollar for each dollar of revenues, but rather, one dollar for the likely retention of revenues. This is why it is common to see a discount factor applied to revenues, like 85 cents on the dollar for internal transfers of equity. If this firm was doing $6 million in annual revenues, and you used a more or less standard factor of 85 percent to arrive at an adjusted value, that value would be $5.1 million. In this case, using a multiple of salary for all partners would cash out the firm at a greater price than it was worth in the market by $900,000 ($6,000,000 minus $5,100,000).

This last scenario is the less damaging of the two when it comes to the possible overvaluation of a firm using the multiple of salary method. The greatest chance of overvaluation using this method comes from the practical reality that everyone doesn't retire at the same time, which is the basis of the first scenario. In reality, the typical CPA firm doesn't retire a partner every year (although very large firms retire many partners in a given year), many firms have never retired a partner, and it is usually the most senior partner in the firm who is the next partner expected to retire. When you consider firms with fewer than 25 partners, the idea that it is the most senior partner about to retire is significant because that partner is likely the highest paid partner in the firm (or second highest paid, but at the very top of the food chain). As well, that senior partner in a firm with fewer than 25 partners is likely to have a great deal of influence about what his or her compensation is each year. Given this, it also makes sense that with each retirement, the firm is retiring one of its highest paid people only to skew the valuation even higher than in the first scenario we covered previously.

Considering table 5-1, if the partners went out in alphabetical order, then we would retire partner A at $1.2 million. Because partner B would be next in line, and because partner B would now be one of the most influential partners and would cherry-pick some of the best clients that became available due to partner A's retirement, when partner B retires in the next few years, his or her salary would likely go up, and that is generally what happens in the real world. Each senior partner who retires is among the highest paid of all the partners. Under the salary method, you are not considering all partner wages converted to a retirement benefit (which may be close to the fair market value of the firm), but rather, retiring each partner at that partner's highest rate of earnings. Each partner is earning one of the highest salaries in the firm at the time of their retirement. Under this method, it is not uncommon for us to see a $4 million firm selling at a value of $5 million to $6 million over the course of multiple retirements.

In a firm with 25–30 partners or more, many senior partners are not the highest paid in the firm; and because only a few partners have much influence over their compensation (except through performance, rather than voting or position power), this greater arm's length determination of compensation allows the multiple of salary method to fall more easily into line with market value and is certainly far easier to implement. In our experience, the greatest potential overvaluation using this method comes when firms with 5–15 partners are using it.

Using Ownership Percentage Times Revenue as a Valuation Method

As we've stated previously, ownership percentage times revenue, although not really applicable to EWYK firms or firms with a very strong EWYK profile, really does make sense for BAV firms. We particularly believe that this method is suitable for the small- to medium-sized BAV firms (up to about $30 million to $40 million in revenues). For one thing, it isn't as easy for a couple powerful partners to manipulate buy-out values under this method as it is under the multiple of salary method. For another, you have to work hard to overvalue a firm's retirement package using this method because it factors in average revenues, the outstanding retirement benefit owed to currently retired owners, and a discount factor.

The potential problems under this method (all the methods have problems—just different problems) lie in the distribution and often necessary redistribution of equity ownership among the partners. We cover that in chapter 7, but suffice it to say for now that ownership interests held should be aligned with the overall contribution of the owners to the firm. Otherwise, the firm can end up paying large buy-out sums strictly due to entitlement because low-performing partners were simply in the right place at the right time, accreting ownership ratably, on autopilot every time an older partner retired. Additionally, under this method, the firm can end up owing large retirement benefits to partners who are leaving no value behind because the firm was sloppy at allocating and reallocating ownership.

The real value in this method is that it allows the firm to have highly compensated partners who have limited vote (that is, a say in the firm's strategy, policies, processes, and budgets) and limited retirement benefits because of the relative value that endures for their efforts after they retire. It also provides for partners who earn an average level of compensation, but who are the real leaders in the firm, to focus on doing what is best for the firm first. They not only have a great deal of voting influence, but they also can earn a higher reward upon retirement for the organization they so caringly built.

Now that we've explained in more depth why we like this method, let's consider another caveat. It is important to recognize that this method of valuation begins to become more and more problematic as the incidences of EWYK behavior and operations increase. The less the firm is operating under a BAV business model, the less sense this makes, because this method, like the multiple of salary method, sets a value that is owed to a partner regardless of annuity stream changes that occur after the partner retires (unless the partner failed to follow the transitioning policies and processes in place for retiring partners). The less consistent the business practices (that is, the less the firm is operated as one firm, rather than a group of practices under one roof), the more you will be putting your firm at risk using this method, because the firm could easily be saddled with retirement payments for value it never even came close to receiving.

Even in firms that are predominantly BAV in their approach to business, we've seen problems with this approach. For example, a partner may choose to specialize in what we call an *island service*, which is a specialized niche that often isn't (1) closely related to the work that the rest of the people perform or (2) something any of the remaining partners want to continue to do. To make matters worse, these island services, particularly in small- to medium-sized firms, don't always end up being leveraged through other professionals. As if that's not bad enough, much of the work done in these niches is not annuity work, unlike traditional accounting services, and it has to be resold continually. When you consider all these factors, what you have is a partner who often wants the benefits of the firm's BAV retirement package, but who

- will not be leaving the firm with a continual stream of income that can be used to pay his or her benefits,
- hasn't developed anyone who can continue to do the work after the partner retires, and
- will likely end up trying to continue that line of business on his or her own postretirement because no one else in the firm is positioned or inclined to do it.

Again, any of the methods in this chapter could make sense in the right circumstances, but common sense and professional judgment is needed to be sure that your firm chooses the right method of valuation for its current circumstances and then continually updates its buy-sell agreements as the firm evolves and conditions change. For example, right now, you may be a growing EWYK firm that agrees to a first right of refusal to buy out any retiring partners on retention. However, three years from now, it may be appropriate because of your size and partner commitment to the BAV business model to switch to the equity method for valuing retiring partners benefits. Fifteen years from now, due to organic growth and mergers, it may be time to switch to the multiple of salary model. (Some reading this might say the idea that a buy-sell could change this much is ridiculous, and they could be right. The key, however, is that the buy-sell valuation and method need to be changed because the firm has changed, not because a senior partner could benefit more from one approach than the other.)

As well, the underlying theme of volume 1 is that the policies and processes that make up the support infrastructure of the firm need to be aligned to protect the firm and its partners but not the partners at the expense of the firm. Another idea to consider is that without manipulation (which, unfortunately, is rare) and with partners always doing what is best for the firm (which is just as rare), an employee's benefits under each of these models could end up being about the same. As you will see in chapter 7, where we discuss equity distribution and redistribution, when we work with firms to restructure their equity, we look at past compensation, book managed, book originated, a partner's competencies, a partner's leadership qualities, and more to come up with a fair share of suggested equity ownership. We know that when we look at the typical leaders in a firm, there will be a lot of alignment among these factors. The difficulty comes when assessing talented, self-serving partners. Book, compensation, and ownership don't align because these partners constantly game the system, rather than focus on doing what is best for the firm.

For many partners within a firm, it doesn't matter what method you use. Each partner will end up generating about the same benefit because they will

- properly transition the clients and referral sources,
- develop people to replace them,
- hand off clients (and all the compensation that goes with them) to other partners and managers because it is in the best interest of the firm as well as in the best interest of the clients,
- follow policy regarding the kind of clients and work the firm is looking for and will bring it in at profitable rates,
- leverage the book they manage by properly delegating work to non-partners,
- commit the time and firm resources to building a right-side-up staffing pyramid while closing competency gaps,
- get other people involved with their clients and referral sources so that they build loyalty from those groups to the firm, rather than just to an individual, and
- support a governance structure that holds everyone, including partners, accountable to strategy, process, policy, budgets, and much more.

Similarly, they won't

- constantly try to game the system,
- create an island service book of business that only they can handle,
- milk the cash cow, but rather, they will constantly reinvest profits in the firm's technology, marketing, and training functions, and
- take advantage of his or her partners because he or she has specific skills the firm needs (a dedicated partner will make sure other people in the firm are being groomed for succession).

We don't go to this effort for the benefit of the unselfish partner dedicated to the firm's success. Rather, we go to all this trouble because there are too many partners who put their self-interest so far ahead of the interests of the firm that it is essential for the firm to find a way to thrive and survive beyond the selfish partner's departure. This situation is frequently exacerbated when historically unselfish partners become selfish in their final years before retirement. This occurs because their egos flare if they feel that their partners are not showing adequate respect for their contribution to the firm. They then shift from asking for a reasonable retirement benefit to demanding an unreasonable one if the remaining partners ever expect them to leave. In the end, most of our clients' firms will have from 30 to hundreds of people remaining after someone or a group of partners retire. We believe it is important that each firm identify a fair buy-out that compensates the retiring partners well for their contributions while simultaneously securing the future of the firm for the remaining loyal staff and partners.

Tools and Resources

Additional Learning Resources

As you know from the materials at the end of the first chapter, additional self-study CPE courses are available for your review. Many of them are all-video courses developed from our streaming video webcasts, and others were created from the various books we have written. These courses can be found at www.successioninstitute.com/PMRC.

Remember to take advantage of your discount by entering the word "succession" into the coupon code field.

Here are two courses we recommend that could provide you some additional insight into choosing a retirement benefit or sell or merger price for your firm.

- The Succession Management Landscape (all-video)—Learn about our findings from the 2012 PCPS/Succession Institute Succession Planning Survey regarding common valuation and terms
- Show Me the Money—Determining the Value of Your Firm

Building Your Firm's Robust Succession Plan

We are now back to the succession planning development phase. As we have covered before, once you complete this last section of each chapter, by the time you finish the book, you will have written down foundational ideas to review with your partners. Once you pull together these final sections, you will have identified your recommendations about how to handle each succession planning area (or, at a minimum, questions the partner group needs to answer), and you will have a document that can be presented for discussion, modification, and eventual approval that will guide the changes in policy, agreements, governance, and culture your firm will undertake to implement this succession plan over the next few years.

Now that you have considered the idea of setting up an appropriate retirement benefit or selling price for your firm, think about some of the changes you might suggest to your partners. Respond to the questions that follow to articulate your thinking about this topic.

Retirement Benefit or Sale Price Changes

Describe which method you feel is most appropriate for your firm given the way you operate it now, with consideration for the changes you will be making through this succession planning process.

- Book of business based on retention
- Multiple of salary
- Discounted equity ownership times average net revenues
- Hybrid or your own special method

_____

_____

_____

_____

_____

_____

_____

_____

_____

Depending on the method you chose and described previously, please note the valuation approach. If you chose book of business, what is the valuation of revenues retained ($1, less than $1, more than $1) and why? If you chose multiple of salary, what multiple did you choose, and why? If you chose the equity method, what is the discount factor to be applied, and why?

_____

_____

_____

_____

_____

_____

_____

_____

If you chose the multiple of salary method, what number of years will you consider to determine the average salary, what period of time will be considered, will any years be thrown out (removing the high and low during that period, averaging them all, and so on), and why? In other words, describe how you determine the average salary that will be multiplied to determine retirement benefits. If you are using the equity method, which years and how many years will be used to determine net revenues?

_____

_____

_____

_____

_____

_____

_____

_____

_____

What number of years are being suggested over which to pay the retirement benefit, and why? This question applies to all methods being considered.

_____

_____

_____

_____

_____

_____

_____

_____

_____

Will interest be charged? If so, please explain under what conditions and why.

_____

_____

_____

_____

_____

_____

_____

_____

Is vesting part of the determination of the retirement benefit? If so, share the number of years an employee is required to be a member of the firm or a partner and why you have chosen that number of years. As well, describe the age required to vest and at what vesting amount for each age, and explain why you chose those discounts.

_____

_____

_____

_____

_____

_____

_____

_____

_____

If you have suggested a vesting schedule, what notice has to be given, if any, to be able to access those benefits? In other words, if you suggested a 50-percent benefit at age 60, would the full 50-percent benefit be available to the partner with a 90-day notice, a 2-year notice, and so on? Or, if less notice than the amount of required notice is given, would the vesting option disappear, be subject to an additional discount, and so on? Explain this package of options and why you are suggesting them.

_____

_____

_____

_____

_____

_____

_____

_____

_____

Should your firm have a mandatory date for the sale of a partner's ownership based on a specific age if he or she does not voluntarily retire prior to that age? If so, share the suggested mandatory age of sale and why you chose that age.

_____

_____

_____

_____

_____

_____

_____

_____

_____

Based on everything we have covered so far, what situations will affect the retirement benefits, and how? If you are having trouble remembering what some of these commonly are, consider rereading this chapter in both volumes, reviewing the 2012 PCPS/Succession Institute Succession Planning Survey, or watching the all-video course "The Succession Management Landscape." Here are a few of the most common issues to consider:

Should transition of clients and referral sources affect the retirement benefit? If so, how?

_____

_____

Should competing with the firm affect the retirement benefit? If so, how?

_____

_____

Should taking clients affect the retirement benefit? If so, how?

_____

_____

Should taking staff affect the retirement benefit? If so, how?

_____

_____

Should behaving unethically or in a way that would affect the firm's reputation after retirement affect the retirement benefit? If so, how?

_____

_____

Should being critical of the firm publically after retirement affect the retirement benefit? If so, how?

_____

_____

Should lawsuits, or the loss of a lawsuit, over past acts of the retired partner affect the retirement benefit? If so, how?

_____

_____

Should uncollectable WIP or accounts receivable or unapproved payables that were not known at the time of retirement affect the retirement benefit? If so, how?

_____

_____

What benefits are you suggesting the partners receive if they have not vested and are leaving or have been terminated? For example, the most common benefit is the partner's capital account or equity share of accrued net book value. Other ideas might also include a severance package or other benefits. Share what you believe this package should be and why.

_____

_____

_____

_____

_____

_____

_____

If repayment of capital or ownership interest in accrual net book value or similar is part of your benefits package, describe the terms of repayment (number of years, paid how often, with or without interest, and so on) and why you chose those terms.

_____

_____

_____

_____

_____

_____

_____

Chapter 6: Establishing Roles and Responsibilities

Key Themes from *Securing the Future, Volume 1: Building Your Firm's Succession Plan*, Chapter 6

- Enabler no. 1: Decision-making authority
- Enabler no. 2: The standard operating procedures (SOP) foundation
- Enablers and synergy
- Enablers and firm size
- Decision-making authority—voting control properties
- Decision-making authority—organizational infrastructure properties
- SOP properties

Depending on your firm size, the business model you are using, and where your firm is headed, you will have different options available to you to address decision making and standardization of roles, responsibilities, and procedures.

In this chapter, we address roles and responsibilities in more detail as well as provide you with some examples to build upon. But before we go any further, we need to explain how we classify and characterize clients because we use that short-hand terminology throughout our books.

Client Classification Scheme

In order to more fully explain the role and responsibilities outlined previously, we need to define for you what we mean when we refer to "A," "B," "C," and "D" clients:

A   An *"A" client* is often defined as one of the 15 percent to 20 percent of the clients that make up 70 percent to 80 percent of the firm's revenues. If you sorted your clients by revenues for your most recent fiscal year, you would quickly identify those clients or client groups that generated substantial fees for your firm. An "A" client is one that you are probably adequately serving that will continually have new projects for you to do and generates sizable revenues for your firm.

B A *"B" client* is one that you are right now most likely underserving but that has an opportunity to generate sizable revenues for your firm. For example, you might have a business client for whom you only do tax returns, but, based on what you know of the business (for example, they might be $5 million in size or have 100 employees), you could easily provide them thousands of dollars more in needed services, help them grow, and create stronger loyalty to, and satisfaction with, your firm.

C A *"C" client* is a client that does not have much additional service opportunity other than what you already do, and the revenues generated by the client are normally relatively small. But, they are good clients, do not have complex situations, pay you on time, pay average or better fees, and are pleasant to work with. The best description of this group of clients is that they are your typical individual tax-return-only clients. Don't confuse the "C" rating with the traditional school performance ratings (where C = 70 percent, B = 80 percent, and so on) and assume that they need to become "B" clients to be good clients. A firm can have all "C" clients and do very well.

D A *"D" client* could fall into any of the preceding classification; however, these clients present at least one of a number of possible problems. They most likely are unprofitable to the firm as a result of poor rates, realization, utilization, service line, and so on. They might be hard to work with because they are abrasive, late payers, or never timely, so they always create scheduling problems. They may always want special accommodations, require services that are too difficult to provide (for example, the client that requires the one governmental audit you perform, which is very inefficient work for you), or only pay your last bill as an incentive for you to start their next project.

None of these issues alone automatically classifies someone as a "D" client. For example, you might have someone that always pays you late, but you charge premium fees for their work, which makes him or her an acceptable client. Or, someone may constantly negotiate fees, but nevertheless, involves you in big projects that are profitable. Generally speaking, most firms know quickly who falls into their definition of the "D" category. At the end of the day, you do not want any "D" clients. This means that your objective is to either find a way to convert them into "C" clients or better or introduce them to your fiercest competitor. In the latter instance, you are looking for these clients to expend your competitor's resources instead of yours, freeing you up to spend more time as your key clients' most trusted business adviser.

Marketing and Its Impact on Roles and Responsibilities

Client Relationship Management and the Marketing Component

Partners, and in some firms, managers, need to take their responsibility for client relationship management seriously. In most firms, this role is purely an economic assignment. However, we believe that the role of relationship management is the foundation of the firm's success and should be formalized, with CPAs being held accountable for doing it properly.

For example, consider the tax partner—the walking tax library for the firm. When this partner is the relationship manager for a client, he or she cannot decide to only talk about tax-related issues. If the tax partner is the partner in charge of a client relationship, then he or she is obligated to understand that client's top priorities, both strategically and tactically, across all services all the time. The partner also is obligated to report that information to the firm in some systematic way, and he or she is responsible for finding ways to help the client, when possible, through extending firm services, referring work to other professionals, staying involved as the client's advocate, and so on. This involves some marketing in the form of functioning as the clients' most trusted business adviser, being their sounding board, and helping them find solutions for their issues.

Marketing—Active or Passive?

Any discussion of partners' roles and responsibilities, including that of being the most trusted business adviser, will necessarily include some coverage of marketing. CPA firm marketing can be broken down into two types of marketing—active and passive. We define *active marketing* as in-person marketing, which usually is accomplished with either face-to-face or over-the-phone contact. It typically includes any conversations that a CPA or CPA firm professional has with a client, referral source, or prospect.

On the other hand, *passive marketing* is marketing that is conducted indirectly through mediums such as postcards, newsletters, newspapers, agencies, telemarketing, website presence, e-mail blasts, and so on. We refer to this type of marketing as *passive* because it can be done through the CPA firm's marketing machine (its administrative support people and systems) and is built around a one-to-many relationship (that is, one letter or e-mail blast sent to many clients).

Active Marketing for "A" and "B" Clients

The most fundamental role of a partner, and in some firms, of the managers, is centered on client relationship management. This critical function involves acting as the most trusted business adviser, specifically including the following:

- For "A" and "B" clients, a partner or manager should be assigned as each client's "relationship manager."
- Quarterly update meetings should be scheduled for all "A" clients and at least semiannual meetings for all "B" clients. At some point, these meetings will become billable, but in the beginning, the investigation necessary to fulfill the role of relationship manager can be done through a breakfast or lunch meeting that is off the clock.
- Each relationship manager, through regularly scheduled meetings, should be able to rattle off each of their key clients' top 5 priorities for the coming 18 months. Client relationship managers should know "what's keeping their clients awake at night" (that is, the concerns and opportunities they are trying to address at this time). Think of the relationship manager as the general contractor. For issues that the firm can address, the contractor brings in his or her own people to complete. For issues the firm cannot address, subcontractors (or friendly outside professionals) are referred to provide the necessary assistance.
- Referral sources should be rated as well as clients. "A" and "B" referral sources should have a relationship manager assigned to each with the expectation of regularly scheduled contact similar to what we have suggested for key clients.

The previously described contact and reconnaissance are accomplished through active marketing. The firm is in danger of losing its "A" and "B" clients when a partner or manager in charge of these relationships cannot at least articulate each client's priorities because the firm is not paying enough attention to these clients and providing those clients with the personal attention and care they need. Although the firm will not likely incur these losses overnight, you can be sure that unmet critical client needs ultimately will attract attention from competing service providers, and with each passing day, with CPA firms continuing to broaden their scope of services, the competitors are more likely to be other CPA firms.

When we discuss the need for CPAs to build and maintain strong referral networks, we're often surprised by how many CPAs expect other professionals to refer business to them but do not reciprocate with referrals to these other professionals. Providing a referral for a needed service helps the client (he or she gets access to needed skills), helps the firm (referrals out create more referrals in, and helping the client increases loyalty and satisfaction), and underscores why the CPA is the clients' most trusted business adviser (because the client can easily access the relationship manager's professional network).

Marketing for "C" Clients

For "C" clients, passive marketing is the best way to keep that group enlightened about the firm's service offerings. For example, e-mail blasts, postal mailings, brochures, and so on listing the variety of services you provide or covering a featured service can be good communication means for your "C" clients. Although "C" clients typically only need one service, such as tax preparation, your "C" clients probably have relatives, friends, former classmates, and the like who could take advantage of several of your offerings, even though the "C" clients themselves don't have a need for them. Unless the clients have some idea of the breadth of coverage of your service offerings, they won't be able to refer these other people to your firm.

In addition to passive marketing, you may also want to use active marketing with "C" clients as a quality referral source.

Dealing With "D" Clients

When it comes to dealing with your "D" clients, marketing is not the issue you should be concerned about. If a client is classified as a "D," then the client relationship manager of that client needs to develop a strategy to convert them to a "C" or better. That strategy could be as simple as

- billing them at 95 percent of the standard rates this year and seeing whether they want to remain a client.
- transitioning this client to one of our senior staff to manage and bill because the client's needs are better suited to the senior's experience level and billing rate.

Alternatively, the strategy could be as drastic as the partner informing this client that the account must be paid current and kept that way, or the client needs to find another accountant.

We are not suggesting out-and-out firing or termination of clients. Rather, we believe in holding the client relationship manager and the client accountable for sustaining a profitable and mutually beneficial relationship. If the client wants the relationship to be one-sided (in other words, profitable and beneficial only to him or her), then adjust the policies and billings to where they should be and let them make their own decision. Recognize that many of your "D" clients have become "D" clients because you created an operating environment that steered them in that direction.

Rainmaking and the Referral Process

For most firms, new business comes in through referral. Therefore, the bigger a partner's client base, the more likely that partner will bring in new business (which simply means that the more clients a partner knows, the more referrals that partner is likely to receive, not in percentage, but in raw numbers. Other drivers of referral success are long-standing service (seniority) and position in the firm (such as being one of the named or senior partners). In these cases, there is an extended opportunity for referral simply because

- these CPAs have been active in the community longer (so they know more people),
- the people they met 20–30 years ago are now in high-level management positions or have achieved a great deal of success and can direct opportunities to the firm, and
- these partners are the named or power players in their firms. Therefore, more new clients that no one knows call and specifically ask for them.

Generally, the bigger the book, the more people you know, the longer you have been involved in the community, the higher your status within the firm, the easier it is for you to bring in new business. Now, this doesn't mean that these partners necessarily will bring in business, but these partners don't have to do too much to make it happen.

The Downside of Typical Rainmaker Models

What ends up occurring is that we constantly reap exactly what we sow. For example, in smaller firms, one or two partners can easily generate all the new business needed to maintain constant growth. Because the issue then shifts from attracting new work to focusing on getting it done, the partners start recruiting future partners who are more technically oriented, and most likely, are happiest working in the office all day cranking out work, rather than meeting with people. This model works great, and the firm continues to grow for a while. But the problem is that it will grow to a point, and then all of a sudden, revenues slow down and start flattening out.

So, what happens to cause that? Well, the one or two rainmaking partners are still bringing in as much business as they ever did, but the situation has changed. Consider the impact of attracting $300,000 of new business in a year when the firm has net revenues of $1 million. That is 30-percent growth—fantastic! Now consider the impact of bringing in $300,000 of new business when the firm has net revenues of $5 million—that is only 6 percent growth. The bad news about a number as low as 6 percent is that this amount might only be enough to offset the business that was lost that year. In other words, clients die, projects end, businesses are sold, and through no fault of the firm, work is lost. At $5 million in revenues, it often takes 5-percent growth or more just to replace the normal shrinkage that will occur from year to year.

Although you absolutely can operate a successful firm with one or two rainmakers and a number of technical partners, this model has limits. The limits are simple: Once those rainmaking partners have committed all their available time to the growth of client management activities (the amount of time they are willing to work towards this objective), the firm is done growing. In fact, we've seen situations in which the partners won't bring in more business because they have a short-sighted view of what it means for the long-term success of the firm, and they feel they are busy enough without the new work. At this point, rainmaking skills become a scarce and unavailable resource. This problem is compounded by the fact that a partner's book of business plays such a large part in the power structure of most small- to medium-sized firms. In order to free up more of the rainmakers' time, they would have to give up some of their book of business, which they are unwilling to do because that is both a source of power and compensation. Therefore, at a certain book size, the rainmakers' time will be completely utilized, and the firm's growth will stagnate. Firms will have to decide whether to expand their current model or consider using a new one.

Growth by Adding Rainmakers

If you continue with the old rainmaker model, you will start focusing on finding another rainmaking partner. In other words, you will look for another superstar to come in and drive the firm (which, by the way, is the most common choice). The problem with this approach is that every time you add a superstar, it doesn't take long before he or she either (1) holds you hostage for money and power (the "I am better than everyone else so I need special accommodations" approach), or (2) once firmly established in the community, splits off and runs his or her own firm. So, we see firms typically between $5 and $15 million in revenues grow, then split off a partner or partners, then grow, then split off a partner or partners, and so on. We've worked with firms in which half or more of the competitors in their local geographic area were spin-offs or were made up, at least partially, of former partners from the original firm.

Growth by Adding Infrastructure and Emphasizing Partners' Roles and Responsibilities

To help you grow through this threshold size barrier and stay connected as one firm, recognize that it is not about rainmaking, but about client account management and marketing infrastructure (which brings us full circle, back to governance, roles, and responsibilities). If your firm is under $10 million in size, it likely doesn't have room for more than one or two technical partners at most, if any. Therefore, it is not about one or two partners bringing in $300,000, but about every partner growing his or her book by extending services to their existing clients every year. It is about every partner staying on top of the needs of their key clients to either find new work or stay top-of-mind with those clients to leverage referrals. Simultaneously, it is also about the firm investing in marketing infrastructure and making sure the firm's name and services are constantly in front of their clients, friends, and professional networks. The firm has to make a financial investment every year to support passive marketing, and the partners have to make the commitment and be held accountable to the active marketing or client account management.

This is why in bigger firms, personal rainmaking skills are often less important. Because marketing becomes process driven, it has significant administrative support, and it permeates the job responsibilities that managers and partners are all held accountable to achieve. Although one or two people in a firm being the rainmakers can work well for a time, it rarely works well for firms above a certain size. Marketing, just like technology, and just like training, needs to be a firm-wide function. Marketing success is more easily sustained when every partner and manager has a responsibility to perform certain marketing activities and play a role in the process. It is about transitioning the firm's culture from focused on the rainmaker to focused on marketing as a function of everyone's role and responsibility. The sooner marketing becomes a core process of the firm, the more quickly your firm will start pushing through its previous revenue barriers. It is critical for you to focus on robust roles and responsibilities that define essential activities, such as marketing, for your owners if you are looking for long-term growth, profitability, and success at your firm.

With this in mind, let's consider a sampling of roles and responsibilities for a few owners or committees and an example of a firm policy. The illustrations are samples based on our work with numerous firms; however, the specifics, limitations, authority, and scope of these roles and responsibilities will vary widely based on firm size, resources, number of partners, and so on. As well, when governance is involved, notice how authority is granted, as well as limited, to ensure sustainable success.

Because employees fill consistent roles in this illustration, rather than roles constantly being customized around employees, hopefully, it becomes clear why this approach allows for a more seamless transition when it is time for leadership changes to occur.

Tools and Resources

Illustration of Partner Roles and Responsibilities

The Roles and Responsibilities of a Client Service Partner

Following is a quick summary of the roles and responsibilities normally expected of a partner that fills the role of "client service partner" in a CPA firm. These partners are responsible for

- maintaining client satisfaction with, and loyalty to, the firm.
- continuously updating their understanding of clients' priorities.
- meeting with "A" clients at least four times a year and with "B" clients at least twice a year.
- identifying additional services that would be beneficial to those clients.
- providing a high-level oversight of the work performed for those clients.
- billing and collecting fees.
- passing down the regular contact, together with billing and collection responsibilities of "C" clients and, potentially, some low level "B" clients to managers.
- maintaining a constant connection with key referral sources by meeting with them periodically (similar to meetings with your key clients).
- leveraging the work being performed for the clients you manage. Partners should be doing client management first; managers should be doing project management first; and staff generally should be doing the detail work.
- focusing on developing all your people and building a right-side-up pyramid.
- implementing firm strategy.
- pricing projects above firm-established minimum levels of realization.
- moving "D" clients up or out, and preventing the firm from getting clogged with bad work.
- actively promoting and complying with firm-wide initiatives.

Clearly, in order to live up to this role, partners have to spend time meeting with, listening to, and trying to understand what keeps their top clients awake at night (that is, understanding the concerns and opportunities they are trying to address at this time). It's not so much about selling services (which you will), and it's not about pushing specific services your firm offers (which will happen). What it really entails is acting as your clients' sounding board and helping them uncover issues they should address, regardless of whether you are able to resolve them.

The great news here is that simply by understanding the needs of your clients, you can live up to our profession's mantra of being your clients' most trusted business adviser. You become the first point of contact when your client has a business problem. Most CPAs are already the first point of contact regarding a financial or tax problem, but that is far different from being your client's most trusted business adviser. By understanding what is keeping your clients awake at night, you position yourself and your firm as having the most potential (1) to help them, (2) to refer other professionals to help them, or (3) to just be supportive of them. All of this builds stronger client loyalty as well as higher satisfaction.

Different Roles for Different Partners

When you are a client relationship partner, regardless of your technical specialty, you take on the role of being that client's general contractor for professional services—that is, his or her most trusted business adviser. If you are unwilling to fulfill this role, then you shouldn't be a client relationship manager, you should be a technical partner. We define these two roles broadly as follows.

Client Relationship Partner: This is a person in the firm who is assigned the duty of understanding the needs and priorities of specific clients and helping them address those needs through

- providing advisory services to assist the client in putting together an action plan or approach to solve those problems.
- providing additional firm services that can directly resolve the identified issues.
- referral of other professionals that can provide the necessary assistance.
- simply being a concerned, objective third party that listens and has an interest in them and their business.

The Litmus Test for Client Relationship Partners

How do you know who is living up to his or her obligation of being a client relationship partner? Just walk up to any partner, identify one of their "A" clients, and ask him or her to list that client's strategic or tactical priorities for the next 18 months—not just that client's tax or audit priorities, but rather, holistically as an organization or as a person, their bigger picture priorities. If the partner can't answer this question off the top of his or her head or after quickly referring to recent notes, then that partner is not fulfilling the duties of a client relationship partner.

Technical Partner: This is a person in the firm that is highly technically competent and whose professional focus is on the following:

- Being the firm's preeminent resource in specific technical areas
- Providing advice and counsel to other partners (and staff) in those technical areas
- Taking on the oversight and project management of the firm's most complex technical work
- Overseeing quality systems, processes, and training to ensure technical standards are maintained regarding the firm's work product

How do you know if a partner is a technical-only partner? Technical-only partners tend to

- always prioritize the work on the floor (in the office) more highly than meeting with clients.
- focus primarily on cranking out work product.
- only talk to their clients about the service they specialize in providing (for example, a tax partner might fully service a client's needs in the tax area, but ignore that same client's needs in other areas).
- emphasize the development of their technical skills and have little regard for soft skills development in themselves or others.
- avoid developing others.
- have a tough time delegating lower-level work to others (although some client relationship partners suffer from this, as well).

Functioning as Both a Technical Partner and a Client Relationship Partner

Can a partner be both a technical partner and a client relationship partner? We believe that one can indeed be both a technical partner and a client relationship partner. As a matter of fact, with firms with less than six to eight partners, this combined role should describe every partner. As firms grow larger, they can begin to afford the overhead of maintaining technical-only partners. Unfortunately, the reality of most CPA firm partners is that they provide lip service to their role of client relationship partner and bury themselves in their role of technical partner.

When small firms start allowing partners to become technical-only partners, they create a long-term success and profitability problem. We find that technical partners typically just function as managers with more experience. If the partners are so busy cranking out the work, then who is

- taking the time to make sure their clients are satisfied and being adequately serviced?
- finding new opportunities to help grow the firm, or at a minimum, replace the natural client attrition that will occur due to no fault of the firm (death, sale of the business, and so on)?

It is poor firm strategy to judge satisfaction and service based solely on whether clients call to complain or ask you to forward their files to some other CPA firm. Technical partners tend to wait for the phone to ring before help is offered, and even then, usually only offer help when the request for service falls into their specialty area. How can we look in the mirror and see ourselves as our clients' most trusted business advisers when the only time we advise them is when they call us or the only questions we want to talk about are their tax returns or financial statements? Client relationship partners proactively seek out what is "keeping their clients awake at night." They care enough about their clients in general that staying in touch has a higher priority than personally doing their work.

Small firms rarely have the luxury of having technical-only partners, which means they have to focus on developing good technical managers. (Even as a solo practitioner, you should think hard about starting to develop someone into a manager level position over the next few years so you are better positioned to serve your clients adequately). The managers should be groomed to take on the responsibility of managing the "C" level and some low level "B" clients. They should also be the project managers for much of the "A" and "B" clients' work. This is the type of organization that firms need to build to free up the owners' time to perform those tasks that only they can do.

Illustration of Managing Partner Roles and Responsibilities

The managing partner is the partnership's CEO. The managing partner is responsible for managing the operations of the partnership and directing its people, within the limitations set forth by the board of directors (board), in a way that the partnership can achieve the directives, policies, and strategies of the board.

Authority:

- Is a member of the board of directors.
- Is accountable only to the full board, not individuals on the board. Therefore, the relationship between the managing partner and any individual board member is collegial, not hierarchical.
- Is accountable for the firm meeting specific expectations as set forth by the board. The managing partner is responsible for the achievement of firm-wide goals, including overall profitability and any other metrics and objectives that are part of the firm's strategic and related operating plans.
- All department heads within the firm report to the managing partner.
- Assigns signatories for partnership banking and other vendor relationships.

To summarize, the managing partner is responsible for the following:

Administration:

- Works closely with the chairman of the board on the firm's strategic plan development and revisions to that plan.
- Implements the strategic plan as approved by the board. This includes developing the strategy implementation plan.
- Presents recommendations to the board on matters requiring board approval
- Keeps the board informed of the firm's financial results. Reviews the firm's financial statements and reports to the board on important matters.
- Continually reviews the services and activities of the partnership to ensure the firm is maintaining a competitive edge.
- Meets regularly with the department heads to provide direction regarding priorities and lead strategic efforts.
- Facilitates and monitors partnership-wide internal communications.
- Ensures that the needs of major clients are being satisfied.
- Resolves serious client complaints.
- Resolves or addresses conflicts between partners.
- Authorizes firm expenditures and purchases within approved budget.
- Plans and facilitates partner retreat and three quarterly board meetings annually.

Human Resources:

- Assuming there is no Partner Compensation Committee, the managing partner develops a draft partner compensation framework (which includes the compensation methodology or formula) and related semi-monthly draw distribution schedule (all to be modified, if necessary, by board suggestion, with final approval required by the board of partners).
- Keeps the board informed of the effectiveness of the compensation system.
- Develops individual partner goals and monitors progress against those goals.

- Develops and monitors key performance metrics for the partnership.
- Develops and reviews the human resources plan for new hires, terminations, and transfers.
- Approves and participates in the hiring process of appropriate staff.
- Approves and participates in the termination process of appropriate staff.
- Approves salary bands for staff.
- Approves framework for bonus or performance plans for staff
- Approves the firm's CPE program.
- Makes recommendation of department heads.

Quality Control:

- Through quality control committees, participates and provides direction for firm policies, procedures, and processes for board approval. This includes SOPs and partner policies and procedures.
- Through quality control committees, participates and provides direction for departmental controls and procedures to be in place to ensure quality and consistent work product is produced.

Scheduling:

- Has oversight over partnership-wide scheduling and ensures the efficient utilization of staffing resources.
- Reviews and approves departmental transfers.

Marketing:

- Participates in professional associations, attends association meetings, and stays abreast of changes in the profession.
- Develops and maintains relationships with managing partners of competing and non-competing firms.
- Participates in community associations, attends association meetings, and ensures the firm maintains a presence in the community.
- Keeps the board informed of the status of new business development and competitors in our target markets.
- Has oversight regarding the overall firm marketing plan and its implementation within budget.

Generally, the managing partner will manage a book of business of up to $700,000. As well, the managing partner will have client charge hour expectations of less than 700 hours.

Partner Group Roles and Responsibilities

Ultimately, the partner group, acting as a board of directors, is responsible for the firm's vision, setting its direction, and creating the framework (for example, budget, policies, procedures, powers, and limitations) to carry out that direction.

To summarize, the partner group, acting as a board

- coordinates firm-wide operations by establishing objectives, formulating policy, and approving goals and programs.
- advises management of the policies it has adopted to ensure their effective implementation.
- protects the partners through the proper management of the firm's assets. This involves the continual evaluation of all financial affairs and management practices.
- provides for proper communications among the people involved.
- creates partner group (board) committees to assist with definitions and objectives of strategic issues.

Matters Requiring Board Approval

- The sale, merger, dissolution, or matters of insolvency or bankruptcy of the firm (in addition to partner approval)
- The filing or settlement of lawsuits
- Insurance coverage limits
- Admission or dismissal of partners (refer to voting methods)
- The strategic plan and amendments to it
- Appointment of chairman of the partner group, officers, and committees
- The firm-wide operating and capital budgets
- Per transaction expenditures in excess of $50,000 per occurrence that are outside the currently revised budget
- Leases of office space
- Firm-wide policies and procedures
- Firm-wide marketing plan

Tax Department Head Roles and Responsibilities

The tax department head is responsible for managing the operations of the department and directing its people within the limitations set forth by the managing partner.

Authority and Accountability:

- Reports to the managing partner.
- Is to be held accountable for the department meeting specific expectations as set forth by the managing partner.
- All tax department leads report to the tax department head.

To summarize, the tax department head is responsible for the following:

Administration:

- Develops the tax department strategic plan, including ongoing revisions to that plan. Communicates the strategic plan to the managing partner and gains approval of the plan.
- Implements the tax department strategic plan. Reports progress to managing partner.
- Presents recommendations to the managing partner on matters requiring managing partner approval.
- Keeps the managing partner informed of important department matters.
- Facilitates regular meetings with the department leads to provide direction regarding priorities and lead strategic efforts.
- Facilitates and monitors department-wide internal communications.
- Ensures the tax needs of major clients are satisfied.
- Resolves serious tax-related client complaints.
- Authorizes department expenditures and purchases within approved budget.
- Maintains required software, software relationships, library, research materials, and other required tools.

Human Resources:

- Establishes annual tax staff projections.
- Oversees recruiting process and makes recommendation of hiring tax staff to the managing partner.
- Makes recommendations of tax staff promotions to the managing partner.
- Makes recommendations of tax staff terminations to the managing partner and participates in those terminations.
- Develops and oversees annual performance review process.
- Delivers annual performance reviews of department leads.
- Develops individual tax staff goals and monitors progress against those goals.
- Develops career paths for tax staff. Mentors staff and identifies and guides future leaders.
- Oversees tax staff training and CPE.
- Makes recommendations of tax staff salaries, raises, and bonuses to the managing partner.
- Develops initiatives to increase retention, job satisfaction, and development of tax staff.

Quality Control:

- Drafts department policies, procedures, and processes for managing partner approval.
- Monitors department policy, procedures, and controls to ensure quality and consistent work product.
- Ensures proper file documentation and engagement letters are in place for all appropriate engagements.
- Ensures consistent presentation of tax returns and related correspondence.
- Maintains current knowledge of tax laws and proposed changes.
- Analyzes client problems and designs and implements solutions.
- Anticipates, identifies, and resolves complex client issues.
- Oversees appropriate tax return technical review.
- Makes recommendations of tax department policy changes to the Tax Policy Committee.

Scheduling:

- Oversees department work allocations and proper staffing assignments.
- Implements and establishes appropriate guidelines for tax engagement budgets.
- Works with other department heads to ensure effective allocation of work between departments to maintain timely and effective client service.

Marketing:

- Participates in professional associations (for example, state society, AICPA, CPA firm associations), attends association meetings, and stays abreast of changes in the profession.
- Identifies additional firm services to existing clients.
- Reviews proposal letters for new tax engagements.
- Develops and promotes industry expertise and profiling of firm.
- Assists in development of firm marketing materials.
- Oversees technical content on website and client promotional materials.

Policy Committee's Roles and Responsibilities

The policy committees are responsible for the quality of our professional audit and tax services. The policy committees are responsible for the following:

Administration:

- Select and maintain required software, software relationships, library, research materials, and other required tools.
- Settle professional disagreements between partners.
- Establish and update documentation methodology and implement training.
- Plans and provides for CPE for all audit and tax personnel. External CPE to be allocated as appropriate.

Quality Control:

- Drafts policies, procedures, and processes for board approval.
- Monitors policy, procedures, and controls to ensure quality and consistency of work product.
- Ensures proper file documentation and engagement letters are in place for all appropriate engagements.
- Ensures consistent presentation of audit reports, tax returns, and related correspondence.
- Maintains current knowledge of GAAP, GAAS, state, and federal tax laws and proposed changes.
- Anticipates, identifies, and resolves complex client issues.
- Works with other department heads to ensure effective allocation of work between regions.

Audit Policy Committee:

- Maintains compendium of internal audit research for future reference.
- Prepares standard disclosures for general use to include new accounting pronouncements.
- Schedules and executes periodic peer review.

New Client and New Work Acceptance SOP

In the past, only new client projects went through the client acceptance process. However, both new clients, additional work from existing clients, or change in scope of current projects now fall under this policy.

All non-partners will go directly to the managing partner for approval of all new work:

A partner can accept a new client or new work from an existing client on his or her own if the project fee is less than $5,000, and (1) is NOT an attest service, or (2) is within the general scope of the services already provided by the firm. However, even though the partner can accept this work, the same paperwork needs to be filled out and turned in to the managing partner for staff scheduling and work management purposes.

If the project is an attest service or not within the general scope of the services already offered, the project must have approval by the managing partner. If the managing partner does not approve and the partner is not satisfied with the decision, the partner may bring the request before the executive committee, if applicable, or before the partner group.

If the potential project fee is $5,000 or more and (1) is within the general scope of the services provided or (2) if it is an attest service of any size, then the acceptance process requires the partner to do the following:

- Prepare a time budget (a time budget is not required if the engagement letter says the work will be billed out at actual hours worked at standard rates with no prearranged fixed price).
- If the client work to be performed falls between January 1st and April 15th when resources are limited, the work must be approved by the managing partner.
- If the managing partner has work falling within the preceding parameters, the chair of the board of partners or whomever is the designated person in the partner group for this responsibility will provide acceptance or rejection of the managing partner's client work.

The client acceptance form found on the following page will be used to document the evaluation process. This client acceptance form will be maintained by the managing partner.

The Succession Institute's New Client and New Work Acceptance Form

Client Name: _____

Industry/Service Area: _____

Type of work (audit/review/comp/tax/consulting/other)_____

Start Date of Work:_____ Due Date:_____

Total projected hours and fees:

	Hours	Composite Rate	Estimated Fees
Partner Time Budget	_____	_____	_____
Staff Time Budget	_____	_____	_____
		Total Budget:	_____

Specific Staff Requested: _____

Pertinent facts about the client's operations, management, integrity, and so on that would affect our relationship with the client: _____

_____

_____

_____

Rationale for acceptance:_____

_____

_____

_____

_____   _____
Signature of Partner   Date

If Required:

Circle One: Acceptance   Decline Acceptance

Rationale for determination:_____

_____

_____

_____

_____   _____
Signature of Managing Partner   Date

Additional Learning Resources

As you know from the materials at the end of the first chapter, additional self-study CPE courses are available for your review. Many of them are all-video courses developed from our streaming video webcasts, and others were created from the various books we have written. These courses can be found at www.successioninstitute.com/PMRC.

Remember to take advantage of your discount by entering the word "succession" into the coupon code field.

Here are two courses we recommend that could provide some additional insight into choosing a retirement benefit or sell/merger price for your firm:

- Implementing Roles, Responsibilities and a Competency Framework in Your Firm
- Introduction to the Eat What You Kill and Building a Village Models of Operations (all-video)

Building Your Firm's Robust Succession Plan

We are now back to the succession planning development phase. As we have covered before, once you complete this last section of each chapter, by the time you finish the book, you will have written down foundational ideas to review with your partners. Once you pull together these final sections, you will have identified your recommendations about how to handle each succession planning area (or, at a minimum, questions the partner group needs to answer), and you will have a document that can be presented for discussion, modification, and eventual approval that will guide the changes in policy, agreements, governance, and culture your firm will undertake to implement this succession plan over the next few years.

Now that you have thought more about governance and key roles and responsibilities required within your firm, think about some formalization as well as changes you might suggest to your partners about this topic area. Respond to the questions that follow to articulate your thinking about this topic:

For which positions or committee structures should you have defined roles and responsibilities? (Place a mark beside each position that you want to formalize or define.)

_____ Managing partner

_____ Client service partner

_____ Technical partner

_____ Line partner (that is, when you have no delineation between client service and technical partner)

_____ Chair of the board or chair of the partner group

_____ Department heads or practice leaders

_____ Specialized niche leaders

_____ Retired or MSO partners

_____ Assurance quality and policy committee

_____ Tax quality and policy committee

_____ Compensation committee

_____ Executive committee

_____ Board or partner board

_____ Other_____

_____ Other_____

_____ Other_____

_____ Other_____

_____ Other_____

_____ Other_____

_____ Other_____

Roles and Responsibilities

In this section, for each preceding person or group that you marked, formalize a draft for board review of the roles and responsibilities prescribed to those positions. Focus on what is expected from that person or group, what authority and responsibilities they will be granted, and within what limitations they will have to work. In this section, create a draft for each.

Position or Committee: _____

_____

_____

_____

_____

_____

_____

_____

Create an Organization Chart for Your Firm

If your firm has fewer than 125 people, in this section, display an organizational chart of your firm, from board, committees of the board, managing partner, department heads, and line partners down to at least all managers. If your firm has more than 125 people, this set of charts should show all offices, departments, and line partners. Show positions as they appear in the hierarchy. For example, partners leading areas of the practice would display in a higher position than a principle or manager filling a similar role in a different practice area. In other words, the organizational chart should provide clarity about who is responsible for what and who is accountable to whom. We have included a skeleton of an organizational chart in figure 6-1 found on the following page to help you get started drawing your own.

Position Election or Replacement

For each major position on your organizational chart, from members of committees to chairs of committees, from managing partner to office partners in charge to department heads, draft the terms of those positions, how those people are elected or appointed to those positions, what it takes to remove them from those positions, and so on. We will address these issues and more regarding the managing partner position because it is critical to get this right, so if you want to wait until after you have read chapter 8 before completing this section, the materials covered there might give you some additional ideas to make finishing this for all the other positions a little easier.

Position or Committee: _____

　　Term: _____

　　How Elected or Appointed:_____

　　_____

　　_____

　　_____

　　_____

　　_____

　　_____

　　How Removed (and transitioned to new position, if applicable):_____

　　_____

　　_____

　　_____

　　_____

　　_____

　　_____

Figure 6-1: Example of a Small Firm Organizational Chart

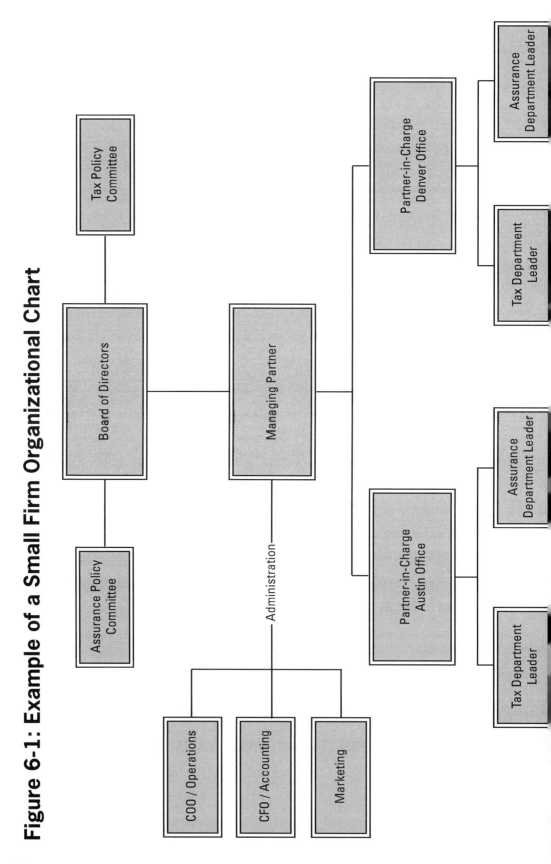

Standard Operating Policies and Procedures, Part 1

In this section, first, create a list of areas that you believe are in need of clarity about firm processes or procedures.

What areas could use formalization or development of firm processes or procedures? (Place a mark beside each position you want to formalize or define.)

_____ Compensation

_____ Timely recording of time—chargeable

_____ Timely recording of time—non-chargeable

_____ Client and project acceptance

_____ Client billings

_____ Client collections

_____ Timeliness of expense reporting

_____ What expenses will be allowable by partners or staff as well as what will require advance approval versus reimburses in the ordinary course of business

_____ Marketing and business development

_____ Nepotism

_____ Severance packages

_____ Employment agreements protecting the firm from managers and staff who are leaving and taking clients or staff

_____ Social media

_____ Telecommuting (what requirements must be met to be able to work at home and under what conditions)

_____ Standard personnel policies, including paid time off, comp time, and so on

_____ Other_____

_____ Other_____

_____ Other_____

_____ Other_____

_____ Other_____

_____ Other_____

_____ Other_____

Standard Operating Policies and Procedures, Part 2

For each area marked previously, draft a policy for review by the partner group.

Process or Procedure:_____

_____

_____

_____

_____

_____

_____

_____

_____

_____

_____

_____

_____

_____

_____

_____

_____

_____

_____

_____

Chapter 7: Establishing Voting Rights, Decision Making, and Equity Distribution or Redistribution Processes

Key Themes from *Securing the Future, Volume 1: Building Your Firm's Succession Plan*, Chapter 7

- The need to call for a vote
- Formal and informal voting
- Equity interest versus one-person, one-vote methods
- Equity ownership and why it matters
- The what, why, and how of equity reallocation

The process of voting on decisions is really quite simple and straightforward. To some extent, the idea that equity needs to be held in relation to one's entrepreneurial contribution is also a fairly simple concept—people who have the most business savvy and are doing what's best for the firm ought to hold a larger share of ownership and have a greater say in the direction of the firm. But, in our experience, many firms (quite often, inadvertently) end up with serious control problems and dysfunction when it comes to equity ownership and voting. Unwinding what has slowly taken place over many years often creates anxiety, but if it is handled properly, that anxiety can be reduced, and the firm will be better for it.

In this chapter, we walk you through our process for reallocating equity to assure that those who do the most and care the most are in a position to have the most say in decisions for the firm.

Tools and Resources

Voting When a Partner Is Removed From the Vote

The mechanism for voting when a partner is removed from the vote is an important policy to understand and put in place. For most votes, all partners, logically, are eligible to vote; however, for votes that pertain to specific partners, it is also logical to exclude those partners from the vote. Two such votes quickly come to mind. The first is termination. It doesn't make sense for the partner that is perceived to be violating firm policy or consistently underperforming to be able to vote on whether his or her termination is appropriate. A second situation would be regarding the removal of a partner from the role of managing partner and placing that person back into a line partner or equivalent position. In both of these cases, as well as others, depending on the firm, removing specific partners from specific votes is a natural and logical thing to do.

This might seem conceptually obvious, but in reality, you need a policy in place to make sure that a minority vote of the partners doesn't become a controlling vote of the firm. For example, let's say you need to consider terminating the managing partner and returning him or her to a line partner role. Let's assume the current managing partner owns 25 percent of the firm's equity. If you were to remove the managing partner from the vote, the remaining 75 percent of equity, at least for this vote, now represents 100 percent of the ownership voting on this issue. If a 65-percent majority of equity interests is required for a vote to pass, then 65 percent of the remaining 75 percent of equity, or 48.75 percent of equity, is all that's required to approve this decision. This results in a minority interest in the firm (less than 50 percent) controlling the termination of a partner from a very important position within the firm. Consider the scenario in figure 7-1, where three shareholders vote for dismissal of the partner from the managing partner role and one votes against, with the current managing partner removed from the vote.

Here is a case, similar to the preceding example, in which less than 50 percent of the equity interest in the firm would dictate the removal of the managing partner from office. Because of this kind of possible outcome, we suggest that the firm have a policy providing guidance for any votes taken when an owner will be removed from a vote. This policy would create a two-tier threshold to pass any votes of this nature. The first requirement is the standard one when the vote has to meet the required voting threshold. In our preceding example, a raw 49.9 percent of 75 percent would exceed a 65-percent voting requirement and pass the first threshold. However, we recommend an additional threshold for approval to provide a sanity check and to be sure that such decisions truly represent the will of the majority of equity interests. Thus, the second threshold to meet, assuming the first one is met, is the requirement for the raw vote to at least be a majority vote of the total ownership of the firm. Considering this second threshold, using the immediately preceding example, the vote to remove the managing partner would fail inasmuch as 49.9 percent would not meet the required threshold.

Figure 7-1: Succession Institute's Example Situation: Assume Equity Interest Voting

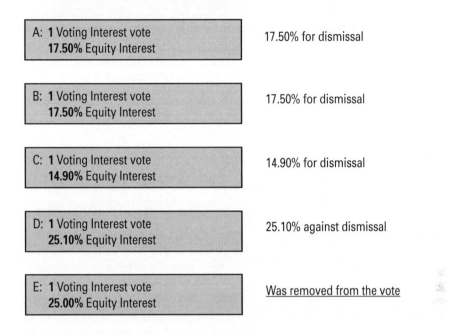

A: **1** Voting Interest vote
17.50% Equity Interest — 17.50% for dismissal

B: **1** Voting Interest vote
17.50% Equity Interest — 17.50% for dismissal

C: **1** Voting Interest vote
14.90% Equity Interest — 14.90% for dismissal

D: **1** Voting Interest vote
25.10% Equity Interest — 25.10% against dismissal

E: **1** Voting Interest vote
25.00% Equity Interest — Was removed from the vote

Raw Totals: 49.9% for Removal, 25.1% Against Removal

Equity Reallocation

Although this process relies on a great deal of professional judgment, it is easily replicable. It contains four steps, with three steps required before we can begin to brainstorm about what equity allocation is fair based on a partner's overall contribution, including leadership, to the firm. The reason why equity allocation is so important in firms that are less than $30–40 million in revenue is that some individual owners will still have a significant vote, and you need to make sure that this voting power is in the right hands (that is, in the hands of the partners who put the firm first and work to make the firm stronger, rather than just to make themselves more money).

As we discussed in volume 1, chapter 7, at some size, firms may shift the real governance to a small group of partners and call that smaller group the board or the executive committee. But, if a firm that takes this step is smaller than $30–$40 million in revenue, the executive committee's governing power indicates that the firm has become sloppy in dealing with equity or voting privileges. The firm tries to make up for its errors by setting up this structure so no day-to-day decisions or compensation issues ever get placed in front of the full partner group.

By now, you probably know that in our opinion, band aid approaches are fine as short-term solutions, but you shouldn't let them become your long-term answers. Fix the real problems. When consulting, we see constantly that the real problems always rise to the surface at the most inopportune time and create a giant mess anytime key players start to retire, leave, spin-off to compete, and so on. It's a common reason people hire us.

If you don't vote on every matter, then start now. If partners have voting power out of line with their contribution, address that. Don't get caught thinking that you and your firm are stuck with what you have. You can change anything if you have the will to deal with it now. You *will* eventually have to deal with any problems you are sweeping under the carpet, and it is almost always less damaging to the firm to address it now rather than wait until there is no room left under the carpet.

Four-Step Process for Equity Reallocation

Step 1

In the first step, we normally begin by having partners anonymously rate one another on several factors, such as those shown across the top of the spreadsheet in figure 7-2 (found on the following pages.

Following receipt of the partners' input, we summarize the data and talk individually with each partner to explore the reasoning behind his or her ratings in a sort of contrast and compare discussion to see if they want to change any of their ratings. For example, someone might have rated partner A as a 9 (on a scale of 1–10, with 10 being the highest score) on business development skills. The same person rating partner A as a 9 may have rated partner E as a 9, as well. However, if during the interview it seems that partner E is held in much higher regard in this competency, we would ask why the two are rated the same. In many cases, these quick discussions create more separation in the ratings as the person doing the rating explains the rationale for his or her answers.

Once we have the final numbers regarding the evaluation of each partner's competencies, we summarize them, excluding consideration of how each partner rated himself or herself.

Step 2

We ask partners to complete step 2 right after they have filled out the detailed partner ratings we just discussed regarding competencies, and in that sense, it's similar to a part B for step 1. We set up a spreadsheet showing the current ownership of each partner (see figure 7-3 on the following pages, for example). Typically, this process is done with the goal of reallocating the equity of a partner who is about to retire. Sometimes, we go through this process when the firm is about to make substantial changes in its operating model or partner agreement, and there is no additional equity to reallocate, and in that case, we approach this exercise to see if the group feels that shifting the partners' current equity is appropriate. This might be done because a new retirement benefit is being put in place, and the current equity of senior partners is out of line—either too much or too little—with their contribution. The process also might be triggered because the firm is considering adding a couple of partners, and there is a need to determine whether the new shares will be taken pro rata from everyone or from specific partners due to their lack of performance over time. We always suggest that our clients go through a process like this anytime 25 percent or more of the ownership in the firm will change over a two- or three-year period, because those retirements and the transfer of that 25 percent of ownership will most likely forever change the power structure within the firm. For that reason, the reallocation of the retiring owner's equity interest needs to be addressed and voted on in advance of those retirements, not after those retirements (because the votes will have already changed pro rata upon retirement if no specific proactive actions are taken as soon as the shares of the retiring partners are purchased by the firm and put back into treasury).

Figure 7-2: Succession Institute's Shareholder Rating Form

Rater: _____

Name	Technical Ability	Relationships	Delegation	Trusted Business Adviser	Project Management	People Development	Business Savvy	Marketing & Business Development	Fitness to Lead in the Future
Equity Shareholders									
A									
B									
C									
D									
E									
Principals									
F									
G									
H									
I									
J									

Each person completes this first, then we summarize totals, calculate averages, etc., and enter in "summary" (see 3rd worksheet).

Rating Scale

Each shareholder will be rated under each of the criteria described above, using a 10-point rating system, with "1" being low and "10" being high. Following are guidelines for assigning ratings to shareholders:

Blank	Leave the box blank if you have had no occasion to observe this person's behavior with respect to this particular area.
1	Unacceptable performance.
4	Needs improvement. Below average performance, with significant potential for improvement.
7	Proficient. Performance is sufficient to meet minimum requirements, although some improvement would be necessary to reach a superior level of performance.
10	Excellent performance. Performance exceeds expectations and represents a standard of excellence other should strive to achieve.

This form is due no later than xx-yy-zz.

Note: Your responses will be summarized with all other responses for anonymity. No responses will be attributed to any individual.

95

Figure 7-3: Succession Institute's Recommended Ownership Allocation Percentages

Rater: _____

DO NOT COMPLETE THIS FORM UNTIL YOU HAVE COMPLETED THE RATINGS SHEET

Name	Present Ownership %	Your Recommendations for Ownership Percentage
A	20.00000000%	**Each person completes this after the 1st sheet,**
B	20.00000000%	**Then we summarize totals, calculate averages,**
C	20.00000000%	**etc. and enter into "summary"**
D	20.00000000%	
E	20.00000000%	
F	0.00000000%	
Rounding	0.00000000%	
Totals	100.00000000%	0.00000000%

Upon completion of this form, please save with your name in the file name and email the file to dom@successioninstitute.com

Please call us if you encounter problems or have questions—512-338-1006, Ext. 104

This form is due no later than xx-yy-zz.

Note: Your responses will be summarized with all other responses for anonymity. No responses will be attributed to any individual.

Some partners will say that you can't take equity from an existing partner. They're right; the firm can't take equity away from a partner, but the firm can certainly fire him or her for underperformance, which, in our opinion, is a much harsher action than simply adjusting his or her power to coincide with his or her value to the firm.

So, during this step, list everyone's current ownership and include the unique variables for your current situation (which might include new partners listed with a specific minimum ownership percentage, retiring partners with their share removed, and so on). If no new partners are being added, you might have a column showing current ownership and a column to the right of it showing proposed ownership that will automatically total to 100 percent, with the request for the partners to work on that spreadsheet until they have determined how all 100 percent of the ownership should be allocated.

If new partners are being added, list those partners on the spreadsheet. Most of the time, we recommend that new partners are admitted at a consistent ownership level and that ownership be allowed to increase or grow based on consistent performance over time. If you know the ownership percentage each of the new partners is to receive, then show those numbers as fixed in the reallocation column, but if new owners can be assigned any ownership percentage, just leave those cells blank for allocation like every other partner.

If a partner or several partners are retiring over the next few years, you can also do this exercise to create a pathway to a final reallocation and then work backwards to see how each retirement would be reflected. For example, consider that one of the remaining partners might currently own 6 percent of the equity of the firm and, as a result of this exercise, the partner group feels he or she should own 14 percent after the retirement of the next three partners. Now that you know the equity starting and ending point for this remaining partner, you could easily determine what adjustments should be made after each of the first two retirements to position him or her at 14 percent by the end of the third retirement.

When we take this "multiple retirement over several years" reallocation approach, we have always recommended to our clients to give notice that management might propose another reallocation process if anyone's performance expectations are deemed significantly different, better, or worse than anticipated because this exercise would be allocating future available ownership based on anticipated performance (versus the preceding examples, in which we are allocating currently available equity based on past performance).

Regardless of the drivers for this exercise (new partner, reallocate among the same partners, allocation near-term for future available shares), the spreadsheet is set up to contain a listing of each remaining partner and his or her current shares in the first column, with another column to the right requesting allocation, and reallocation if desired, for the full ownership of the firm to the remaining partners. For example, the remaining shareholders might only represent 72 percent of the ownership in the first column with the requirement to not only allocate the retiring 28 percent of ownership but also give the group the right to suggest reductions of any partner's current ownership as part of the same exercise.

There are a couple of points to consider regarding this particular exercise. First, we always throw out each partner's allocation of ownership to themselves. We look at it and consider it as a factor, but we drop it from the summary statistics. Otherwise, everyone could be easily motivated to allocate most of the available ownership to themselves just to skew the averages. Although the partner's self-allocation is not considered in the overall averages, it does factor into the bigger picture in this exercise. For example, when a partner is viewed as being self-serving, unrealistic about his or her own contributions, exhibits poor leadership skills, and so on, and then that same partner overallocates ownership to himself or herself, it is just another data point to consider when making final recommendations regarding the equity allocation process.

The second point to consider is bringing in an outsider to at least do some of the tabulations or both the summary tabulations and interviews (which are part of step 3). When potentially negative feedback is being gathered, the value of taking these steps can easily be watered down, especially the data pertaining to the person who will see the raw data and calculate the summaries (or whoever the internal person works for that is preforming this function) because no partner wants to make an enemy of a very powerful partner. For instance, no one is going to be very critical of the managing partner if the managing partner will be looking at the raw data. As well, there is the perceived risk of leaks occurring about who said what about whom anytime negative raw data is made available to an internal employee. But when all the partners see is the summary data, even if the information is negative or critical of someone, it represents the view of the group, rather than the view of a specific partner.

Third, it is common to have the retiring partner chime in on this process. Sometimes, this process is driven by the retiring partners in recognition of their not having paid attention to this all along. If this is the case, then the retiring partners will be voting in this process. An argument could be made that the remaining partners can simply change it back as soon as the senior partners retire, and that is totally correct; but, we often find that this rarely happens because the remaining partners who are disgruntled with the results of the reallocation process don't have enough of the vote to change the equity in place. Had the process not been done prior to the retirement of the senior partners, they might have had enough votes to retain the status quo. Finally, in a recent situation, the partner group compared the results based on the responses by the full partner group to those of just the remaining partners to see how they differed. They ended up choosing the allocation suggestion that included the retiring shareholders.

Once you have gathered the equity suggestions of the partners and summarized them (remembering to remove each partner's suggested allocation for themselves), you are ready to move on to step 3.

Step 3

Gather key data about each partner's performance. That data is typically tied to the metrics you currently use to drive your partner compensation system, which commonly includes statistics such as generated book or managed book, realization, collections, annual business developed, ownership, and so on. As well, take a look at the last three years of compensation for each partner. If the person you are looking at is a new partner, a recently promoted partner, a partner who has inherited a much larger book to manage or a greater job responsibility (such as tax department leader), then the most recent year's compensation, or even the current year's expected compensation, may be a key focal point in this step. For partners that have been doing roughly the same work for three years, then you might consider a straight average, a trend, or weighting (such as averaging the three years of compensation and giving last year's pay three times the weight, pay for the year before that two times the weight, and the compensation from three years ago only one times the weight, and then averaging that). The point is to try to normalize each partner's compensation to determine what number best reflects his or her likely consistent earnings under your current compensation system. The completion of this summary marks the end of step 3 and the start of step 4.

Step 4

This final step is the evaluation step. We have put together three groups of data points to consider. The first is an average of each partner's competencies, which drills down into how each partner provides value. The second reflects the average of what each partner believes the other partners should own and also how much influence they should be able to wield, which is their way of assigning a value to the contribution perceived. For example, we commonly find a partner who might be perceived as one of the smartest partners in his or her field, one that should be among the highest compensated in the firm, but one that no one wants to be in a position to follow. In other words, he or she does great work and makes the firm money, but the partners don't trust him or her to be in firm decision-making positions because of that partner's selfishness. The third data group shows statistics about how partners have been performing in the current environment.

This step is where the process becomes subjective and involves a little bit of art. You have to decide how to weight this data and how it ends up driving a final suggested equity ownership number. We typically give the greatest weight to step 2 (the direct suggestions regarding ownership), then we look at step 1 to see how our averages from step 2 should be tweaked based on those who rose to the top for this evaluation as well as those who fell to the bottom. Finally, we consider the data in step 3 for any final adjustments. We don't use a formula for this, just experience. Because we are mostly looking at data, along with commentary from the partners during our discussions, we try to align that information so the perceived leaders of the firm are in a position to have influence over the direction of the firm. Figure 7-4, found on the following page, is a shortened example of a spreadsheet format we've used.

Before we unveil our suggested equity allocations, we share the preceding information with the entire partner group. Often, some of the partners will want to revisit the ratings and equity distribution percentages they provided and make some modifications. Some of the partners who ended up being rated poorly want to discuss with the group why that occurred because they are often shocked by that realization. But, to be fair, the rest of the partners are often equally shocked that the negatively-evaluated partner didn't know this was coming. After more discussion, and sometimes one round of evaluations just from step 2, the group normally comes to an agreement. In some cases, rather than redo the exercise, compromises are negotiated with a partner or two and then proposed to the group. Those who are performing well are clearly highlighted, and those who are not are quickly in the middle of conversations that should have occurred years ago.

Additional Learning Resources

As you know from the materials at the end of the first chapter, additional self-study CPE courses are available for your review. Many of them are all-video courses developed from our streaming video webcasts, and others were created from the various books we have written. These courses can be found at www.successioninstitute.com/PMRC.

Remember to take advantage of your discount by entering the word "succession" into the coupon code field.

We recommend the course "Moving From Eat What You Kill and Building a Village Models of Operations" (all-video), which could provide you some additional insight into the equity reallocation process.

Figure 7-4: Succession Institute's Example Overall Summary of Shareholder Allocation Calculations

Equity Shareholder	A Average Compensation (Last Three Years' Average Compensation)	B Equity Shareholders' Ratings	C Equity Shareholders' Suggested Allocations	Average of A+C Compensation, Suggested Allocations	Average of A+B Compensation, Ratings	Average of B+C Ratings, Suggested Allocations	Average of A+B+C Compensation, Ratings, Suggested Allocations	Succession Institute Suggestion
A	18.707%	21.150%	19.405%	19.056%	19.928%	20.277%	19.754%	19.500%
B	20.622%	18.686%	21.715%	21.169%	19.654%	20.200%	20.341%	20.500%
C	14.980%	19.576%	15.246%	15.113%	17.278%	17.411%	16.601%	16.000%
D	25.020%	22.519%	25.564%	25.292%	23.769%	24.041%	24.368%	24.500%
E	20.671%	18.070%	18.070%	19.371%	19.370%	18.070%	18.937%	19.500%
	100.000%	100.000%	100.000%	100.000%	100.000%	100.000%	100.000%	100.000%

	Total	Percent of Total Equity Shareholder Ratings*	Equity Shareholders' Suggested Allocations*	% Ratings without Retiring Shareholders*	Suggested Allocations without Retiring Shareholders*
A	309	21.150%	19.405%		
B	273	18.686%	21.715%		
C	286	19.576%	15.246%		
D	329	22.519%	25.564%		
E	264	18.070%	18.070%		
	1,461	100.000%	100.000%		

*Excludes self ratings

SUMMARY OF RATINGS AND SHAREHOLDERS' SUGGESTIONS FOR ALLOCATIONS, EXCLUDING ALL SELF RATINGS

Name	Technical Ability	Relationships	Delegation	Trusted Business Adviser	Project Management	People Development	Business Savvy	Marketing & Business Development	Fitness to Lead in the Future
Equity Shareholder-(Minus Self Ratings)									
A	35	35	32	35	35	35	32	35	35
B	36	28	32	30	19	36	32	30	30
C	32	32	35	30	30	32	35	30	30
D	35	40	33	39	36	35	33	39	39
E	30	29	21	34	31	30	21	34	34

SUMMARY OF OTHER METRICS
Last Three Years' Average Hours

	Charge	Non-Charge	Total	Last Three Years' Aver. Personal Production	Last Three Years' Aver. Book of Business	Last Three Years' Average Bad Debts	Last Three Years' Aver. Realization	Average Capital Account, April 20xx-20yy
A								
B								
C								
D								
F								

Building Your Firm's Robust Succession Plan

We are now back to the succession planning development phase. As we have covered before, once you complete this last section of each chapter, by the time you finish the book, you will have written down foundational ideas to review with your partners. Once you pull together these final sections you will have identified your recommendations about how to handle each succession planning area (or, at a minimum, questions the partner group needs to answer), and you will have a document that can be presented for discussion, modification, and eventual approval that will guide the changes in policy, agreements, governance, and culture your firm will undertake to implement this succession plan over the next few years.

Now that you have thought more about voting, the importance of equity being aligned with a partner's contribution to the firm, and the equity reallocation process, think about some formalization as well as changes you might suggest to your partners about this topic area. Respond to the following questions to articulate your thinking about this topic.

How do you vote? Place a mark by the description that most closely reflects your process:

_____ We don't really vote on anything until we think everyone agrees, and then we vote, which always results in unanimous agreement.

_____ We don't really vote on anything unless someone needs to be told we are not going to do what he or she want to do, and then we formally vote his or her issue down.

_____ We typically vote on everything, with each person having one vote, and generally, all of our votes require a majority vote to win.

_____ We typically vote on everything, with each person having one vote, and with most issues requiring a majority vote and a few requiring a higher threshold.

_____ We typically vote on everything, with each person having one vote. Most issues require higher than a majority vote, and only a few require just a majority vote.

_____ We typically vote on everything, with each person voting his or her equity ownership, and generally all of our votes require a majority vote to win.

_____ We typically vote on everything, with each person voting his or her equity ownership. Most issues require a majority vote, and a few require a higher threshold.

_____ We typically vote on everything, with each person voting his or her equity ownership. Most issues require higher than a majority vote, and only a few require just a majority vote.

_____ We typically vote on everything, with some issues requiring a one-person-one vote system and other issues, typically more impactful financial issues, being voted on based on equity ownership. Generally, all of our votes require a majority vote to win.

_____ We typically vote on everything, with some issues requiring a one-person-one vote system and other issues, typically more impactful financial issues, being voted on based on equity ownership, with most issues requiring a majority vote, and a few requiring a higher threshold.

——————————— We typically vote on everything, with some issues requiring a one-per-son-one vote system and other issues, typically more impactful financial issues, being voted on based on equity ownership. Most issues require higher than a majority vote, and only a few require just a majority vote.

Voting Processes and Your Culture

Based on what you have read in volumes 1 and 2 regarding the topics in chapter 7, describe the culture you want to create regarding voting (it could be the same or vastly different, formal or informal, or a combination of these, depending on the topic being voted up). Describe how you believe voting should be handled as part of your governance process:

The Culture Our Firm Should Create With Respect to Voting

———————————————————————————————————

———————————————————————————————————

———————————————————————————————————

———————————————————————————————————

———————————————————————————————————

———————————————————————————————————

What Are Our Minimum Thresholds Regarding Voting?

The following are some common issues that firms regularly vote on. What are the minimum thresholds you feel should be established to pass each issue at your firm? A majority or a supermajority (66 2/3) are both common thresholds, and although many firms have higher thresholds for approval than supermajority, we believe that supermajority should be the highest level of approval in most firms. There are some circumstances when we suggest otherwise, but as a general rule, as you start getting above a supermajority threshold, you start allowing the minority "No" vote to become more important than a supermajority "Yes" vote. That situation is very dangerous for the firm because it almost guarantees marginal performance from a number of partners as well as the likely creation of factions within the firm working together to protect the self-serving interests of that subgroup.

We suggest higher than supermajority voting in cases in which one partner in a three- or four-partner firm owns more than a supermajority of the firm or when two partners in a seven-partner or larger firm own more than a supermajority. In these situations, we have supported some issues (such as retirement or termination) requiring a higher-than-supermajority vote. But, usually when these situations occur, rather than trap a firm for all time with a ridiculous voting threshold, we might suggest to its lawyers (for example, assuming the firm had seven or eight partners) to write that as, "The voting requirement to pass this issue is 66 2/3 percent (a supermajority), with a minimum of three partners supporting the vote."

This way, the voting threshold is more reasonable and sustainable, but given the current circumstances, the "three partners in agreement" requirement creates some balance as well as provides an appropriate benchmark to meet.

Some common areas that require partner voting are listed subsequently. This is not meant to be an all-inclusive list, but a sampling of topics to consider. As you continue reading the text, add areas to this list that you want to bring to the attention of your partner group. In the left-hand column, note your recommendation for a voting threshold you believe should be required to approve or make changes. Indicate in the right-hand column with the letter "E" that you believe the issue should be decided by an equity vote of the owners or with an "O" that you believe the issue should be decided by a one-partner-one-vote process.

% Vote	E/O	
_____	_____	Changing roles and responsibilities of various positions, groups, and committees
_____	_____	Electing the managing partner or shareholder
_____	_____	Dismissing the managing partner or shareholder
_____	_____	Admission of a nonequity shareholder
_____	_____	Admission of an equity shareholder
_____	_____	Termination of a partner or shareholder
_____	_____	Determining price for the purchase of new or additional shares
_____	_____	Determination of retirement benefits
_____	_____	Determination of retirement requirements (vesting, years of service, and so on) to be eligible for retirement benefits
_____	_____	Buy-sell terms for a departing partner or shareholder who will *not* be taking clients or staff or competing with the firm
_____	_____	Buy-sell terms for a departing partner or shareholder who will be taking clients or staff or competing with the firm
_____	_____	Determination of death benefits for active partners or shareholders
_____	_____	Determination of benefits for total or partial disability for active partners or shareholders
_____	_____	Determination of life insurance or disability coverage limits
_____	_____	Approval of sale or upstream merger of the entire firm
_____	_____	Approval of sale or upstream merger of a line of business of the entire firm
_____	_____	Approval of the purchase or merger of an entire firm into your firm
_____	_____	Approval of the purchase or merger of a partner or line of business from another firm into your firm
_____	_____	Determination of the maximum payout of deferred compensation for retired shareholders
_____	_____	Approval of changes to the transition process for retiring partners
_____	_____	Approval of changes to the partner compensation framework or process
_____	_____	Approval of changes to the special compensation framework or process for retiring partners with two years or less before retirement
_____	_____	Approval of rights, benefits, and privileges to be allowed to retired shareholders

_____	_____	Approval for general operational decisions
_____	_____	Determination of the purchase price of other companies owned by the firm
_____	_____	Approval for standard operational policies like client acceptance policies, collection policies, and so on
_____	_____	Other: _____
_____	_____	Other: _____
_____	_____	Other: _____
_____	_____	Other: _____
_____	_____	Other: _____
_____	_____	Other: _____

Note: Any policies identified in the "Standard Operating Policies and Procedures" section at the end of volume 2, chapter 6, should be included in this list.

Equity Reallocation

Based on what you have read in chapter 7 of volumes 1 and 2 regarding equity reallocation, describe what you believe is appropriate or inappropriate for your firm to consider regarding the equity reallocation process. Remember, the process doesn't require you to change the current ownership, it only gives the firm insight about how well the current equity distribution is tracking with the value delivered by the various partners. Describe your position regarding the following:

Equity Reallocation as It Pertains to Our Firm Right Now

_____
_____
_____
_____

Equity Reallocation as It Pertains to Our Firm Before Our Next Senior Partner Retires

_____
_____
_____
_____

Equity Reallocation as It Pertains to Our Firm Before Our Next _____ Senior Partners Retire

_____
_____
_____
_____

Equity Reallocation Process You Recommend That the Firm Follow

Based on our discussion in this chapter regarding the four-step reallocation process, what is your recommendation to your partners about the process you want to follow (are you suggesting following the entire process, part of the process, your own process; with or without outsiders involved in the tabulations and summaries; and so on)? Describe your approach.

_____

_____

_____

_____

_____

_____

_____

_____

_____

Equity Reallocation in Relation to the Valuation Method for Retirement Benefits

Based on your recommendation regarding the valuation method for determining retirement benefits at the end of volume 2, chapter 5, if you recommended the equity method for determining retirement benefits, how would the equity reallocation process need to be integrated with that change? For example, you could suggest that the near-term retiring senior partner be excluded from the reallocation process, or exclude certain partners because they will retire under the old benefit calculation, or suggest that certain vested partners would also have minimums established regardless of their calculation. The point here is that if you have chosen the equity method for valuation of a partner's retirement benefit, describe if there are any exceptions to certain partners depending on where they are in the retirement transition process or for partners that have given notice of their pending retirement.

_____

_____

_____

_____

_____

_____

_____

_____

Chapter 8: Defining the Managing Partner Role

Key Themes from *Securing the Future, Volume 1: Building Your Firm's Succession Plan*, Chapter 8

- A quick definition of the role of the managing partner
- Why the managing partner is charged with implementation and accountability
- Electing and dismissing the managing partner
- Managing partner compensation

The role of the managing partner will vary from firm to firm, but the role and responsibilities—the expectations for the position—should be based on what makes good business sense. The job should not be carved out based on one person's strengths and weaknesses but should represent current best practices for the position. Similarly, the compensation scheme used for the managing partner's position will need to be based on the firm and its needs at the time.

Structuring the Managing Partner Position

For an illustration of the roles and responsibilities of the managing partner, please refer back to the "Tools and Resources" section of chapter 6. An exercise at the end of this chapter will ask you to think through any modifications you might suggest for the role you drafted back in chapter 6 of volume 2.

Once you have a sample of the managing partner's roles and responsibilities, it is time to determine the framework around electing and dismissing the managing partner. As you know from volume 1, chapter 8, we don't believe that everyone is suited to be the managing partner. As well, we believe it is a critically important position for the firm's long-term success, not some unimportant administrative role. Therefore, we certainly suggest that the firm should determine who it is that has the skillset to manage the rest of the partners, the willingness to hold them accountable to the strategy the group sets, and the desire to build a better firm (not just a desire to work with and bill clients), rather than defaulting to assigning the managing partner position to the largest shareholder or the partner with the biggest book.

The person who is likely to be the best fit as managing partner of your firm is the person who

- enjoys working with the other partners.
- has earned the respect of the other partners.
- will come to work every morning happy to think of your CPA firm as his or her top client.
- is excited about making the firm better, faster, and stronger.
- can effectively implement change. This is the position that is charged with implementing whatever change the partner group sets, not the position that sets the vision or direction of the firm.
- is comfortable with technology because that is a critical tool to integrate throughout the firm.
- wants to recruit and develop great people while constantly managing them.

Many times, the managing partner baton passes to the partner with the largest client base or the best client service partner. This is all well and good if that partner wants to focus his or her time on the firm and pass on most of his or her client relationships to other partners; however, that often is not the case until a firm grows to about $15 million or more in size. In fact, most managing partners we encounter manage one of the largest books of client work in the firm when we first meet them while consulting. This leads them to manage the firm after hours, and even worse, after their "real" clients get taken care of.

There is no question that the managing partner position is a prestigious one. This is a major part of the problem. If managing partner wasn't considered the top position in a firm to hold, then it would be far easier to get candidates applying for that position who actually want to do the job required by that position. We usually suggest that the top client service partner, if he or she would really rather continue to serve clients, take on the role of chair of the partner group or chair of the board. This also is a very prestigious position but doesn't require nearly the time and internal focus that the managing partner role does, so it doesn't require that client service partner to shed clients in order to have time to fill this role. With the person who doesn't want to shed his or her client responsibilities stepping back from the managing partner role, the firm then can take a hard look at who would really be the *right* candidate—not the next senior person or the person with the second biggest book—but the best person for the job.

As a recap from volume 1, chapter 8, we believe the minimum term for managing partner should be 5 years because it takes at least 3 years to implement any major changes in the firm and a couple years to learn how to do the job. Therefore, because it takes time to learn how to excel at doing the work of a managing partner, we would not suggest passing the baton to any partner who is about 5 or 6 years out from retiring. The stage is set to pick just about anyone else, from the most junior partner to any partners that still plan to work 8 or more years before retiring.

With all of this in mind, the "Tools and Resources" section includes sample roles and responsibilities of the chair of the board or partner group, because these are the common positions into which to transition the top client service partner. As well, we have included some language regarding hiring and firing the managing partner. Keep in mind that although this is a fairly short chapter, getting this process right is one of the most critical steps in influencing the long-term success of your organization.

Tools and Resources

Chairman of the Partner Group Roles and Responsibilities

The chairman (chair) of the partner group (partners) is responsible for the functioning and management of the partners when they meet as a governing body. The chair does not have a separate voice from the partners and is bound to represent the position of the partners, even if he or she does not agree with a decision of the partners.

To summarize, the chair

- schedules all partners' meetings (or assigns this duty to the managing partner as his designee).
- presides over all partners' meetings (or assigns this duty to the managing partner as his designee).
- sets the agenda for the partners' meetings (or assigns this duty to the managing partner as his designee).
- utilizes Robert's Rules of Order to conduct business so that the meetings are run efficiently and foster participation.
- votes on all matters before the partners (even though this doesn't conform to Robert's Rules of Order) or breaks tie votes (select one).
- works closely with the managing partner on the firm's strategic plan development and on revisions to that plan.
- takes the lead in working with the partners to set the managing partner's goals and monitors progress against those goals.
- represents the firm and provides leadership in strategic, professional, and community-related activities.

Electing or Dismissing the Managing Partner

In order to elect or dismiss the managing partner, a vote of 66 2/3 percent of the equity interest is required. The partners being considered for this position are not eligible to vote on this matter (depending on the size; for both small and large firms, this last provision requiring those running for the position to be removed from the vote is often eliminated).

The managing partner is elected for a term of five (5) years and shall have a compensation plan unique to that position focused on carrying out the strategic and tactical objectives of the firm.

Because of the substantial administrative role and duties of the managing partner and the natural shifting of client service responsibilities to other partners that occurs during his or her term, should the managing partner step down, voluntarily or involuntarily, the firm commits to transition him or her back to a line partner position with a workload, client load, and compensation package similar to that of other line partners of similar seniority or ownership. He or she will be permitted three years (the "rebuilding period") to build a consulting, administrative, or other service niche practice that is considered to be valuable to the firm. The firm agrees that during this rebuilding period, although the former managing partner can earn more compensation than in previous years, the firm will not adjust compensation downward by more than 10 percent per year unless the average of all line partners' compensation for a year has declined by an amount greater than 10 percent.

If the average line partner's compensation has declined by an amount in excess of 10 percent, then the firm can adjust the former managing partner's compensation down a commensurate percentage to the average earnings decline of the entire partner group. After the rebuilding period, or at a time that the former managing partner has been put in a position commensurate with his or her peers regarding ability to earn compensation, the former managing partner will be evaluated and compensated based on his or her contribution to the firm, just like any other line partner.

Notice of Retirement Required by the Managing Partner

When the retiring partner is also the managing partner, three years' notice is required instead of the traditional two years' notice because of the additional time required to transition this important role. Once three years' notice is given by the retiring managing partner, as of three years out from retirement, a new managing partner will be elected by the firm. Because the managing partner is retiring rather than being removed, the first year of this three-year period is the managing partner role transition period. During this year, the retiring managing partner will still fill the role of managing partner, and the newly elected managing partner will use this period to become acclimated to the duties of the job. At the end of the first year, the newly elected managing partner will become the managing partner of the firm, and the retiring managing partner will step aside and begin transitioning all of his or her other duties and client responsibilities.

During the retiring managing partner's final two-year transition period, the newly elected managing partner will be responsible for determining the necessary transition activities required by the retiring managing partner, as well as updating him or her about progress regarding plan achievement, and is also responsible for the final determination to be presented to the board right before the departing managing partner's retirement as a summary of successes and failures of that transition plan.

Managing Partner Election Process

At the expiration of the term of the current managing partner (every five years), due to notice given by the current managing partner that he or she will be stepping down, or because the partners have removed the current managing partner from his or her position, an election will be held to select a new managing partner as part of a scheduled partners' meeting. The timeline and process will be as follows:

- Nomination—Two months prior to the scheduled partners' meeting, there will be a call for nominations. Nominations must be made by an equity partner, and each equity partner can only nominate one person. Self-nomination is permitted. The nomination period will be established by the board but will be no less than two weeks.

- Any person accepting his or her nomination will then prepare a profile to be circulated to the voting partners.

- At the scheduled partner meeting, when the managing partner election is to be held, one person will be selected by vote as the elections commissioner. This person cannot be a nominee.

- At the scheduled partner meeting, the nominated individuals will each be given 10 minutes to address the partner group, followed by a 10-minute question and answer period. Only nominees may address the group and are to restrict their statements to their own qualifications and desires, not compare and contrast their plans against those of their opponents.

- Immediately after completion of nominee presentations and question periods, the election will be opened, and voting will commence.

- Partners will vote their equity by submitting a piece of paper to the election commissioner noting their name, their equity interest in the firm, and their choice for managing partner. Regarding equity, if a partner owns 10 percent of the firm's equity, his or her vote will be the equivalent of 10 votes. A partner cannot split his or her votes between multiple nominees.

- Partners may vote for themselves, or, depending on your firm's size, nominees may not vote in this election. (Choose the appropriate option for your firm.)

- Once the voting is closed, the votes will be counted by the election commissioner, and summary results will be announced.

When the summary results are announced by the election commissioner, no specifics about who voted for whom will be shared—only the raw tabulation of votes. The specific pieces of paper handed in to the election commissioner will be destroyed without anyone knowing who voted for whom.

Additional Learning Resources

As you know from the materials at the end of the first chapter, additional self-study CPE courses are available for your review. Many of them are all-video courses developed from our streaming video webcasts, and others were created from the various books we have written. These courses can be found at www.successioninstitute.com/PMRC.

Remember to take advantage of your discount by entering the word "succession" into the coupon code field.

Here are a few courses we recommend that could provide you some additional insight into the equity reallocation process:

- How to Build a Partner Compensation System that Supports Accountability (all-video)

- Implementing Roles, Responsibilities and a Competency Framework in Your Firm (all-video)

- Implementing the Partner Goal Process: Step-by-Step Instructions (all-video)

Building Your Firm's Robust Succession Plan

We are now back to the succession planning development phase. As we have covered before, once you complete this last section of each chapter, by the time you finish the book, you will have written down foundational ideas to review with your partners. Once you pull together these final sections, you will have identified your recommendations about how to handle each succession planning area (or, at a minimum, questions the partner group needs to answer), and you will have a document that can be presented for discussion, modification, and eventual approval that will guide the changes in policy, agreements, governance, and culture your firm will undertake to implement this succession plan over the next few years.

Now that you have thought more about the managing partner's roles, responsibilities, powers, and limitations, as well as considered electing or removing someone from that position, think about some formalization as well as changes you might suggest to your partners about this topic area. Respond to the following questions to articulate your thinking about this topic.

Within the context of what we have explained about business models and their effect on the managing partner role, consider the role of your managing partner. Which of the following best describes the managing partner role that you plan to propose to your partner group?

1. We want our managing partner to be building consensus among the rest of us about how we should address day-to-day operational issues.

2. We want our managing partner to run the firm unless an owner objects to a specific issue or direction, at which time we will call a meeting to discuss it.

3. We want our managing partner to establish the budget, set compensation, and run the firm.

4. We want our managing partner to run the day-to-day operations within the budget, policies, and powers established by the board.

I am suggesting that our firm operate as described in item _____ . Here are some of my reasons for making this choice:

_____

_____

_____

_____

_____

_____

_____

_____

_____

Changes to the Managing Partner's Role, Responsibilities, Powers, and Limitations

Given that you drafted the managing partner roles and responsibilities at the end of chapter 6 and based on what you considered rereading in chapter 8, volume 1 and ideas processed thus far, are there any modifications you might propose to your sample draft? Use the space that follows to note any changes you might suggest to the work you did in chapter 6 to develop what you believe the managing partner's role, responsibilities, powers, and limitations should be.

_____

_____

_____

_____

_____

_____

_____

_____

Transition Changes Required by the New Managing Partner

Assuming you have a new managing partner in place or you are contemplating a change from the current role of the existing managing partner to a new role, what changes need to be made for the managing partner to be most effective in this position? The following are some common steps that managing partners need to consider.

Client Transition

Current Client Book: _____

      Reduce Client Book by _____ date _____

      Reduce Client Book by _____ date _____

      Reduce Client Book by _____ date _____

Describe the process you will use to drive this change.

_____

_____

_____

_____

_____

_____

_____

_____

_____

_____

The following is a sampling of important areas for the managing partner to address or significantly improve. These will vary based on your circumstances and your firm's overall strategy. Put a mark by the areas that your firm's managing partner needs to focus on.

_____ Ensure that the firm is always operating under a board-approved strategic plan and budget.

_____ Set goals for the partners based on the firm's strategic plan within the budget, policies, and processes established by the partner group.

_____ Hold each of the partners accountable for achieving their goals and adhering to firm policy and processes.

_____ Develop competencies for all levels within the organization and put programs in place to develop people and create capacity.

_____ Achieve at least the minimum partner profit goals established by the budget and approved by the board.

_____ Recommend policies and processes to the board that will help the organization become more efficient and effective.

_____ Complete the succession plan draft and present it for changes, then update it and present it for approval.

_____ Review partner agreements and propose updates if the current agreement will create hurdles for the changes the partner group wants to put in place.

_____ Create a client acceptance policy or other policies that will help the firm manage the peaks and valleys of its operation as well as improve profitability.

_____ Institute employment agreements for each manager and staff member who has client contact to protect the firm from those people taking clients or staff if they leave.

_____ Establish a policy that will guide the terms and conditions of how retired partners can continue to work for the firm.

_____ Create a pay for performance system for managers and staff.

_____ Increase the leverage ratio for all partners who manage a book of business.

_____ Ensure that all of our partners and managers are regularly scheduling in-person meetings with the firm's top clients to ensure loyalty and find ways to help them.

_____ Verify that the top 15 percent of the firm's clients are satisfied with the service provided by both the partners and the firm.

_____ Put together a plan for presentation to the partner group about how the firm can better leverage technology, if possible.

_____ Put together a marketing plan for presentation to the partner group about how the firm can organically grow its revenues.

_____ Other: _____

_____ Other: _____

_____ Other: _____

_____ Other: _____

_____ Other: _____

_____ Other: _____

Now for the most important part. For those areas you noted previously as issues or priorities for the managing partner, describe changes in the way you operate that need to take place to provide the person filling the managing partner role with the powers and the time necessary to accomplish any of it.

_____

_____

_____

_____

_____

_____

_____

_____

Chapter 9: Building Capacity for Long-Term Sustainability

Key Themes from *Securing the Future, Volume 1: Building Your Firm's Succession Plan*, Chapter 9

- The importance of building capacity through your people
- Developing real people-management skills
- Learning how to develop people more quickly
- Motivating your people
- Culture and people development
- Competencies form the foundation for people development
- People development in three steps
- Setting people up for success with clear expectations
- The effect of your expectations on others' performance
- The importance of values
- Reporting models

If you want to focus on just one area that can give you a competitive advantage and create a greater range of opportunities for succession management at your firm, you need to address people development—at all levels, from the bottom to the top of the firm. In this chapter, we provide you with ideas you can use to create a more robust process for the development of your number one asset: your people.

Annual Performance Reviews Are a Waste of Time

We suspect that your human resources (HR) professionals will disagree with the title of this section, but just consider how much time is devoted to conducting periodic performance evaluations and how little comes out of it. To be fair, the employee personnel files are updated by adding the evaluation reports to them (which are often erroneous), and decisions regarding bonuses or raises are arguably supported by the paper trail thus created (with the bonuses based less on performance and more on status quo). In other words, more bonuses are given based on this statement: "Well, our people are expecting at least X amount of bonus, so we probably need to start there and see what we can afford" than this one: "Here are the clear expectations I set at the beginning of the year and, therefore, based on my evaluation of that performance, he or she should at least earn Y."

As for calling evaluations "erroneous information," we find in the vast majority of cases, poor performers are not evaluated as poor performers, but instead, as satisfactory performers. No one has taken the time to actually watch those employees close enough to identify specific issues that need to be corrected, nor have they taken the time necessary to actually manage them. The standard practice becomes one of noting on paper that a marginal employee is acceptable, rather than openly admitting that as the poor performer's manager, you have been too busy to do this part of your job.

With this in mind, let's come full circle and discuss why the clearly challenging title of this section, "Annual Performance Reviews Are a Waste of Time," is appropriate. We agree that annual performance reviews as a concept are *not* a waste of time, but the way most organizations do them makes them ineffective. There is a great deal of confusion over complying with HR requirements and people development in many organizations. An annual performance review might be all that is needed to comply with your firm's HR policies, but true, measurable changes in performance, if they occur, are rarely the direct outcome of most performance appraisals. If you want to really improve your people, you need to change your thinking and your processes.

The new way of thinking and doing with respect to employee performance improvement looks something like the following:

1. You identify which competencies are needed at each level of position within the firm, from entry level through equity partner positions.
2. You document the competencies to show staff what their career path can be if they do their part (and you do your part).
3. Next, you compare the actual, observed competencies of each individual with the competency definitions for his or her level of position within your firm, and you note which areas could use some improvement.
4. After identifying these competency gaps, you sit down with employees in one-on-one discussions to review your individual perceptions with respect to desired competencies and map out a plan to begin to work on one or two weak areas.
5. You take an active role in lining up informal and formal training, as well as developmental assignments for staff, to improve those competencies you deem to be both important and in need of some growth.
6. You continually monitor and coach employees, checking in approximately every 30–60 days, to review what they've accomplished, provide feedback, reset expectations, or set new expectations. These actions should result in significant performance improvement in those tightly targeted areas.
7. As they get those improvements under their belt, you continue to identify the next area or two for growth, and then you run through this same process again.

Periodically, you can conduct formal performance evaluations, garnering feedback from other people in the firm to whom an individual reports on a project level or other basis; however, these periodic evaluations should not present any surprises. This is because the process outlined here, together with real-time feedback on projects on which they're working, should have the staff on the same page as you regarding their progress, strengths, and any developmental needs they may have. By creating or using tools such as those illustrated in this chapter, your firm can much more quickly move people along the learning curve and grow your own 6- to 10-year professionals in something closer to 3–6 years.

You will most likely need to modify the behavior of partners and managers to make this work effectively. We cover how that works in chapter 15 of both volumes when discussing accountability and compensation. The effort required to develop someone is far greater than the effort required to comply with HR policies. These two processes do not need to be at odds with each other, but we do want to point out that HR compliance and people development, although often lumped together under the same management umbrella, have little in common regarding their focus. The simplified focus of the former is to make sure you are not discriminatory in the way you operate or, more clearly, that you are treating your employees fairly. The focus of the latter is to make your people better, faster, and stronger (and preferably, to implement people development processes in a way that is better and faster, as well).

Tools and Resources

Succession Institute's What You Can Start Doing Now to Develop Your People Checklist

This checklist was created to help you think through what you might want to do to improve your people-development processes. It should help you see any major gaps you might need to fill. If you feel that your firm is making sufficient progress in the area, then the right-hand column can be left blank. If you feel an area needs some additional work, put a check in that column by the statement that triggered your concern.

Issue	Check if area "Needs Work"
1. *Give people throughout the organization the power and responsibility to do their jobs autonomously within established limits and boundaries.* • This doesn't mean that each functional area should set up its own rules and regulations; in fact, that is not recommended. • Instead, create a corporate structure that enables all staff—and particularly, potential leaders—the chance to develop the kind of intuition and gut instinct, usually created through making mistakes and learning from them, that will serve them and the firm well in the future.	
2. *Chart your firm's skillsets.* • Reflect on what kinds of talent and experience your staff possesses and whether they reflect the firm's future needs. • Reflect on whether your staff's skillsets will help achieve your strategic goals. • Skillsets should be developed in line with your strategic goals. • In other words, ensure you have secured the proper staffing—or hiring and promotion plans—to support current and future client needs.	
3. *Identify managers or other staff with potential.* • Once you have staff members working independently and you understand what kind of talent you have, the firm should develop formal or informal processes for judging how well younger staff manage people and situations. • You should also consider providing training for the most promising candidates.	
4. *Understand the difference between a top-notch manager and a leader.* • Partner candidates should have not only strong technical skills but also entrepreneurial instincts and demonstrated leadership talent. • Partner candidates should have unwavering ethics and be trusted by everyone around them. • They should constantly demonstrate the difference between doing what they want versus doing what they should. • Most of all, they should hold themselves accountable to the same standards, rules, and processes that they expect everyone else to follow. • Leaders in accounting firms have to embrace the idea that although technical knowledge is important to our delivering quality service, CPA practices live and breathe on the success of partners forming and maintaining close relationships with their clients and an understanding of their clients' priorities, aspirations, and goals.	

Issue	Check if area "Needs Work"
5. *Mentor promising staff.* • Employees need good technical skills, but they also must understand what it means to handle clients and run a business if they are to take over the firm one day. • Give them responsibility, and if they run into problems, let them work through those problems (with occasional guidance, if necessary) so they can develop into stronger and more valuable employees. • Don't lock them up in the office. Introduce them to clients and to the kinds of challenges that come up in the field.	
6. *Don't just talk about mentoring and client contact; get partners actively involved.* • This step is avoided at many firms because partners want to maintain client relationships without intrusions from outsiders. Although this might seem prudent in the short run, it is a bad long-term policy for the firm. The practice will stagnate if younger CPAs aren't introduced to existing clients and taught how to bring in new ones. • Although the firm should help younger firm members learn to handle client contact, it may turn out that some of them may not have a talent for building client relationships. If that's the case, we may need to rethink whether they are partner material in the first place, bring them in as technical partners (with clear limitations about what that means), or demote them to a non-equity owner status. • In the end, client service partners should always drive CPA firms, not technical ones. CPA firms are in the client service business, and it is difficult to build and sustain a successful practice unless you develop partners that can establish and maintain client relationships. Too many senior partners create an organization of technical partners to assist them in managing their books of business, which, after the partner's retirement, limits the few remaining entrepreneurial partners because the technical partners do not embrace some basic tenets of running a successful practice. • Clean up your partnership house now and start developing all your partners so that they are ready to take your firm to a higher level, not a lower one.	
7. *Include junior staff in decision making.* • Although key decisions must still be made by top leaders, consider how the firm can include younger staff in selected decisions and perhaps delegate some choices to them. • This not only offers them greater responsibility but also improves morale and aids in the retention of talented people.	
8. *Set your firm's requirements, financial and otherwise, for new partners.* • Determine what size book of client relationships employees should be managing, at a minimum, to begin the partnership process. • Determine what level of realization they need to maintain and what kind of staff leverage they should have in the work they do. • As well, determine how much they will need to come up with for a capital account and under what terms.	

(continued)

Issue	Check if area "Needs Work"
9. *Get formal leadership training for the appropriate firm members.* • Leadership training should complement, but not replace, day-to-day coaching and mentoring by senior leaders. It is key to make sure that senior leaders who are coaching the incoming leaders have formal training in this area. • Many mentors try to teach their mentees to be exactly like them. However, what firms should be striving for is to build better leaders, not just mirror what exists today. Firms have to strive to be better, faster, and stronger, not worse, slower, and weaker.	
10. *Set up a timetable for new leadership.* • Determine, for example, whether the new managing partner, will take over when all the senior partners have retired or if the reins will be passed sooner than that. Many consultants recommend that a new managing partner be installed while older partners are still on the job. These older partners should offer advice and support without trying to interfere with the new leader's authority. • The true test of leadership is whether the senior partners put in a system of governance to which they adhered and held themselves accountable during their later years. "Follow my lead" is a far more powerful motivator than "do as I say, not as I do."	
11. *Adequately estimate the amount of time it can take to groom a new partner.* • Some CPAs believe it can take as long as five years to nurture the requisite leadership abilities. When planning for a transition, the firm should allow enough time for the person to qualify for, and grow into, his or her new role. • Also consider that some people chosen to be leaders will not make the grade. • Don't set up a system that defaults to people being named partners just because they were selected for a "partner-in-training" development slot. The test of a partner is whether he or she will embrace and adopt the roles and responsibilities of a partner, allow themselves to be held accountable to the firm, have the personal integrity to be trusted, work to do what is best for the firm, and be willing to work within the governance and SOP systems in place.	
12. *Create a compensation plan.* • A clear-cut compensation system offers the kinds of incentives and rewards that help retain staff and motivate promising future leaders. • Compensation systems should be performance based but change with strategy. • They should include both objective and subjective elements. • Every person should have personal goals that are monitored and constantly updated to help that individual meet his or her objectives while supporting the overall firm's strategy. • Because compensation drives implementation and implementation drives attainment of firm's objectives, it should be no surprise that established compensation levels and programs also support a successful succession plan.	

Examples of Competency Definitions

As we discuss in great detail in chapter 9, volume 1, if you want your people to get better, faster, and stronger, it is essential to have a clear idea of what that means. We have developed a competency model that many of our CPA firm clients use. It provides competency definitions for 8 levels of employees, covering 15 competency areas. We are not suggesting that this is the only model you should consider using; many of the firms we work with develop their own or get models from other sources. Regardless of whether you create one or buy one, you should define what competencies you expect for each level in your firm and what it takes to move up to the next level, and share that information with everyone in the firm. We have included samples of competency definitions for a CPA firm from our model to provide some additional perspective. The first competency example that follows, expanded upon from the corresponding example in this chapter of volume 1, is about job competency for someone filling an associate- or staff-level position in your firm. Notice the competency expected in the left column, which states that the person needs to "demonstrate excellent skill and experience in his or her technical area for an associate level." This is just one competency definition shown as an example. In the right-hand column are some specific behaviors you would look for at that level.

Associate Level—Competency Area: Job Competency

| Demonstrates excellent skill and experience in his or her technical area at the associate level of firm operations. | **General:**

Does this person understand general accounting—basic accounting concepts, such as double-entry accounting, how processes or transactions are recorded, and so on?

Is he or she able to use Microsoft Excel and Word effectively in the technical work assigned to him or her?

Is he or she functioning effectively when using the firm's working paper system and other firm technology platforms?

Does he or she effectively use firm standard working papers and file formats?

Does he or she make sure documents, working papers, and files are all complete and organized for good information flow, numbers tie out, and so on, prior to submitting for review?

Does he or she understand the processes, working papers, and techniques he or she is using on an accounting or tax job, and why?

Audit and Accounting:

Does this person understand the differences between different levels of service (that is, audit, review, and compilation)?

Can he or she work effectively, with normal supervision, on segments of a project, such as cash, receivables, inventory, notes payable, and so on?

Tax:

Can he or she effectively complete uncomplicated individual returns and simple small business returns? |

Senior Level—Competency Area: Judgment and Decision Making

Our second example comes from the competency area dealing with judgment and decision making and is for a senior accountant in the firm. In this example, unlike the previous one, we show in the left column that you can have multiple expectations for a competency, all of which are completely different from one another (that is, competency definitions will likely have multiple expectations) and with more specific detailed questions in the right column to help you consistently and fairly evaluate anyone who fills this same role in the firm.

Is able to make timely decisions.	Does this person have the capacity to review facts and make a decision related to routine situations that commonly arise in his or her level of work in a timely manner?
	When dealing with this person, do you feel he or she readily takes on decisions that can be addressed at his or her level or avoids them?
Is able to deal with complex issues and cause-and-effect relationships.	Does this person appear to have the ability to break down complex problems into their root causes?
	Does he or she seem to know where to start to resolve complex issues, or does he or she tend to become overwhelmed as the complexity increases?
Offers solutions that effectively address problems.	When this person makes a decision, does it appear sensible and on target, even if you may disagree with it?
	Does he or she routinely show good judgment in decision making?
	Can you see the logic behind this person's decisions?

Technical Manager Level—Competency Area: Business Savvy

Here is a sample from the competency area we call "business savvy" for a technical manager (that is, a manager-level employee who manages projects but who doesn't spend a lot of time developing people [except when teaching various technical skills on the job]).

Minimizes write-downs and charge-offs.	Does this person monitor projects appropriately to avoid billing surprises and unexpected write-downs at the end of the projects?
	Does he or she negotiate change orders in advance of doing out-of-scope work?
Acts as a good steward of firm resources.	Does this person obtain optimum value for expenditures of firm resources?
	Does he or she effectively operate within budget?
Manages overall efficiency and profitability of client relationships and projects he or she oversees.	Does this person focus on executing work profitably and maintaining profitable relationships with clients?
	Does he or she monitor profitability of jobs and clients?
	Does this person look for ways to improve profitability while continuing or creating value-adds for clients?

Owner Level—Competency Area: Leading Change

Finally, here is a sample from the competency area we call "leading change" for an owner in a CPA firm. As you can see, the help text on the right is there to structure the expectation so that each person who fills the same role and level within the firm is being assessed based on the same criteria.

Knows when it is necessary for the firm to initiate significant change.	Is this person willing to implement a significant change when it becomes evident that the change is necessary? Is the person willing to champion and manage a change effort even though it may be unfavorably received or resisted by some partners and staff?
Provides the leadership and motivation for substantive changes to be embraced.	Is this person a capable motivator for change? Does he or she possess the skills to persuade and encourage partners and staff to embrace and adopt substantive changes?
Can effectively express the compelling reasons for change.	When this person initiates a change process, can he or she make a convincing argument for the necessity of the change? Does he or she make sense? Are the reasons credible and well-substantiated?
Knows how to manage and implement change.	Is this person adept at keeping the change process on track? Does he or she know how to set up a structure and process to maintain momentum, deal with resistance, incentivize behaviors, and bring the change initiative to completion?

Next, we move on to a sample from our 360° assessment report, which is tied to the competency model. Utilizing a 360° assessment is not a requirement, but it does provide partners or managers with some great insight into how the person being developed is perceived by others across each competency area. If you are like us, a view from those people who work directly for the person you are developing, as well as from your peers, who may be more objective about some of the person's attributes, is helpful even for an employee whom you closely monitor (anytime you are developing someone, you naturally have a chance of losing a little bit of perspective as you become a champion for that person's improvement or dismissal).

In the following 360° report example, you'll see an overall summary of scoring for this owner on the assessment. It breaks down the scoring to show scoring by the person completing it for himself or herself as well as by feedback groups. Thus, you'll see scores from the evaluated person, from that owner's direct reports, and from the owner's peer group (other owners). If this were an assessment of a manager, for instance, there would likely be one more summary score, from the category of "boss." Generally speaking, except when someone clearly has a direct boss to whom he or she reports, we don't show results from any other group than "boss" individually. Additionally, unless there are at least three responses from a group, we don't display those results because when there are two or fewer, unfortunately, we have too often found those being assessed more inclined to aggressively confront those individuals they think might have unjustly scored them. For that same reason, for many CPA firms (that is, those without a clear hierarchy and those that hold a more collegial view of working relationships between line partners and the managing partner), we don't utilize the "boss" category, but instead, include the managing partner's assessment of each partner in the same grouping ("peer") as all the other partners. This often reduces the potential for direct hostility between the partner and the managing partner because the managing partner's individual ratings of a partner are not singled out.

In figure 9-1, the competency areas shown in dark grey are considered the highest priority strengths based on the assessment results, and the areas shown in black are competencies that are perceived as high priority areas needing improvement.

Figure 9-1: Succession Institute's Sample Report Pages From a 360° Assessment

Performance Assessment

Report Card

Your Performance Index™:

83

Succession Institute Benchmark Comparisons

	Percentage
Direct Report	86%
Self	68%
Peer	82%

Total Distribution: 10 **Total Participants:** 10
Percentage: 100%

Group Name	Participants
Direct Report	5
Self	1
Peer	4

Capabilities

Direct Report

Coaching/Mentoring	87%
Ethics/Integrity	96%
Leadership Image	88%

Self

Marketing Focus	79%
Vision and Strategy	80%

Peer

Vision and Strategy	85%
Coaching/Mentoring	84%
Leadership Image	85%
Execution	86%

Constraints

Direct Report

Communication	82%
Vision and Strategy	80%
Building Teams	85%
Industry Knowledge	86%

Self

Execution	58%
Communication	66%
Business Savvy	66%
Building Teams	63%
Judgment/Decision-Making	66%

Peer

Most Trusted Business Advisor	78%
Communication	70%
Developing a Following	69%

Figure 9-2: Succession Institute's Example Action Plan

How do your results compare to these best practices?

55% positive score on having an unwavering resolve to achieve goals
18% positive score on setting clear, prioritized goals
36% positive score on establishing measurements for success
27% positive score on aligning organizational resources
27% positive score on positive score on monitoring progress against goals
27% positive score on assigning clear accountability
36% positive score on allowing self to be held accountable
18% positive score on willingness to confront performance issues
45% positive score on demanding measurable results

What is your plan for improvement in this area?

Action Item	By When	How Success Will Be Measured
Begin to better manage projects under my control by full use of firm tracking systems	5/20/XX*	More timely turnaround of projects; fewer last minute rushes and/or slipped deadlines
For items I delegate, I will set clear expectations as to deliverable expected, budget for the work, deadline for completed product	5/20/XX*	Better staff efficiency, fewer write-downs over time, fewer last minute rushes and slipped deadlines
I will appropriately monitor progress on delegated tasks, roles, activities, with frequency	5/20/XX*	Better staff efficiency, fewer write-downs over time, fewer last minute rushes and slipped deadlines
Work closely with the scheduler to plan and anticipate personnel needs for projects	5/20/XX*	Less ambiguity when it comes to staffing jobs resulting in better planning for the work
Step up and take responsibility for what works and doesn't work under my management	5/20/XX*	Partners will see me as being held accountable
Will be addressing unsatisfactory performance through regressive cycle interventions on tasks, jobs, etc. I have delegated.	5/20/XX*	Staff efficiency and output will be improving, as will staff skills

*Starting dates, but efforts will be ongoing here.

To show some of the details of the 360° report, we have included the summary of scores for the competency area we call "business savvy." This shows the behaviors expected within that competency as well as summary scores by expectation by group ("all," "direct report," "self," and "peer," in this example). Once again, this is just an example, and there are many instruments you can utilize or develop on your own. We are just providing the kind of information that we find valuable when we are developing or coaching others to give you a perspective of what you might want to build or utilize in your firm.

Assessments such as this one are just a tool to help you develop someone else. The assessment cannot take the place of active, continual, and consistent management. The opinion of others might be helpful for you to confirm your opinions, or in many cases, to challenge your thinking, leading you to more investigation, but in the end, your judgment as the person responsible for developing someone else has a far higher priority than a tool like this. Regularly meeting with those you manage, providing them with an action plan for development, monitoring their performance, and having regular conversations with them about their progress is paramount. Tools like this don't take the place of the work you need to do to manage and develop someone—they aid in the process.

Example of an Action Plan

Individual development won't occur unless actions are taken to create improvement in certain areas. Figure 9-2 is a sample of an action plan created to enhance a competency area. This only represents one area from a potential number of areas that have been designated for improvement. In this case, it applies to someone with supervisory responsibilities who needs to improve his or her execution. This is an example when the supervisor of the person being evaluated garnered some great information to confirm the supervisor's opinion that a lot of work needed to be done. Therein lays a key benefit of an objective 360° assessment based on established criteria established in advance by a competency framework. When it's time to confront poor performance, the evidence is there to support your position.

In order to create a people-development culture and implement processes that will allow you to develop a traditional 6–10-year experienced employee in 3–6 years, there are a number of steps to follow.

1. Create a competency framework for each level within your firm. Don't try to roll it out all at once. Focus the initial effort on the group that can provide the biggest gain for the effort spent. We most commonly recommend that the first group for roll out should be the partners. How can partners hold others accountable for performance according to a competency framework if they don't know anything about it or have any experience working with it themselves? So, for changes as dramatic as this one, "tone being set at the top" is important.

2. Once you have a competency framework established, make sure you share it with all the people being held accountable under it. Just as important, make sure that all the people charged with development of others understand it as well. This is not a situation in which each developmental manager gets to customize the competency model to suit his or her preferences. The case here is that we are trying to put together an assembly line production process that identifies the component parts of the product being manufactured, how each of those parts are expected to

perform when they are isolated, how each of those parts will perform when working together, the specific actions necessary to build that product, and the oversight, monitoring, and feedback required to ensure the product is being developed at the quality desired and on the timeline projected. Now apply this analogy to people development because it is the same process we are trying to develop for consistent minimum competencies at every level within the firm.

3. Someone (that means *one* individual) needs to be charged with the task of being the developmental manager for each person you want to develop. Generally speaking, someone can manage up to about 10 people in this capacity. As we covered in chapter 9, volume 1, we believe that everyone needs to report to someone when it comes to development and performance evaluation. Not everyone is well suited to be a good developmental manager. Doing this well takes time, and efficiencies are gained when developing more than one person, so don't just assign everyone as a development manager. Pick those at each level who are best suited for the job, make this effort part of their performance pay, and assign multiple people to each developmental manager.

4. The developmental manager needs training. In our experience, most people don't know how to manage people in our profession; they know how to manage projects. There is a difference. Make sure the developmental manager receives help in learning how to manage and develop people. Spend time and resources giving them training in this critical, foundational skill. The Situational Leadership® training is a great starting point. This is a management course developed by Dr. Paul Hersey and Dr. Ken Blanchard, based on Hersey's best-selling book called *Situational Leadership*, which really created the field of organizational development.

5. Make sure the people you charge with development have some time set aside to perform the important process of establishing expectations, creating action plans, monitoring performance, and providing timely feedback ("timely" can be considered, at maximum, every 60 days, but more frequent feedback is better). Don't confuse this feedback process with HR compliance. This is developmental activity that needs to be ongoing and consistent. As well, the developmental manager should not become totally administrative in nature. For example, if we are setting expectations for a technical manager in a firm, we might expect 1,500 hours chargeable (because they basically don't develop people except by teaching them technical skills; they predominantly manage projects). However, for a supervisory manager (a manager in a CPA firm who has developmental responsibility), maybe 1,200–1,300 chargeable hours, depending on the developmental load, would be reasonable.

6. When appropriate, leverage tools such as a 360° assessment to provide additional insight regarding performance to the person being developed as well as to the developmental manager.

7. Someone needs to provide oversight to anyone in the development role. In CPA firms, it is easy for developmental managers at every level to get overly focused on charge hours and put off the developmental efforts until they have free time, which is often never. Oversight must be provided to those who are charged with people development to ensure that

   • competency expectations are being shared early and often,

   • action plans are being timely developed and communicated, including external and internal training, along with on-the-job exposure to experience-based learning,

   • frequent monitoring activities are occurring, and

- timely feedback regarding performance is being provided, with action plans being updated and communicated at appropriate intervals based on progress.

This simple process closes competency gaps at and between every level, creates talented capacity at every level, and builds an army of personnel that are better, faster, and stronger. We suggest creating a developmental organizational chart. Although it might just mirror the firm's organizational chart, we call it a "developmental organizational chart" because the focus is on who reports to whom for development and evaluation, taking away the requirement of worrying about status in the firm and, when pools are utilized (which is common), keeping a labor pool intact—in other words, people are assigned to the best person who can help them grow and develop.

Additional Learning Resources

As you know from the materials at the end of the first chapter, additional self-study CPE courses are available for your review. Many of them are all-video courses developed from our streaming video webcasts, and others were created from the various books we have written. These courses can be found at www.successioninstitute.com/PMRC.

Remember to take advantage of your discount by entering the word "succession" into the coupon code field.

Following are courses that could provide you with some additional insight for your people-development process:

- Dynamic Leadership™ Part 1 (all-video)
- Dynamic Leadership™ Part 2 (all-video)
- Dynamic Leadership™ Part 3 (all-video)
- Implementing Roles, Responsibilities and a Competency Framework in Your Firm (all-video)
- Interpreting Your Everything DiSC© Management Profile (mainly video)
- Interpreting Your SIPA™ Assessment (mainly video)
- Managing for Accountability (all-video—1–3 partner firm)

Building Your Firm's Robust Succession Plan

We are now back to the succession planning development phase. As we have covered before, once you complete this last section of each chapter, by the time you finish the book, you will have written down foundational ideas to review with your partners. Once you pull together these final sections you will have identified your recommendations about how to handle each succession planning area (or, at a minimum, questions the partner group needs to answer), and you will have a document that can be presented for discussion, modification, and eventual approval that will guide the changes in policy, agreements, governance, and culture your firm will undertake to implement this succession plan over the next few years.

Now that you have thought more about developing your people, as well as the steps you might want to take to enhance your firm's culture and accountability in this area, complete the following exercises to capture your thoughts.

Six Steps To Creating Your People Development Culture

1. Do you plan on utilizing or developing a competency framework for each level within your firm? If so, are you planning on making (building) one or buying (licensing) one? What is the timeframe in which you plan to roll out this competency framework? Describe to which groups you want to roll this out and when.

_____

_____

_____

_____

_____

_____

_____

_____

_____

2. Describe your approach to ensuring that the competencies are adequately communicated to those being developed. Describe your approach to ensuring that the developmental managers all understand how the competencies are to be evaluated and what process they will follow to manage and coach their people. List the steps you plan to have each developmental manager follow (including what kind of action plan template you want everyone to utilize, the frequency of feedback, the process for monitoring progress and improvement, and how it all will be communicated to both the person being developed as well as to the person who is overseeing the developmental manager).

_____

_____

_____

_____

_____

_____

_____

_____

_____

3. Who will be assigned to manage each person in your first roll-out group, second, and so on? Show this by sketching a "Developmental Organizational Chart" in the space provided.

4. Describe any parameters you plan to include, such as identifying the maximum number of people that can be assigned to any developmental manager, number of charge hours expected while performing this additional function, and the developmental performance metrics you plan to monitor to ensure these people are spending adequate time executing this function.

_____

_____

_____

_____

_____

_____

_____

_____

_____

_____

5. What training do you plan to provide to get your people developers better skilled at managing people? What tools do you plan to use (competency framework, assessments, time entry time codes, checklists, software, and so on) to support your developmental managers in accomplishing this task?

_____

_____

_____

_____

_____

_____

_____

_____

_____

_____

6. Now that you have determined the first group for this developmental project and created an abbreviated organizational chart to show who will be responsible for developing whom, expand the organizational chart in the space provided to show the hierarchy. Include names of personnel who will be required to oversee that the developmental managers are spending adequate time performing this function, which includes communicating competency expectations, action plan generation, monitoring, and feedback.

_____

_____

_____

_____

_____

_____

_____

_____

_____

_____

Chapter 10: Transitioning Client and Referral Relationships

Key Themes from *Securing the Future, Volume 1: Building Your Firm's Succession Plan*, Chapter 10

- Why you need solid transitioning
- Benefits of proper transitioning
- A transitioning process
- Penalties for not transitioning
- Referral sources
- Sample transitioning plans
- Transition compensation plan

Transitioning Relationships

In a true BAV business model, outgoing partners will be required to properly transition clients and referral sources. In the transitioning of clients, the outgoing partner will be entering into a state of "systematic incompetence," such that, in year two of a two-year (for very large clients, maybe three) transition period counting down to the retiring owner's departure date, the retiring partner's focus should be on making sure the incoming client-service partner or manager (CSM) is always brought into the full client conversation, both business and personal. Towards the end of year two, the retiring partner should be publicly deferring to the CSM and no longer answering questions without involving the CSM. In year one (that is, the last year of transition—the year before the partner departs) of the transition process, the retiring partner's conversations should be solely personal, and he or she should avoid business issues altogether. If the retiring partner is trapped by a client who insists on seeking advice or information from the retiring partner, generally speaking, the retiring partner should sell the skills of the CSM while admitting that he or she doesn't want to answer because he or she has not been staying as current.

Under the BAV business model, we advocate occasionally shifting clients from partner to partner based on the needs of the firm, the needs of the clients, and who is most appropriate to manage the relationship of the firm with the client. This approach allows a shuffling of clients so by the time a partner is ready to retire, he or she is not doing so with a book twice as large as everyone else's (which only makes the transition process that much more difficult to manage). Managing a larger-than-average book of clients in a partner's final years as an owner only provides him or her with more leverage for negotiating a special deal for retirement or for staying on after retirement. Founding fathers usually want special privileges to transition their books, anyway. Most of them won't want to transition completely because they want to keep a good-sized client base to force the remaining partners to pay them after retirement to stay around and maintain those accounts or to slowly transition the rest over to other partners. They have all kinds of reasons why they don't transfer the clients, from "that partner will just run off my client" to "that partner doesn't have the skills to do the work," and so on.

Proper operation within Continuation Mode (for more on Continuation Mode, see chapter 4, volume 1) will stop this from happening. First, the firm will have SOPs that don't allow partners to keep books after they have retired, and if partners do keep books, their payout is reduced. Second, if it's true that a partner will drive away the clients if the clients are transitioned to them, then this mode puts the emphasis on transitioning early. If partners repeatedly can't retain client relationships transitioned to them, then why are they partners? Why would a firm want key partners who are retiring to leave several weak partners for the remaining partners to carry on their backs?

Continuation Mode delivers a consistent message: Deal with it now. We tend to find that the partner whom other employees think will run off every client he or she gets is much better than everyone thinks he or she will be, and he or she does just fine. The partner might treat the clients differently, but in many cases, that is not a bad thing. In the rare instance that a partner can't keep clients, but the firm decides to retain them as a partner due to some extraordinary off-setting skill (it is very, very rare that this justification is reasonable), the firm needs to know early on that the partner can't keep clients. In this way, the firm can make sure this unique partner's role and influence in the organization is minimized, and he or she doesn't have the ability to sabotage the firm and its next generation of leaders by the example set for them.

Sample Transition Plan

The sample partner's transition plan located in the "Tools and Resources" section of this chapter will help your managing partner create a reasonable, realistic plan of transition for outgoing partners at your firm. The managing partner, working with the retiring partner, would create a set of transition instructions for each client, showing what specific steps the retiring partner will perform over what timeframe and to whom the retiring partner will be transitioning the client.

Periodically—at least quarterly—the managing partner will be meeting with the retiring partner to review the status and note any issues of noncompliance. Typically, smaller clients don't need as much time for transitioning as the larger, more complex clients, but you'll still want to keep a record of transition activities performed with them, as well (see some sample instructions for using the transition template in the "Tools and Resources" section).

Similarly, this same type of form (modified to fit your situation) and process should be used to assist with transitioning referral source relationships to others within the firm.

Tools and Resources

The key to transition is the action plan that the transitioning partner needs to follow for each client. As we covered in chapter 10, volume 1, you will see how those instructions get communicated through the transition process template.

For a small tax client, the directive could be as simple as enacting a one-year transition and turning it over to the person assigned to take over that account. For example, the action plan might be something like the following:

- Get on the phone and introduce Cheri to personal tax client A in December, or have her meet the client, if the client comes in and drops off his or her information.
- Have Cheri conduct the tax return interview for client A.
- Allow Cheri to manage the entire tax return preparation process for client A.
- When client A comes in to pick up the tax return, have the client meet with Cheri to go over it.
- During that meeting, come down and pop into the meeting for no more than five minutes. In the meeting, mention that you are happy to see the client and comment about how excited you are that you were able to get them assigned to Cheri, whom you believe is one of the most talented people in the firm.

As you can see, this action plan is about getting out of the way and being supportive of the change being made. It only covers about a four-month period in the entire two-year transition plan, which is all that might be needed for smaller clients. On the other hand, for larger clients, the transition process might take the full two years to execute, and the instructions might be broken down into shorter periods, such as every six months, to provide more relevant directives (for example, consider a larger client for whom the firm does planning and consulting). Following is what the action plan for the first six months of the transition period might resemble.

- Take John along and introduce him in either a breakfast or lunch meeting with the client as the partner taking over his or her account within the first 30 days of the two-year transition process.
- Set it up so that John has a reason to interact with the client as part of the preparation process for the client's current year executive retreat.
- John should be there to observe the entire two-day retreat facilitation.
- Coach John in advance on leading some part of the facilitation process during the retreat so that the client can see him in action and get comfortable with his participation.
- Have John follow up with the client on his own within three weeks after the retreat to go over the notes taken, actions identified, and assignments made.

In this situation, while the retiring partner is still in control of the engagement for the first six months, the actions are all about allowing the client to become comfortable with the skills and involvement of the new partner.

Given the preceding discussion, let's convert this information to the sample Transition Form document (Figure 10-1).

Figure 10-1: Succession Institute's Sample Transition Form

Partner Name: _____

Planned Retirement Date: _____

Years Until Retirement (3, 2, or 1): _____

Client or Group Name: _____   New Client Service Partner: _____

Planned Action/Activity: _____

Start By: _____ Completed By: _____ Done Properly (Y/N): _____

Planned Action/Activity: _____

Start By: _____ Completed By: _____ Done Properly (Y/N): _____

Planned Action/Activity: _____

Start By: _____ Completed By: _____ Done Properly (Y/N): _____

1st Qtr	2nd Qtr	3rd Qtr	4th Qtr	5th Qtr	6th Qtr	7th Qtr	8th Qtr

Client or Group Name: _____   New Client Service Partner: _____

Planned Action/Activity: _____

Start By: _____ Completed By: _____ Done Properly (Y/N): _____

Planned Action/Activity: _____

Start By: _____ Completed By: _____ Done Properly (Y/N): _____

Planned Action/Activity: _____

Start By: _____ Completed By: _____ Done Properly (Y/N): _____

1st Qtr	2nd Qtr	3rd Qtr	4th Qtr	5th Qtr	6th Qtr	7th Qtr	8th Qtr

Partner Name: Dom Cingoranelli   Planned Retirement Date: 12/31/2015

Years Until Retirement (3, 2, or 1): 2

For smaller tax clients, the directive could be as simple as those described subsequently and really only only affect about one year of a two-year transition. As you can see, this action plan is simply about getting out of the way and being supportive of the change being made. Notice that while I used the preceding form as a template, you will want to change this form so that it works for you and the client transitions that need to occur.

Client or Group Name: 1040 Tax Only Clients (see list that follows)

New Client Service Partner: Cheri Martz

	Done Properly:	
Joe Smith	Done Properly:	Y
Jack Thomas	Done Properly:	Y
Sue and Tom Raines	Done Properly:	
Bill and Mary Fowler	Done Properly:	Y
Michelle Pearce	Done Properly:	Y
Rob and Laura Christenson	Done Properly:	Y
Mike and Beth Tomlinson	Done Properly:	
Pat and Stan Winters	Done Properly:	
Rory and Gerry Calhoun	Done Properly:	Y
Jan and Rick Houseman	Done Properly:	
Nicky Houseman	Done Properly:	Y
Billy Houseman	Done Properly:	
Roger and Anita Moore	Done Properly:	Y

Planned Action/Activity: Get on the phone and introduce Cheri to each personal tax client in December, or have her meet the client, if the client comes in and drops off their information around that time.

Start By: December 1, 2014   **Completed By:** January 15, 2015

Planned Action/Activity: Coordinate with Cheri a time that will work for both of you for the tax return interview. When a client scheduled to work with Cheri comes in, be in the room to personally introduce Cheri, tell the client how lucky he or she is that you were able to get him or her assigned to Cheri, and after a few minutes of rapport building, excuse yourself and let Cheri handle the interview. If she needs something, she will call you, so stay around the office during these appointments.

Start By: December 1, 2014   **Completed By:** April 15, 2015

(continued)

Planned Action/Activity: Allow Cheri to manage the entire tax return preparation process for this client. In other words, don't take over for her. If you see a problem, first talk with Cheri. If you don't agree to the same resolution, bring the issue to the managing partner for a final resolution of the matter.

Start By: December 1, 2014   **Completed By:** April 15, 2015

Planned Action/Activity: Cheri will go over the tax return with clients who come in to pick it up. If those meetings are scheduled, rather than just walk-ins, make sure you are in the office at the scheduled time to stop by and say "Hi." But, if a client asks a question while you are in the room, refer them to Cheri, even if you know the answer, so that she has the opportunity to assure the client they are in good hands. Even if Cheri doesn't know the answer and you do, allow her to defer the answer and share your insight with Cheri after the client leaves, then Cheri can follow up with the information requested.

Start By: December 1, 2014   **Completed By:** April 15, 2015

Planned Action/Activity: After the December 1, 2014, kickoff for this transition group, any time one of these clients asks you tax questions, whether they call you at the office or see you in a personal setting, refer them to Cheri by saying something like "Let me talk with Cheri; she is more familiar with your situation, and one of us will get back to you this afternoon or tomorrow." Have Cheri follow up with the answer unless she asks you to interact for her because of lack of timely availability. The point is that once December 1, 2014 arrives, don't undo the transition process by undermining Cheri as a result of answering client questions that would allow her the opportunity to build more rapport.

Start By: December 1, 2014   **Completed By:** December 31, 2015

In this situation, because we put in a placeholder to check off each client, the quarterly boxes shifted from an acknowledgement of how the plan was being followed to a note that five quarterly reviews have been held, and the status of each client in this grouping was shared with the retiring partner at that time.

8th Qtr	7th Qtr	6th Qtr	5th Qtr	4th Qtr	3rd Qtr	2nd Qtr	1st Qtr
Held Review	Held Review	Held Review	Held Review	Held Review			

Now, let's consider the transition directive for a single larger client. Consider that this is a client that engages the firm for both planning and consulting. The transition plan, because of the number of instructions, might only cover six months at a time or the first year, but if someone wanted to spend the time mapping out all the steps, it could be for the entire two-year transition period. With larger clients like this one, it is hard to say what the right steps should be nine months from now because we need to understand how well the transition is working to determine if more or less interaction is required. So, consider the following action plan for the first six months of the transition period:

Client or Group Name: Winters Construction, LLC
New Client Service Partner: John Cameron

Instruction Period   June 1, 2014 through December 31, 2014

Planned Action/Activity: Take John along and introduce him in either a breakfast or lunch meeting with the client as the partner taking over his or her account within the first 30 days of the two-year transition process.

    Start By: June 1, 2014   **Completed By:** June 30, 2014   **Done Properly (Y/N):**

Planned Action/Activity: Set it up so that John has a reason to interact with the client as part of the preparation process for this year's executive retreat in August.

    Start By: July 1, 2014   **Completed By:** August 10, 2014   **Done Properly (Y/N):**

Planned Action/Activity: John should observe and participate in the entire two-day retreat facilitation. Identify and coach John in advance on leading some part of the facilitation process during the retreat so that the client can see him in action and get comfortable interacting with him.

    Start By: **Completed By:** August 31, 2014   **Done Properly (Y/N):**

Planned Action/Activity: Make sure John, assuming an opportunity arises, is assigned during the meeting some part of the normal follow-up work that you normally do to complete the planning process.

    Start By: **Completed By:** August 31, 2014   **Done Properly (Y/N):**

Planned Action/Activity: Have John follow up with the client on his own within three weeks after the retreat to go over the notes taken, actions identified, and assignments made.

    Start By: August 31, 2014   **Completed By:** September 21, 2014   **Done Properly (Y/N):**

Planned Action/Activity: Have John lead the planning meeting in which you are working through the draft plan and beginning to integrate it with the budget in preparation for the planning summary meeting with the entire executive team.

    Start By: October 15, 2014   **Completed By:** November 15, 2014   **Done Properly (Y/N):**

1st Qtr	2nd Qtr	3rd Qtr	4th Qtr	5th Qtr	6th Qtr	7th Qtr	8th Qtr

It is up to the managing partner to monitor the performance of the retiring partner and determine how well action steps have been accomplished. Notice at the bottom of the large client example the blocks with labels "8th Qtr" through "1st Qtr." This worksheet assumes that the managing partner is going to evaluate the transition plan performance each quarter (however, if you are using a two-year semiannual review process, change and retitle the blocks accordingly). Assuming the retiring partner is performing as expected, you would enter a "Y" in that quarter's block, or, if not performing, an "N." In the end, if the retiring partner has an N denoting the retiring partner's lack of transitioning of a specific client, should that client leave the firm, we recommend one year's average annual fees be deducted from the retiring partner's retirement benefit. If there is a Y in the last block for a client, regardless of whether that client leaves the firm, there should be no penalty to the retiring partner.

One commonly asked question is, What if someone had Ys for almost all the quarters and then got Ns in the last few? It seems like the managing partner has too much power over this situation. For the record, if someone has Ys in most of the blocks and Ns in the final few, one of two bad things has happened. Either the managing partner has become totally unethical in his or her evaluation (which we have never seen and would likely be overruled by the partner group, were it to happen) or, more likely, the retiring partner took actions with his or her clients that totally reversed the transition process. Consider this real life example. At one firm, the retiring partner, in his last few months of the transition period, told all of his clients that they should move to a different firm because his remaining partners were idiots and did not know what they were doing.

Because the retiring partners have so much to lose if they do not transition their clients properly under this approach (one year's annual fee deducted from their retirement benefit potentially anytime during the benefit payout period) and so much to gain by simply following the process (regardless of whether the clients leave, their benefit is protected), our experience is that they will follow the plan. But, the managing partner has a critical role to fill in this situation, as well. If the managing partner does not identify the action steps for each client in advance (do the work laid out previously), does not monitor whether the retiring partner fulfilled those expectations, and does not meet with the retiring partner on some consistent basis to provide feedback about progress (that is, assess either quarterly or semiannually whether each client or client group is considered to be on track to being properly transitioned at that time), then this process won't work. This is about two-way accountability for both the managing partner and the retiring partner.

If you follow this process, you will find one of two things. First, if it flows smoothly, you will be preventing the single most commonly violated process in succession management, and you will experience proper client transition. Second, if the process is being ignored, you will find out much earlier that the retiring partner is not going to properly transition his or her clients, and you can start taking action to salvage whatever relationships you can. The good news is that even if you can't salvage those clients, you at least will have an offset against the retiring partner's retirement benefit to ease the financial burden on the firm.

As you look at each client or group of clients, remember to modify the transition form to fit whatever you think will provide the best instructions for your retiring partners to help them understand what you want them to do and when to transition each client or client group.

You may be wondering if this process takes a lot of time. Yes, this process will take time. Consider the following:

- Consider any policy changes you want to make to give the transition process greater accountability and motivate retiring partners to comply with the process.

- Think about how to approach transitioning the client book the retiring partner is managing—which clients will have an instruction set and timetable as a group and which will be handled individually.

- Decide who will be charged with taking over each account.

- Determine what steps you should outline to make sure a client is properly transitioned. For example, if a particular client is a personal friend of the retiring partner, a large client, and someone the retiring partner often meets with socially, you will need to include steps in the plan to make sure that social outings don't undermine the transition work going on during the business week. This could include instructions as benign as "When you are out with client X socially, if questions are asked about the workplace, whenever possible, do not answer those questions but defer them by saying, 'Let me get with the partner taking over for me, get his or her thoughts, and get back to you.'" Or, those instructions could be direct and aggressive (in situations when you know the partner does not want to hand off this client), such as, "If we are made aware of conversations occurring between you and client X during your social activities that are critical of the firm or of the partner taking over, regardless of the actions you take in your transition plan, this client will be considered improperly transitioned."

- Come up with a plan for communicating the transition process to the retiring partner, deciding how you are going to monitor it, determining at what frequency the feedback will occur, and what documentation will be considered adequate (just verbal commentary from the retiring partner versus commentary with both the retiring partner and the partner taking over) and so on.

- Lay out an effective and efficient process for escalating the determinations made by the managing partner about whether a client has been deemed improperly transitioned.

- Verify that the partner taking over is actively involved and providing the necessary time and support to this process because effective transition requires action by both the retiring partner as well as the partner taking over.

- Establish trickle-down transition plans. For every person inheriting clients from a transition process, it is probable that those people will need to transition some of their existing work to others in order to free up enough time to take on this higher level workload being assigned. Therefore, once the initial transition plan for the retiring partner is conceptualized, abbreviated plans will need to be established so that the appropriate capacity is freed up throughout the organization for the transition process to work.

- Establish compensation performance goals tied to the transition process for each person involved to ensure accountability and execution of the plan.

- Monitor all the transition plans in place, provide timely feedback, and enforcing accountability through compensation adjustments up or down based on performance for each person involved in the transition process.

But, if you take the time to do this right, you will find that you

- protect the value of your firm (by penalizing retiring partners who don't leave the value of their work in the firm).

- ensure a logical and orderly phasing out for the retiring partners.
- help the younger partners or managers build strong relationships with the firm's client base.
- begin to get those same younger people to step into their place as future leaders of the firm.

Additional Learning Resources

As you know from the materials at the end of the first chapter, additional self-study CPE courses are available for your review. Many of them are all-video courses developed from our streaming video webcasts, and others were created from the various books we have written. These courses can be found at www.successioninstitute.com/PMRC.

Remember to take advantage of your discount by entering the word "succession" into the coupon code field.

Here are a couple of courses we recommend that could provide you some additional insight into strengthening your transition process.

- Retirement Issues and Strategies (all-video)
- Pulling It All Together with a Partner/Shareholder Agreement (all-video)

Building Your Firm's Robust Succession Plan

We are now back to the succession planning development phase. As we have covered before, once you complete this last section of each chapter, by the time you finish the book, you will have written down foundational ideas to review with your partners. Once you pull together all these final sections, you will have identified your recommendations about how to handle each succession planning area (or, at a minimum, questions the partner group needs to answer), and you will have a document that can be presented for discussion, modification, and eventual approval that will guide the changes in policy, agreements, governance, and culture your firm will undertake to implement this succession plan over the next few years.

Now that you have thought more about the transition process and steps you should be taking to create clarity about how it should work, policy changes you might want to suggest to give the process more teeth, and how you want to roll this out, respond to the following questions to articulate your thinking about this topic.

Are you recommending any firm policy changes to provide the transition process greater accountability and motivate retiring partners to comply with the process? For a reminder, consider the agreement ideas shared in chapter 10, volume 1.

_____

_____

_____

_____

_____

_____

_____

_____

Segment the clients of the retiring partner into relationships or groupings. Then, as you consider the instructions to be followed for client transitions, group those clients with identical instructions together. Describe the process you are recommending, incorporating the previous forms, if appropriate, the firm uses to provide clear instructions and expectations to the transition partner.

_____

_____

_____

_____

_____

_____

_____

_____

_____

Draft a policy covering how you would recommend the following:

- Communicating transition plans to the retiring partner
- How you believe the plan should be monitored
- At what frequency you suggest feedback be provided
- What documentation, interviews, or investigation processes you feel are best to employ for verification of compliance or completion of each client transition
- How that partner's annual performance compensation will be affected by current transition efforts
- What the escalation process should look like to provide final resolution if conflicts emerge between the managing partner and the retiring partner regarding the designation of clients improperly transitioned

_____

_____

_____

_____

_____

_____

_____

_____

Once the retiring partner's transition plan has been created, describe the trickle-down process you are recommending to ensure that capacity is freed up for all levels of people involved in the transition process. As part of this description, share the monitoring, feedback, and incentive process you are suggesting to hold those "being transitioned to" accountable to perform their part of the transition in a timely and proper manner.

_____

_____

_____

_____

_____

_____

_____

_____

_____

_____

Chapter 11: Defining Admission to Ownership and the Development Process

Key Themes from *Securing the Future, Volume 1: Building Your Firm's Succession Plan*, Chapter 11

- Who should become owners in your firm?
- Career paths for prospective owners
- New partner admission
- Admission to equity ownership
- Nurturing new partners
- Dead weight

Knowing When and If to Admit Someone to Partnership—Remove the Guesswork

Firms can mitigate their risk in the new partner selection process by thinking ahead to identify what they're looking for in partners and in the competencies partners should bring to the table. All partners should have some bare minimum level of competency across the wide spectrum covered by a partner's position. In addition to some average level of performance across the full range, they should be developing stronger competencies in some key areas identified through 360° feedback and performance management coaching sessions with their managing partner or group leader.

By identifying in advance what competencies you are looking for, your firm will benefit by

- letting your future leaders know what will be expected of them to be admitted to ownership;
- minimizing the chance of making people partners who should not be partners;

- keeping the high potential, future leaders you need for your firm;
- raising the bar for all partners in the firm (how can you demand new partners to have certain competencies that the existing partners lack?); and
- creating a stronger firm for the future, resulting in more security for retiring partners and the remaining partners.

We have included some sample competencies from our Succession Institute Competency Framework™ in the "Tools and Resources" section that you may want to consider for your partner group, together with a checklist for the development of your partners-in-training.

Getting Your Partners-to-Be the Development They Need

It is one thing to identify competency gaps, but quite another to fill them. In other words, in addition to action planning, monitoring, and follow-up, your leaders, at all levels, probably will need some additional training and development, and most of that likely will be sourced from outside the firm. This is because the subject matter experts for the training that may be required probably don't reside within the firm. There are exceptions to every rule, but that is the way we typically see it done. Topics such as communication, conflict management, appropriate delegation, people development, and other interpersonal skills, which historically have been referred to in our profession as *soft skills*, can be "hard" or difficult to learn without appropriate training from someone who knows what they're doing. Make no mistake about it—leadership skills, including those in the interpersonal skillset, are not learned by reading about them. They require practice to develop and improve them.

Following are some of the most common sources for this kind of training:

- AICPA/CPA society or CPA firm association formal leadership development program
- Formal training or education in delegation and supervision
- Formal training or education in interpersonal skills
- Specialized online CPE courses covering these topics

In addition to external training and development programs, you'll also want to consider some or all of the following options to be sure that the training transfers back to the workplace:

- Experiential assignments chosen to develop competencies
- Coaching by an outside consultant
- Informal coaching by an assigned partner or owner
- Formal mentoring program

Keep in mind that, unless the senior partners are totally behind any developmental programs for managers and newer partners, your firm's return on investment on those programs will fall far short of what it should. Senior partners need to be engaged with their junior partners or managers, or both, as they progress through their leadership programs. An effort needs to be made to find ways to apply in a practical manner what the participants are learning during their leadership programs. This application of new learning needs to be customized to the firm's needs and reflective of its culture, as well. Who knows? The senior partners may also learn a thing or two from the program.

Now that you are considering adding additional partners, let's take a look at the steps you should address as part of the process:

- Decide what alternatives you want to offer regarding partnership in your firm.
    - Are all partners going to be equity partners, or will you have multiple levels of partners (such as income partners, non-equity partners, and so on, in addition to equity partners)? Verify with your state board of accountancy what alternatives are allowed.
    - What voting rights, if any, does each level of partnership carry?
- Develop and coach each partner group so you are building, on average, more complete partners than you might already have.
    - Clarify the roles and responsibilities of each group as well as the expected minimum competencies for each group.
    - Work to continually make your partners at all levels better, faster, and stronger.
    - Once someone is deemed ready to become partner in any level of partnership, determine what general organizational requirements should be met. This might include the following:
        o Certain revenue requirements (for example, the firm has to average more than $1 million per partner)
        o Certain net profit requirements (for example, the partners must average more than $250,000 per partner)
        o Certain planned openings (a new partner can be added within one year of a partner retiring)
        o Meeting minimum business development goals (has brought in at least $250,000 of new business)
        o Client management goals (currently is the client service manager of at least $600,000 of client services)

The point is not that someone needs to meet all of these requirements. This exercise is to formulate a game plan outlining what combination of situations warrants the admission of a new partner once it has been determined that a person is ready to become a partner. Obviously, requirements or combinations of requirements such as these would be developed for each partner group.

- For each partner group (equity, non-equity, income, and so on), decide how they will buy in, how much they are allowed to buy when they come in, over what period are they allowed to buy-in, how they are bought out, and how they are terminated if they don't perform.
- Establish when partners can earn retirement benefits. See chapter 5 of both volumes for insight on retirement value and the "Tools and Resources" section of this chapter for a common policy many of our firms work from when creating their own buy-in policies.
- For partners in any lower category than equity owners, describe a pathway for them to follow to move from one level of partner to the next.
- For owners who want an opportunity to earn more than their pro rata share of equity distributions, describe the factors that will influence how additional equity allocations can be earned.

Tools and Resources

Sample Partner Competencies

Based on our competency framework, sample partner competencies are the 15 areas we assess when considering whether someone is partner material. As we discussed previously, as well as in chapter 11, volume 1, we expect partners to meet a minimum level of competency in all of these categories and excel way above minimum on a number of them. As also previously mentioned, anytime a firm goes through a formalization of their methodology such as this, it will become evident that some, if not most, of the existing partners don't meet the minimum criteria for all the competencies. This is not a problem if the firm adopts a grandfather clause excusing all the existing partners from this expectation. Although no partners would be removed because they did not meet the competency expectations in the short term, if marginal partners did not work on improving their missing skills, they very well might be removed in the future. One common exception when firms establish new robust sets of competencies is to waive the requirement of going through the development process for a partner two or three years from retirement because in the near term, those partners will be focusing their efforts on the transition of their clients and the departure from their leadership positions anyway.

Take a look at those competencies we utilize. As we have said throughout this book, firms may develop their own, utilize templates from other firms, from other consultants, and so on. This list is to get you thinking about what is important to your firm when considering whether someone should be added to the partner ranks.

Vision and Strategy

- Can clearly explain the reason the firm exists—why it is in business
- Understands and respects differences in roles between the board, managing partner or CEO, and line partners
- Has demonstrated a willingness to take reasonable risks with a well-thought-out rationale for doing so

Job Competence

- Demonstrates excellent skill and experience in his or her technical area at the current level of firm operations
- Has been able to transition from tactical to strategic responsibilities, pushing down lower level work to others
- Works in a highly organized and disciplined manner

Industry Knowledge

- Has an in-depth understanding of the industries he or she works in and competently relays that knowledge to the firm's clients
- Stays current on professional trends and events
- Understands the need to know how well the firm is doing compared to other accounting firms and best practices in the profession

Communication

- Has the ability to express complicated ideas in a simple, direct, and clear manner
- Is poised, confident, and competent presenting before groups
- Communicates with a frequency and tenacity that keeps others well informed

Leading Change

- Does his or her part to assist with implementation of firm change
- Can understand and effectively relay the compelling reasons for change to staff
- Understands the need to actively manage and implement change and carries out change implementation as directed by partners

Execution

- Establishes clear measurements for success
- Regularly monitors progress against goals, both his or her own and those of the people working for him or her
- Allows himself or herself to be held accountable for results

Leadership Image

- Leads by example
- Appears comfortable in a leadership position
- Demonstrates personal drive and ambition

Developing a Following

- Is able to gain the commitment of others in the firm to his or her ideas
- Has effective interpersonal skills
- Enjoys engaging with staff, partners, and peers

Judgment and Decision Making

- Is able to make timely decisions
- Is able to deal with complex issues and cause-and-effect relationships
- Offers solutions that effectively address problems

Ethics and Integrity

- Demonstrates that personal ethics guide his or her decisions
- Conducts his or her professional life in accordance with the organizational values and principles of the firm
- Puts the needs of the firm ahead of his or her personal aspirations and agenda

Coaching and Mentoring

- Creates an environment for learning in which he or she takes the time to develop, coach, and mentor his or her people
- Knows when to personally manage projects and when to delegate both authority and control to staff
- Supports a learning environment with the freedom to make mistakes

Building Teams

- Fosters teamwork and collaboration when appropriate
- Acts as a good team member
- Works for the good of the firm as a whole, rather than building a personal empire

Marketing Focus

- Initiates, participates in, and supports practice development activities, including networking, industry associations, and community involvement
- Builds and maintains effective relationships with clients and referral sources
- Actively coaches and develops others in business development activities, including involving them in the selling process

Business Savvy

- Consistently sells work at a pricing level that comfortably allows the firm to complete the work within standard rates
- Bills and collects in a timely manner
- Minimizes write-downs and charge-offs

Succession Institute's Shareholder-in-Training Program Checklist

This checklist was created to stimulate your thoughts and provoke your thinking regarding the creation of a shareholder-in-training program at your firm. It is based on four broad steps, with detailed issues to consider under each step. There's no one right or wrong way to do this, but this outline can help you get started in your process.

Step 1: Identify Program Structure: Selecting and developing prospective firm owners (referred to in this document as shareholders) is not a stand-alone issue. For it to be successful, it has to integrate with many other processes. Following are some of the basic questions you should consider as you develop your partner-in-training program.		
Issue	**Assigned To**	**Date**
a. How are potential shareholders selected?		
b. What are the requirements that need to be met in order for someone to be nominated for the Shareholder-in-Training program?		
c. How does the firm decide how many potential shareholder candidates it can accept? In other words, just because a CPA appears to be shareholder material doesn't mean that it makes sense for the firm to admit another shareholder. What process identifies the need for, or the "making room for," a potential new shareholder?		
d. What changes (job duties, expectations, compensation, and so on) occur once a person is admitted to the firm's Shareholder-in-Training program?		
e. What alternatives are there for a person nominated for the Shareholder-in-Training program who declines the offer?		

Issue	Assigned To	Date
f. How long does it take to go through the Shareholder-in-Training program (does it take a minimum period of time, is there a maximum, can someone stay in it indefinitely, can someone be kicked out, and so on)?		
g. Is there any status change for someone entering a Shareholder-in-Training program (new title, added to a leadership group, public announcement, and so on)?		
h. Is there more than one shareholder definition (for example, are there technical shareholders, client relationship shareholders, or non-equity shareholders)?		
i. How are annual goals and expectations of shareholders (and personnel, in general) established, monitored, and evaluated?		
j. Are there minimums for being a shareholder (book size, project management skills, personal billings, years of experience)?		
k. How are potential shareholders developed (education curriculum, training, skills, project management, leadership, becoming aware of internal firm issues, management)?		
l. How are potential shareholders mentored and evaluated?		
m. How often do the shareholders-in-training receive formal reviews and feedback from others, rather than just from their mentors?		
n. What happens to shareholders-in-training who never make the cut?		
o. How long can a potential shareholder operate in this phase before the "in" or "out" decision is made?		
p. How are potential shareholders field-tested (put in action to see how they respond in shareholder situations)?		
q. When a shareholder-in-training is deemed ready to take the next step, what is the process for that to occur (for example, nomination, denial, postponement, acceptance)?		

Step 2: Identify Shareholder Abilities Needed: To begin identifying the shareholder abilities needed at your firm, you need to be able to clearly answer the following three questions.		
Issue	**Assigned To**	**Date**
a. What are the job duties of a shareholder?		
b. What are the characteristics that a shareholder should possess?		
c. What are the competencies expected from a shareholder? (Here are some of the common broad categories of shareholder competencies and characteristics that many firms seek out): • Character • Client relationship management • Coaching and mentoring • Commitment to the firm and selflessness • Communication • Execution • Developing a following • Industry knowledge • Job competence • Judgment and decision making • Leadership image • Leading change • Management abilities • Practice development • Problem solving • Project management • Staff relationships and team building • Technical skills • Training plan • Work ethic • Vision and strategy		

Issue	Assigned To	Date
Step 3: Develop Performance Evaluations: Once you have identified shareholder characteristics and competencies, another key step is the development of a performance evaluation process. This includes personal goal setting, personal development programs, evaluation, mentoring, and so on.		
a. Start by identifying and establishing specific objectives for each of the areas you have identified as measurable competencies or performance objectives at least annually.		
b. Have your shareholders-in-training perform self-evaluations of their performance against those objectives, answering questions such as the following: • What have they done this year to achieve or make improvements in each area? • How do they think they have improved? • How would they rate their performance or accomplishment in each area? • Can they provide commentary about what they did achieve, what they didn't, and why? Additionally, they should have room to expand on what they plan to do to make headway in those areas where they fell short. • How would they rate their performance overall?		
In addition to the previous step, consider the following steps:		
c. Have each person evaluated by people for whom he or she works (bosses), peers, and direct reports. This creates a 360° assessment that will provide additional, valuable insight.		
d. Use an assessment instrument for the 360° process that measures characteristics and competencies necessary for success, with questions such as the following: • Does this person confront low performers?* • Does this person try to balance the firm goals with aspirations of his staff? * • Does this person work in a highly organized and disciplined manner?* • Does this person communicate in a way that keeps others well informed?* *Adapted from SIPATM (Succession Institute Performance Assessment™).		

Step 4: *Address Current Shareholder Deficiencies:* If your current shareholders do not possess these expected shareholder competencies, then they need to be put on a development path and given a timeframe to achieve them. Requiring a shareholder to grow is not the problem; allowing them to stagnate in this top position is.		
Issue	**Assigned To**	**Date**
a. Adapt all the preceding steps to existing shareholders and set up a compensation system and other standard operating procedures to hold them accountable.		
b. Monitor shareholder performance and provide them with advice and assistance in making changes required in their behaviors.		
c. If a current shareholder refuses to go along with the new program, consider parting ways with him or her.		

Admission of Non-Equity Partner Policy

By a vote of 66 2/3 percent (supermajority) of the outstanding equity interest of the firm, a person may be elected as a non-equity partner (or income partner, if that is the designation chosen) of the firm. A non-equity partner or income partner (remove one) shall be an employee of the firm, with such duties and compensation as determined by the managing partner. A non-equity partner shall not have an ownership interest in the firm or its assets nor be entitled to any share of its profits or distributions or to any allocation of its income or expenses.

Share Purchase Policy

When shares are available for purchase or repurchase, they will be offered at the accrual basis book value (assets less liabilities) of the firm as of January 1 of the year of admission as a Partner for new Partners or the award of additional shares to existing Partners. The book value for this purpose will not be reduced by any deferred compensation obligations payable to retired Partners.

When additional shares are sold or purchased and distributed, they are not automatically distributed pro rata to the remaining Partners. The Management Committee will make a recommendation to the Board of Directors for its approval of who will be given the privilege to buy additional shares. Approval of the additional shares to be purchased or distributed will require an equity interest vote of 66 2/3 percent.

Sample Wording for Self-Funding (if That's the Firm's Choice)

Funding of the Share Purchase Price will be the individual responsibility of the acquiring Partner.

Sample Wording for Firm Funding (if That's the Firm's Choice)

The Share Purchase price will be financed through the use of a Share Loan. The Share Loan shall have a maturity date of five (5) years and shall bear interest at the firm's borrowing interest rate, with interest and principal payable in annual installments.

Clarification of Non-Equity and Income Partner Status

In the vast majority of firms around the country that we have worked with or are aware of, there is no distinction between being an income partner and a non-equity partner. This is because these are two labels describing the same position: a partner with no equity in the firm. We have covered why the position exists in volume 1, which is to test potential future equity partners to see how they conduct themselves when operating as a partner or to see if becoming a partner affects their business development capability, whether they put themselves before the firm or vice versa, and more.

In certain states, you can't have income partners, but you can have very low equity partners, which is about the same as having non-equity partners. So, some small- to medium-sized firms might consider their non-equity partners as any partner that owns less than one or two percent of the firm. In other words, their legal voice is almost negligible. As well, some firms, especially larger ones, might want to create three tiers when it comes to partner status; so, income partners might be their entry-level position, non-equity is the second (or *very low equity* might be another term for it), and then equity partner would be a third tier.

Which categories you choose for your firm will depend on the needs of your firm, the current talent you have in your firm, and the laws in your state. The good news is that, with each level of partner, you can create added differentiation. That differentiation might include voting rights (do they have any rights, and if so, what are they?), roles and responsibilities, work expectations, minimum competencies, compensation tiers, and more. There isn't a right or wrong answer here. You might have a greater need for partner tiers today because of your succession management concerns, but then you may need only one level of partner eight years from now. This is simply another tool to help you formalize expectations and manage the talent in your firm, creating a strong, viable, sustainable firm for today and for the future.

Additional Learning Resources

As you know from the materials at the end of the first chapter, additional self-study CPE courses are available for your review. Many of them are all-video courses developed from our streaming video webcasts, and others were created from the various books we have written. These courses can be found at www.successioninstitute.com/PMRC.

Remember to take advantage of your discount by entering the word "succession" into the coupon code field.

Here are some courses we recommend that could provide you some additional insight into strengthening your transition process:

- How to Build a Partner Compensation System that Supports Accountability (all-video)
- Implementing Roles, Responsibilities and a Competency Framework in Your Firm (all-video)
- Implementing the Partner Goal Process: Step-by-Step Instructions (all-video)

Building Your Firm's Robust Succession Plan

We are now back to the succession planning development phase. As we have covered before, once you complete this last section of each chapter, by the time you finish the book, you will have written down foundational ideas to review with your partners. Once you pull together these final sections, you will have identified your recommendations about how to handle each succession planning area (or, at a minimum, questions the partner group needs to answer), and you will have a document that can be presented for discussion, modification, and eventual approval that will guide the changes in policy, agreements, governance, and culture your firm will undertake to implement this succession plan over the next few years.

Now that you have thought more about the types of partners you might include in your organization, the rights of those partners, the buy-in and buyout of those partners, their expectations, what it takes to move from one partner level to the next, and more, think about some formalization as well as changes you might suggest to your partners about this topic area. Respond to the following questions to articulate your thinking about this topic.

Decide what alternatives you want to propose to your partner group regarding partnership or ownership in your firm.

1. I think we should have equity partners only.
2. I think we should have both equity and non-equity partners.
3. I think we should have both equity and income partners.
4. I think we should have equity, non-equity, and income partners.
5. I am recommending this combination: _____

I am suggesting that our firm operate as described in preceding item _____, and here are some of my thoughts and reasons for leaning in this direction.

_____

_____

_____

_____

_____

_____

_____

Voting Rights

Given the choice you want to make regarding levels of partners (before you make the final decision on this, you will want to check with your state board of public accountancy and your attorney to verify whether those choices are allowable within your state), it is time to consider the voting right for each group. In other words, do partner levels other than equity owners have a right to vote, and if so, what does that look like, and when would those votes be applicable? As you know from reading chapter 11, volume 1, we believe you should be very careful about granting any non-equity groups too many rights too early. As well, even if you decide to only allow voting for equity owners, when you vote, is each owner voting his or her equity, or does each owner get one vote regardless of ownership amount, and do these voting rights change based on the subject being voted on? Describe your recommendation regarding voting rights and privileges.

_____

_____

_____

_____

_____

_____

_____

_____

Developing More Complete Partners

Develop and coach each partner group so you are building, on average, more complete partners than you might already have. We have created this section for you to jot down your ideas about appropriate roles and responsibilities for each partner group as well as the expected minimum competencies for each group. You might want to consider leveraging the work you already did on roles and responsibilities in chapter 6, volume 2.

_____

_____

_____

_____

_____

_____

_____

_____

_____

_____

Once someone is deemed ready to become a partner at any level of partnership, what general organizational requirements should be met? In our example, we mentioned minimum levels of revenues, profits, owner retirement openings, client management, business development, and more. This exercise is for you to lay out your thinking about what will generally drive new partner opportunities within your firm once you have a viable candidate ready or close to ready.

_____

_____

_____

_____

_____

_____

_____

_____

_____

Buy-In, Buyout, and More

For each partner group (equity, non-equity, income, and so on), jot down your ideas about how partners will buy in, how will they get bought out, when they will vest in the value of the firm rather than just in their capital accounts, whether you will offer financing, what the terms should be if you do (interest, payment period, installments, and so on), and what type of vote and threshold it should take to terminate a partner at each level.

Buy-in: _____

_____

_____

_____

Buyout: _____

_____

_____

_____

When will they vest, and on what will they base their vesting (years of service as a partner, age, some combination)? _____

_____

_____

Will you offer financing to support partners buying in? If so, what does that look like? _____

_____

_____

_____

What type of vote and threshold does it take to terminate a partner in each partner group?

_____

_____

_____

Developing More Complete Partners

For partners in any lesser category than equity owners, describe a pathway (whatever you plan to use, such as a competency model, higher minimum standards for performance, and so on) for them to follow to move from one partner level to the next (from non-equity to equity, or income to equity, or income to non-equity to equity, and so on).

_____

_____

_____

_____

_____

_____

For owners who want to be offered an opportunity to increase their equity ownership percentage, describe the factors that will influence how additional equity allocations can be earned (consistently exceeding performance goals, exceeding certain standards in specific areas, and so on).

_____

_____

_____

_____

_____

_____

_____

_____

Chapter 12: Dealing with Partner Departures

Key Themes from *Securing the Future, Volume 1: Building Your Firm's Succession Plan*, Chapter 12

- Terminating a partner
- Partners leaving and going to work in industry
- Partners leaving and competing
- Employment agreements and related issues

Any time a firm loses a key player, the firm is at risk. This is particularly true with the departure of partners, for whatever reason, no matter how dysfunctional they may have become. Chapter 12, volume 1 covers our perspectives on what should be done, and how, with respect to partners leaving, whether of their own accord or by virtue of a vote for termination. The "Tools and Resources" section of this chapter provides some ideas for dealing with partners who leave the firm for any reason.

Tools and Resources

Policy on the Termination of a Partner

When your firm decides it is time to terminate a partner or if the partner decides to leave, you need a policy that makes it clear that the terminated or withdrawing partner will sell his or her interest in the firm back to the firm at the agreed-upon terms; that he or she will not harm the firm (severance package); that if the partner takes clients or staff, these events have agreed-upon consequences; and more. Termination or withdrawal of a partner is messy regardless of the situation. You need to have a process clearly outlining the steps for handling this situation professionally, efficiently, and calmly. The more either side decides to make this situation personal, the greater the likelihood that it will escalate into a lose/lose scenario, which, unfortunately, is a common outcome. We covered a number of specific issues that should be addressed, as well as our recommendations regarding the same, in volume 1. In support of that discussion, following is a simple sample termination policy and policies dealing with benefits and penalties when someone leaves as well as some foundational components of a severance policy a firm should consider putting together to tie up any final loose ends when someone leaves. As always, when it comes to legal issues such as this, we recommend that you consult your legal counsel on the best approach for your firm.

Sample Termination of a Partner Policy

A Partner may be terminated by a vote of 66 2/3 percent (supermajority) of the equity votes of the Partners. For the sake of this policy, the Partner being terminated is not eligible to vote on this matter; therefore, his or her equity is removed from the calculation of supermajority equity vote required. However, even if the supermajority equity vote occurs, the raw equity percentage voted to terminate also needs to represent a majority vote of the total equity votes of the firm.

The amount due the terminated Partner will be determined based on whether the partner leaving will be retiring, continuing to work outside of public practice, or continuing to work in public practice.

When a Partner is terminated by the firm, he or she agrees to immediately sell his or her equity in accordance with the firm's policies.

Upon termination, in addition to payment of any retirement benefits earned, the Partner will be paid a severance package of two months of his or her annual budgeted salary (see more about severance packages in the following pages). The terminated Partner will not be entitled to any undeclared or partial year incentive compensation. Receipt of incentive compensation in prior years by the withdrawing or terminating Partner is not a precedent to be considered regarding this Policy. However, if incentive compensation has been declared to be earned prior to termination, the terminated Partner is entitled to his or her earned share of that incentive compensation.

To be entitled to the severance package and payment of retirement benefits due as outlined by the firm's policies, the terminated Partner agrees in advance to execute the firm's severance agreement.

The firm maintains the ability to fire a Partner at will. At any time, the Partners may vote to remove a Partner, for any reason not specifically subject to discrimination governed by law (race, religion, age, and so on).

Partner Leaving Who Will Not Be Taking Clients or Staff

At the time of withdrawal or any termination of a Partner from the firm, whether voluntary or involuntary, the withdrawing Partner agrees to automatically sell his or her equity interest in the Firm according to the following conditions.

The withdrawing or terminating Partner is entitled to the following benefits:

1. The withdrawing or terminating Partner will not be entitled to any undeclared or partial year incentive bonus compensation.

2. The value of a withdrawing/terminating Partner's Equity will be determined by the valuation and vesting policies.

3. If the withdrawing/terminating Partner is to receive any deferred compensation benefits or return of capital, the Partner is subject to adjustments under the Transition Policy as an offset against any deferred compensation or capital repayment owed.

4. The total amount due the withdrawing/terminating Partner will be offset by any outstanding liabilities owed by that Partner to the Firm.

5. The Partner's portion of capital, at the most recent previous year-end is to be considered owed to him or her at the time of departure. The Firm will pay the total capital owed, after deducting any outstanding liabilities or offsets owed by the Partner, in equal monthly payments plus interest over a 60-month period with interest.

6. Any amount owed as deferred compensation, after adjustments and offsets, will be paid to the Partner over a 10-year period without interest.

7. Acts that will immediately cause discontinuation of the payment of deferred compensation include (but are not limited to) …

Partner Leaving Who Will Be Taking Clients or Staff or Both

At the time of withdrawal or any termination of a Partner from the Firm, whether voluntary or involuntary, the withdrawing Partner agrees to automatically sell his/her Equity in the Firm according to these same conditions.

The withdrawing/terminated Partner is entitled to the following benefits (we use the same items as above with the addition of the three points below):

1. For those clients that the Firm loses after the withdrawing/terminating Partner's departure to either the withdrawing/terminated Partner or his/her successor organization through any year in which the departing Partner is receiving Deferred Compensation or Return of Capital Payments, one year's fees collected for each client lost by the Firm will be calculated (there are several ways to calculate this, so your firm should decide whether it should be an average of several years, the last 12 months, or some weighting calculation).

2. For each client lost, the withdrawing/terminating Partner will be charged at the rate of *2 times* the amount of the fees lost.

3. If the withdrawing/terminating Partner takes staff with him/her to his/her successor organization within three years of departure from the Firm, the withdrawing/terminated Partner will be charged *2 times* the Annual Salary for each staff member joining his/her successor organization.

Separation or Severance

This discussion on severance was contributed by R. Peter Fontaine, founding member of NewGate Partners, a firm providing legal and risk management services exclusively to the accounting profession. Peter has nearly 20 years of experience working in the accounting profession and has served as the general counsel of McGladrey and as an assistant general counsel of Arthur Andersen. He can be reached at p.fontaine@newgatepartners.com.

Introduction

The roots of today's separation or severance arrangements can be traced back to early 19th century industrialized England, when labor codes formally emerged to protect workers. Even before that time, it was common practice to terminate employment only after a notice period equal to the frequency of pay (for example, day, week, month) or make a payment in lieu of notice. More recently, with the high demand for skilled workers, particularly in the accounting profession, generous severance policies have become part of a firm's platform for attracting and retaining key employees and partners. Accordingly, separation arrangements are becoming an essential component of an accounting firm's personnel management practices.

Although some partnership or employment agreements include provisions addressing separation, they frequently fail to tackle the details of a partner's or employee's departure. As a result, severance plans and the related agreements are regularly used to properly wind up the relationship between the individual and the firm.

Separation Agreements Generally

Ideally, a separation agreement should be executed in all employment termination situations, but their use is largely limited to cases in which a partner or employee is involuntarily terminated and receives benefits under a severance plan. Severance benefits usually accompany a termination without cause—the individual's position has been eliminated, their services are no longer needed, or things just are not working out. A partner or employee who is terminated involuntarily is more likely to seek some type of redress against the firm. Accordingly, firms offer a severance package in order to obtain a release of claims against the firm. Offering a severance payment also gives the firm an opportunity to reach other agreements with the employee and reaffirm existing employee obligations.

Workers who voluntarily resign rarely take legal action against their employer, unless their resignation is alleged to be a constructive discharge. In addition, if an employee leaves of his or her own accord and is ineligible for severance benefits, the employer has virtually no leverage in obtaining a separation agreement. As a result, separation agreements signed by employees who voluntarily quit are uncommon. That being said, in some situations when a worker leaves voluntarily, offering a small severance payment or other consideration may be advisable to obtain the release and other important terms that appear in a separation agreement, particularly in the absence of an employment agreement.

There is considerable disagreement on whether severance benefits should be paid to partners and employees who are terminated for cause. The notion that a partner or employee can commit "bad acts" and still receive a severance benefit is offensive to some. Nothing is ever clear cut, and employees consistently present facts that weaken the employer's position. The employee's response to a termination for cause is quite often a wrongful termination lawsuit or a complaint to a governmental agency, such as the Equal Employment Opportunity Commission (EEOC). Economically speaking, paying some severance to obtain a release of claims is, in most cases, better than defending a wrongful termination lawsuit that is eventually settled. And, the amount does not need to be the full severance benefit but only enough to obtain and support the consideration requirements of the release. Given today's cost of legal representation and the predilection that courts have for employee's claims—not to mention the consumption of management time—paying severance and getting a full release is usually the right decision.

Separation Terms

Financial Terms. As suggested previously, the centerpiece of the severance agreement are the financial terms. It is the gateway to obtaining the all-important release of claims. To be clear, firms are not legally required to have a severance plan or offer a severance package. Beyond paying compensation for wages earned, reimbursement for expenses incurred, and settling the capital account, firms are not mandated to make severance payments to departing employees and partners. Firms need to ensure, however, that if they provide severance benefits it is done on a nondiscriminatory basis. Even the best drafted releases will not protect a firm against a claim that decisions about severance benefits were made on an arbitrary and discriminatory basis.

A key financial term related to the separation of a partner is the return of capital or the redemption of equity. This should be addressed in the partnership agreement. In the unlikely event it is not, the departing partner and the firm need to agree on the terms for the liquidation of the partner's interest in the firm and document it in the separation agreement. A discussion of the terms for settlement of the capital or equity account of a partner exceeds the scope of this section. Similarly, this section will not address the treatment of a partner's or employee's participation in any deferred compensation, retirement, or other compensation or benefit plans that might be affected by termination.

The financial terms of a severance arrangement generally fall into three categories: incentive compensation, severance payments or benefits, and what may be called "unique circumstances."

Incentive Compensation: The payment of incentive compensation is often the subject of considerable discussion whenever a partner or employee is terminated. Most incentive compensation plans provide for the vesting and payment of bonuses after the close of the fiscal year. If a worker leaves the firm after the bonus vests but before the scheduled pay-out date, it is generally a good idea to pay the bonus and avoid a dispute. However, depending on the circumstances, paying a partial bonus may make sense in any termination, even in for-cause situations. Just make sure that you are consistently applying whatever policy you decide upon.

Severance Benefits: Severance benefits come in both cash and noncash forms. Cash benefits are typically paid in a lump sum based on the number of years of service. The payment may also be made over time (for example, salary continuation) or simply a stipulated amount regardless of years of service (three-months' base salary). Salary continuation is often used to maintain benefits, such as medical coverage, vest other benefits, like retirement or a matching 401(k) contribution, or reduce the individual's tax liability. A stipulated cash payment is often found in an agreement negotiated with a high producing lateral hire who sought protection from an unknown and potentially untenable work situation.

A common severance amount for nonexempt employees is one week of base compensation for each year of service up to a certain maximum—say 8–12 weeks. Similarly, professional personnel often receive one month of base compensation for each year of service, up to a maximum of 6 months for non-partner level employees and 9–12 months for partners. Professionals may also be entitled to a minimum benefit—2 months' salary—regardless of duration of employment. These amounts and how they are structured or paid vary significantly from firm to firm. Although there are no definitive standards or guidelines, there are three important considerations to keep in mind. Is the benefit amount sufficient to attract and retain desired personnel given the competition for talent in the accounting industry? Is the benefit amount enough to obtain the release and avoid a lawsuit? And, third, is the benefit amount adequate consideration to legally support the release of claims against the firm. The numbers suggested previously have proven to be effective in all three areas.

In addition to the traditional severance benefit discussed previously, other cash or cash equivalent payments may also be made. A typical example is a lump sum COBRA subsidy. It may be equal to the amount the partner or employee will pay under COBRA, or it can be limited to the firm's prior contribution. The amount is frequently a function of the number of months used to compute the salary-based benefit. In addition to the COBRA subsidy, the firm may also consider covering some portion of other expenses previously paid by the firm, such as life or disability insurance, car lease payments, or club dues. An accelerated 401(k) matching contribution might also be made if the plan permits. These discretionary benefit "extras" are most often reserved for the most senior or highly compensated partners.

Departing employees and partners may also be offered noncash benefits. Although these benefits may be fairly minimal to the firm, they may, nonetheless, be very helpful to the transition of the former partner or employee. One of the more typical ones is outplacement services. The fess are customarily paid directly to the provider and are relatively low ($1000 per month or less), particularly when the employee or partner finds a new position quickly. Another benefit is retention by the terminated worker of firm-owned technology, such as a laptop computer, tablet, or mobile phone. In all likelihood, this equipment has been expensed by the firm and a generation behind in technology. A final example of a noncash benefit is continued, but limited, access to the firm's resources, such as its e-mail system, office space, or knowledge base. Although this can present some risk to the firm, if properly monitored, the benefit to the transition of the worker can significantly outweigh the exposure for the firm.

Unique Circumstances: From time to time, every firm will have unique circumstances with departing partners and employees that need to be addressed on an individual basis. For illustration purposes, consider the case of the sole practitioner who joins a larger firm as a partner bringing along a sizable book of business. The partner and firm agreed that the partner would receive a minimum salary for three years, plus a significant bonus if the transfer of the clients was successful. For one reason or another, things do not work out, and the partner and the firm go their separate ways after one year. Many of the clients wish to remain with the firm, although some are likely to follow the partner or go elsewhere. The firm and the partner now need to address how the firm will meet its commitment to compensate the soon-to-be former partner for the clients he or she brought and effectively transferred to the firm as well as allowances for clients lost. There are a variety of resolutions to this situation that not only include financial terms related to the client but also future commitments by the partner and restrictions on the partner's activity following termination. Firms need to be prepared to handle circumstances falling outside the scope of a standard separation practice creatively and on a case-by-case basis.

Timing of Payments: In general, there are no specific requirements for when severance benefit payments need to be made. That said, there is a very large exception for older workers (older than 40 years) discussed subsequently, which usually drives payments to all workers.

Firm and Client Information. Accounting firm partners and employees are knowledge workers. They create and handle great volumes of information belonging to both the firm and its clients. At the very least, every firm should already have in place a confidentiality agreement with its partners and employees that protects sensitive firm and client information from disclosure and misuse, both during and after employment. This obligation should be reaffirmed in the termination agreement.

At the end of their employment, partners and employees should be required to confirm in the severance agreement that they have returned or destroyed all firm and client information that they possess or may have diverted to others. This includes any information that may be resident on any equipment (computers, tablets, smartphones, and so on) the partner or employee owned or used in connection with his or her employment. Hopefully, the firm has a "bring your own device to work" policy that defines the terms under which employee-owned technology may be used and that enables the firm to remotely remove firm or client information from the device.

Firm and client information needs to be broadly defined in the severance (and employment) agreement to catch all important data belonging to the firm, regardless of location, form, or source. One of the areas often overlooked is the partner's or employee's social media presence. The firm should have a social media policy that is reaffirmed in the severance agreement. If the firm does not have a policy, the agreement should make it clear that the firm owns any social media accounts and the related content created or enhanced by the employee or partner within the scope of their work at the firm. In addition, it needs to be clear that any information owned by the firm, whether created by the employee or coworkers, and posted on an employee's or partner's individual social media account remains the property of the firm. There have been a number of well-publicized cases involving the ownership of employees' Twitter and LinkedIn accounts and the overlap of employee connections and firm clients. Much of this litigation could have been avoided if the employee and employer had reached an agreement before the employee or partner left.

Unfortunately, many partners and employees leave with valuable firm and client information. It is an unavoidable fact. Although it is difficult to police this behavior, a well-drafted separation agreement establishes a solid foundation for enforcing the firm's right to protect its information after a partner's or employee's departure.

Restrictive Covenants. If the firm's partnership or employment agreement contains restrictive covenants, such as prohibitions against competing with the firm, soliciting coworkers and clients, and performing work for clients, these should be reaffirmed in the separation agreement. If there are no restrictive covenants in place at the time of termination, it is highly likely that any restrictions imposed on a departing employee will be unenforceable, unless the severance benefits are very generous and the restriction period relatively short. There simply is not enough consideration in the average severance benefits package to support both the release of claims and the newly added restrictions.

Cooperation and Indemnification. An accounting firm's partnership and employment agreement should include a provision that requires the partner or employee to cooperate with the firm in connection with current and future matters. A corollary to the duty to cooperate is an indemnification of the partner or employee by the firm against liabilities that might arise that are related to the firm's business. If these terms are contained in the partnership or employment agreement, a simple reference in the separation agreement should be sufficient. If not, they should be adequately covered in the severance agreement along the following lines.

Duty to Cooperate: Partners and employees who leave the firm involuntarily are naturally reluctant to assist afterwards. A provision in the severance agreement requiring reasonable cooperation may give the firm some leverage. Common areas where firms need the assistance of former employees include (i) transitioning clients to other firm personnel; (ii) protecting confidential information or other legal interests; and (iii) asserting or defending legal claims, investigations, or regulatory actions. The duty to cooperate should also include a commitment not to assist third parties in bringing an action against the firm. Obviously, such a restriction could not prevent a former partner or employee from truthfully testifying against the firm if compelled to do so. Firms should agree to pay the reasonable expenses that a partner or employee might incur in connection with assistance they may provide. In addition, in some situations it may make sense to compensate former partners or employees for the work they perform in supporting the firm's interests. If they receive payment, they are more likely to happily assist.

Indemnification: Although indemnification of a former partner or employee may appear to be gratuitous, there is a well-recognized legal obligation for employers to indemnify their employees for actions taken (or omitted) that are within the scope of the employee's duties or responsibilities. Accordingly, an indemnification provision in a severance (or employment) agreement actually places limitations on the underlying indemnification obligation, such as the condition that the worker acted in good faith. In addition, the indemnity encourages employees to cooperate with the firm and gives the firm some control over the handling and resolution of matters.

Confidentiality and Disparagement. In some cases, firms may wish to maintain the confidentiality of the terms of the severance agreement, particularly if the separation arrangement is nonstandard or a settlement of threatened litigation. It is quite possible that the firm or the partner or employee may also want to conceal the circumstances surrounding the termination. In both cases, a confidentiality provision can be inserted into the severance agreement. The confidentiality obligation should be taken seriously by both parties. In a noteworthy case, an executive's severance payments were stopped when his daughter commented on Facebook how lucrative her father's settlement was.

A provision in the separation agreement prohibiting one party from making disparaging statements about the other is commonplace. When employees and employers part company, emotions often run high, and the parties are prone to say negative things about each other. In particular, employees often seek vindication and retribution for being terminated by vocally criticizing their previous firms. Former employees should be cautious about publicly judging their prior employers. Even in the absence of written non-disparagement obligation, former employees can be liable for inaccurate statements about their employers, and they do not enjoy the protection under the National Labor Relations Act that enables coworkers to openly discuss wages, hours, and conditions of employment, even if it is harmful to their employer's reputation or standing. In today's social media world, disparaging comments, even those made in private, about an employer have a way of surfacing on Twitter and Facebook and have been the subject of numerous law suits. As a final note, the same exception for compelled testimony described in the section on firm and client information also applies to the non-disparagement obligation.

Return of Firm Property. The required return of firm property is an adjunct to the return or destruction of firm and client information. It is a perfunctory, but necessary, provision of a standard severance agreement. This part of the separation agreement ought to cover equipment (for example, laptops, smartphones, tablets, external hard drives, and so on), software applications, firm credit cards, building access key cards, manuals, books and promotional material, and any other property furnished by the firm to the employee. It is always a good idea to have an exit interview with the terminating partner or employee and collect firm property at that time as well as give a receipt for returned property.

Release

Although the well-being of the firm's former partners and employees is part of the motivation for offering severance benefits to departing workers, severance payments are largely made as an inducement to obtain the release of claims against the firm. In addition, receipt of severance benefits provides the necessary consideration to support the enforceability of the release.

Releases in severance agreements are typically very broad and cover just about every possible claim that the soon-to-be former employee or partner might have against the firm arising from the employment relationship. The potential claims released by the partner or employee fall mainly into three categories: wrongful termination, constructive discharge, and violation of law. *Wrongful termination*—when the employee is improperly terminated or the basis of the termination is illegal—includes claims such as breach of the employment contract or violation of a personnel policy, retaliation, or discrimination. *Constructive discharge*—the employee resigning because of intolerable or hostile activity in the workplace—includes claims of sexual, gender, religious, or ethnic harassment; bullying; unfounded reductions in pay; and the like. There is considerable overlap between wrongful termination, constructive discharge, and violation of law claims. Most of the wrongful termination and constructive discharge claims are based on a violation of law.

The release also covers multiple standalone violation of law claims. The best example is a claim alleging past racial, gender, or other discrimination that was injurious to the employee's compensation, advancement, and employment opportunity. Another example is a claim, either individually or as a member of a class, for back pay based on misclassification as an exempt employee in violation of federal and state wage and hour statutes.

Concern by the EEOC over release language in severance agreements has been on the rise. Accordingly, the EEOC has established guidance for severance agreements, which is well founded even with respect to matters not before the EEOC. Employers should consider the following:

- The release must be clear, specific, and understandable to the employee given his education, experience, and language proficiencies.
- The release cannot be induced by fraud, duress, undue influence, or other improper conduct by the employer.
- The employee must have reasonable time to consider the severance offer.
- The agreement must advise the employee to consult an attorney.
- The release should not be excessive and overly broad and cannot act as a release of an employee's rights regarding future acts of discrimination.
- The release must be supported by adequate consideration.
- The release cannot inhibit an employee's ability to file a complaint or cooperate with the EEOC in an investigation alleging past violations of employment laws.

Special rules also exist for workers 40 and older under the federal Older Workers Benefit Protection Act of 1990 (OWBPA). Many firms adopt the required OWBPA periods for all workers simply because they are a safe harbor from inquiry by the EEOC, and there is not much downside to delaying payment. The OWBPA rules include the following:

- The release must specifically reference the Age Discrimination in Employment Act.
- The employee must have 21 days from the date of the employer's final offer to consider the release, or 45 days in the case of a group termination. The employee can accept the offer sooner.
- The employee must allow a 7-day revocation period. This 7-day period cannot be changed or waived by either party for any reason.
- The employer must give certain written disclosures regarding the class of employees from which the terminated employee came.

The law with respect to releases in severance agreements changes regularly. Too often, outdated "boilerplate" documents are used that do not conform with the EEOC's requirements or other employment-related laws and court decisions.

Conclusion

The emergence of severance arrangements is certainly not a recent phenomenon. They have existed for over 200 years. There has been, however, an accelerating judicial and legislative trend toward a greater balance between the authority of an employer to freely operate its business and the fair, reasonable, and dignified treatment of workers. In large measure, severance plans have been established by employers to conclusively end the employment relationship, and in particular, to reduce the growing risk of legal action by a former employee.

Accounting firms that do not currently have a severance plan should consider developing one. Periodically, the need to pay severance benefits will arise, and it is wise to fulfill this need in accordance with a written plan, rather than to arbitrarily make decisions about which employees or partners receive benefits and how much. In addition, severance plans are becoming an important tool for attracting and retaining key talent in a generation in which jobs are often short lived. Finally, both the severance plans and related separation agreements need to be well-prepared and regularly reviewed to ensure they meet the employer's objective: to conclude the employment relationship in a manner that represents minimal threat of a legal challenge.

Additional Learning Resources

As you know from the materials at the end of the first chapter, additional self-study CPE courses are available for your review. Many of them are all-video courses developed from our streaming video webcasts, and others were created from the various books we have written. These courses can be found at www.successioninstitute.com/PMRC.

Remember to take advantage of your discount by entering the word "succession" into the coupon code field.

Here are a couple of courses we recommend that could provide you some additional insight into the many issues surrounding either the termination or voluntary withdrawal of a partner.

- Pulling It All Together with a Partner/Shareholder Agreement (all-video)
- Shareholder/Partner Agreement Framework Built on a Standard Operating Procedure Approach (video and text, with support documents created by Peter Meeker, attorney, Reed, Claymon, Meeker & Hargett, PLLC)

Building Your Firm's Robust Succession Plan

We are now back to the succession planning development phase. As we have covered before, once you complete this last section of each chapter, by the time you finish the book, you will have written down foundational ideas to review with your partners. Once you pull together these final sections, you will have identified your recommendations about how to handle each succession planning area (or, at a minimum, questions the partner group needs to answer), and you will have a document that can be presented for discussion, modification, and eventual approval that will guide the changes in policy, agreements, governance, and culture your firm will undertake to implement this succession plan over the next few years.

Now that you have thought more about the termination or voluntary withdrawal of a partner, including what benefits partners are entitled to depending on whether they are retiring, going to work outside of public accounting, or competing with your firm in public accounting, think about some formalization as well as changes you might suggest to your partners about this topic area. Respond to the following questions to articulate your thinking about this topic:

Describe your view of the process to terminate a partner. What voting percentage will be required to terminate a partner? What type of vote will be required (equity, one-partner-one-vote)? Who will be able to vote (that is, will the partner being considered for termination have a vote)?

_____

_____

_____

_____

_____

_____

_____

_____

_____

_____

What a Partner Is Entitled to Upon Voluntary Withdrawal

Using the space provided, describe what a partner is entitled to when he or she voluntarily withdraws from the firm (assuming for now that he or she is moving to a city far away and not competing). Consider in your description how that might differ depending on whether that partner is vested or not. Also consider whether that partner gave you proper notice of withdrawal. Factor in the recommendations you have already made regarding retirement, vesting, notice, and so on in chapter 5, volume 2.

_____

_____

_____

_____

_____

_____

_____

_____

_____

What a Partner Is Entitled to Upon Termination

Using the space provided, describe what a partner is entitled to when he or she is terminated by the firm (assuming for now that he or she is moving to a city far away and not competing). Consider in your description how that might differ depending on whether that partner is vested or not. Because termination doesn't allow for proper notice, how does that affect what the departing partner should receive? Finally, does your response vary if the termination is for cause or "bad acts" versus a situation that is no longer a good fit between the terminated partner and the firm? Factor in the recommendations you have already made regarding retirement, vesting, notice, and so on in chapter 5, volume 2.

_____

_____

_____

_____

_____

_____

_____

_____

_____

Penalties for Partners Leaving

What penalties are you recommending, if any, to your partner group to levy against a partner who is leaving your firm and has decided to compete? What is your recommendation regarding clients taken? What is your recommendation regarding staff taken? What about partners who are vested and due retirement benefits if they were to retire, but instead, compete with the firm? Will your firm void all retirement benefits to partners leaving and competing with the firm regardless of additional penalties that might be due the firm for taking clients or staff? In other words, describe the policy you want to put in place regarding partners who leave the firm and compete, regardless of whether they are vested in retirement benefits.

_____

_____

_____

_____

_____

_____

_____

_____

_____

What penalties, if any, are you recommending to the partner group to levy against any outstanding amounts owed to a partner leaving to work outside of public accounting who did not try to help the firm retain his or her client base; suggested to his or her clients to change CPA firms; or went to work for the firm's largest client and, therefore, significant revenues and profits were lost; or lured away staff to work with his or her new employer? In other words, describe the policy you want to put in place regarding partners who leave the firm, are not competing with the firm, but still damage the firm on their way out. Give special consideration to when the departing partner is owed money by the firm.

_____

_____

_____

_____

_____

_____

_____

_____

_____

_____

Severance Agreement in Combination With Partner Agreements or Policies

Based on what you read from Peter Fontaine regarding severance agreements, what is your position about augmenting your partner agreement with this type of additional support tool? If you are inclined to propose this to your partner group, what sections would you want to include, what amount of severance would you suggest, and so on? For the record, we like the idea of requiring that the departing partner sign the severance agreement as part of the requirements for receiving any benefits due them under the partner agreement. We also like the idea of using a fixed number of months regardless of tenure or a sliding scale based on tenure that might have a total range of two to four months, because we don't want a severance agreement to be just another open spout for spending money when a partner leaves. When a partner leaves, whether it is voluntary or involuntary, the firm already has plenty of pieces to pick up and put back in place. We like the idea of having a final document that creates closure and makes sure all the "i's" are dotted and the "t's" are crossed. Obviously, you need to consult with an attorney before making any final decisions, but for now, use the following space to outline your thoughts on what you think a severance package might look like for your firm.

_____

_____

_____

_____

_____

_____

_____

_____

_____

Chapter 13: Establishing Processes and Procedures for Retired Partners

Key Themes from *Securing the Future, Volume 1: Building Your Firm's Succession Plan*, Chapter 13

- Boundaries are necessary
- Annual contracts
- Retired partner employee compensation

Getting clarity and agreement on the terms governing a retired partner's employment with the firm is a critical factor in avoiding future, unforeseen conflicts over this matter. This chapter provides you with some food for thought about your firm's retired partner employment agreements.

Tools and Resources

The following is an example of some provisions that might be included in a retired partner employee (RPE) annual agreement. The specific services outlined in this agreement will vary based on factors such as the skillset, work habits, technical competencies, and so on of the RPE. The key to this agreement is that it is annual in nature (that is, it expires at the end of the year and does *not* automatically renew). Furthermore, it needs to be customized to fit the needs of the firm first, and the needs of the RPE second. As we covered in chapter 13, volume 1, the RPEs in this role should *not* be managing client relationships, and the RPE should not be part of firm leadership or participate in leadership meetings (unless asked to attend a specific meeting as support staff). Italicized notes in the sample terms should not be included in the wording; these are additional clarifications for your use.

Sample Terms for a Retired Partner Employment Contract Policy

At the time that a partner sells his or her equity interest in the firm, the firm may, at the sole discretion of the firm, choose to continue to employ the retired partner for up to 12 months at a time under terms outlined in this policy. *(Each contract should end, generally, at the CPA firm's fiscal year-end. We recommend that a statement be placed right above the signature line to the effect that "If a new contract is not offered to the RPE before this contract expires, the RPE should assume that his or her services will not be needed in the following year. Without a new contract, the RPE's services will no longer be requested or paid for by the firm as of the first day of the new fiscal year.")* RPEs agree to the following conditions under the terms of their retired partner employment contract with the firm:

Duties and Obligations of RPEs

- Retired partners who continue to perform technical work on client projects as firm employees will continue to be subject to all the same SOPs as all other employees of the firm, including but not limited to, quality control processes and procedures and other administrative processes and procedures.

- RPEs will serve in the roles of technical reviewer and technical adviser. They will not maintain client contact with any existing or new clients of the firm inasmuch as all client contact is to reside with current partners and their designees (which will not include RPEs). *(Note: In some limited cases, depending on the size of the RPE's former book, the nature of the clients served, and other similar factors, some firms will allow the RPE to maintain client relationships with a few, small clients, typically individual tax clients, who are contemporaries of the RPE, but this is usually limited to clients making up no more than $20,000 to $30,000 in annual revenue.)*

- RPEs will conduct their work in an organized manner such that they meet deadlines and leave other firm personnel adequate time to do their part within the clients' deadlines, avoiding last minute rushes and crises in producing deliverables.

- Detailed duties and expectations, within the boundaries set herein, will be outlined for each RPE and may also include business development and representation of the firm on the boards of community service and nonprofit organizations.

- RPEs will be responsible for maintaining the appropriate number of CPE credit hours of CPE in the fields of study required for them to maintain their licenses and conduct the technical work they will be performing. The firm will underwrite the costs of up to 40 hours of CPE for each RPE. To the extent that such CPE is available in-house, the firm will expect the RPE to attend the in-house training sessions in lieu of attending programs outside the firm.

- RPEs are expected to maintain an appropriate professional demeanor within the firm's community or marketplace and act as supporters of the firm when out and about, passing on to firm management any feedback regarding the firm they happen to come by during their activities. Any disparagement of the firm by an RPE will result in summary dismissal of that RPE.

Compensation for RPEs

- RPEs will be paid 35 percent of the net billings (production based on charge hours and standard rates, net of write-downs) for their personal time, charged to the projects on which they perform technical work. The standard billing rates of RPEs will be set and adjusted as necessary by the firm's managing partner, based on the overall firm billing rate structure, the RPE's billing rate prior to retirement, and the nature of work that they are performing as RPEs.
- Finder's fees equal to 10 percent of the first year's fees on new projects sold to people and entities who are not existing firm clients will be paid to RPEs.
- Service on boards and other community activities will be compensated on an arranged fee basis, determined by the detailed nature of the work performed, and will be set by agreement between the RPE and the managing partner, with such agreement including expected attendance and periodic performance metrics. Paid board and community work must be approved in advance by the managing partner or must be outlined specifically as part of the expected and explicitly compensated duties of the RPE.
- Work performed for administrative duties internally at the firm will be compensated based on either an hourly charge rate or total project fee, which has been agreed upon in advance. Services rendered by the RPE to the firm might take the form of internal training, special firm projects, specific administrative duties, and so on.
- The firm will employ its normal pay practices for partners to set the frequency and timing of payment for billable work and community activities (for example, if the firm pays existing partners twice monthly, then the firm will pay RPEs twice monthly).
- Finder's fees will be paid to RPEs within 60 days after the first year's fees from new client work the RPEs sold are determined. Payment of finder's fees is based on collections. Therefore, in the circumstance in which the managing partner authorizes compensation for work sold and then later determines that some or all of those fees are uncollectable, the RPE will either be allowed to reimburse the firm for any overpayment, or if not rectified within 30 days of notice, those fees owed to the firm by the RPE will be taken out of future earnings. If no future earnings are expected to be available within the subsequent 30–60 days, then the shortfall can be taken out of the RPE's retirement benefit or capital reimbursement.
- In addition to pay for services performed, the firm will pay or reimburse the RPE for properly documented ordinary and necessary business expenses, including the following:
  - Up to 40 hours of annual CPE
  - Professional licenses, AICPA dues, and home state society dues
  - Dues for membership in up to two community service organizations that have been stipulated between the RPE and the managing partner, active participation in which has been agreed to between the RPE and the managing partner
  - Other, as determined necessary between the managing partner and the RPE

Employment at Will

The firm's annual contract with an RPE can be terminated unilaterally by the firm at any time, without notice or cause. Upon termination, any balance owed under this contract for billable work, community service participation, or any other agreed-upon activities performed under the annual contract then in place will be paid to the RPE within 30 days of the termination of the contract, with the exception of finder's fees for new business.

Additional Learning Resources

As you know from the materials at the end of the first chapter, additional self-study CPE courses are available for your review. Many of them are all-video courses developed from our streaming video webcasts, and others were created from the various books we have written. These courses can be found at www.successioninstitute.com/PMRC.

Remember to take advantage of your discount by entering the word "succession" into the coupon code field.

Here are some courses we recommend that could provide you some additional insight into the many issues surrounding successfully transitioning partners into productive and valuable RPEs.

- The Succession Management Landscape (all-video)
- Building Your Firm's Succession Plan—Part 2 (all-video)
- Pulling It All Together With a Partner/Shareholder Agreement (all-video)

Building Your Firm's Robust Succession Plan

We are now back to the succession planning development phase. As we have covered before, once you complete this last section of each chapter, by the time you finish the book, you will have written down foundational ideas to review with your partners. Once you pull together these final sections, you will have identified your recommendations about how to handle each succession planning area (or at a minimum, questions the partner group needs to answer), and you will have a document that can be presented for discussion, modification, and eventual approval that will guide the changes in policy, agreements, governance, and culture your firm will undertake to implement this succession plan over the next few years.

Now that you have thought more about setting up policies for RPEs, please respond to the following questions about this topic:

What is your recommendation regarding the duration of the agreement with an RPE? When would it expire, thereby requiring a new agreement to be entered into?

_____

_____

_____

_____

What is your recommendation regarding RPEs being allowed to continue to manage clients? If you support RPEs continuing to manage clients, describe limitations, if any, you would suggest imposing regarding what kind of clients or what size clients they would be allowed to manage. (For example, typically, individual tax clients, who are contemporaries of the RPE, are limited to clients making up no more than $20,000 to $30,000 in annual revenue.)

_____
_____
_____
_____
_____
_____
_____
_____

Would RPEs be required to follow some standardized firm processes and procedures (because in many firms, partners are often allowed to operate with some autonomy regarding their work process)? Would RPEs be allowed to act inappropriately outside of work (under the influence, arrested, DWI or DUI, public criticism of the firm, inappropriate public behavior, and so on) and continue to work for the firm? If they don't, what are the consequences (for example, termination of contract, financial penalty)? Does the managing partner have the power to take action alone, or does it require a partner meeting to make this type of decision?

_____
_____
_____
_____
_____
_____
_____

Do RPEs have the ability to instruct staff to put in overtime to get their projects out? Other than performing project work, do RPEs have the authority to manage anyone?

_____
_____
_____

What perks and benefits will RPEs be entitled to (working space or office type; flexibility regarding CPE, such as conferences in resort areas; expense reimbursement for what types and amount of expenses, and so on)?

_____

_____

_____

_____

_____

_____

_____

_____

_____

How will RPEs be paid? What are the general pay provisions that can be built into an RPE's contract or the firm's RPE policy? As a reminder of what these might be, see the preceding examples and those in volume 1.

_____

_____

_____

_____

_____

_____

_____

_____

_____

Describe the process that you recommend for terminating an RPE. Who specifically has the power to terminate an RPE or RPE contract (managing partner, vote of the partner group at what voting threshold)?

_____

_____

_____

_____

_____

_____

_____

_____

_____

Chapter 14: Defining the Maximum Payout Process and Other Buyout-Related Issues

Key Themes from *Securing the Future, Volume 1: Building Your Firm's Succession Plan*, Chapter 14

- Personal liability of remaining owners for retired owners' full payout
- Specific recourse or solutions should a retired owner not be paid in full
- Sale or merger of a practice
- Ability of retired partners to block mergers or sales unless their retirement obligation is paid in full
- Ability of retired partners to block sale of a line of business unless their retirement obligation is paid in full
- Partially funded retirement plans
- Maximum payout provision
- Purchase price of other companies and real estate

Because we have covered the preceding topics in detail in volume 1, we have a few policies to consider and then formalize for your own use in the "Tools and Resources" section. As a bonus, we have added more information about buying, selling, or merging firms into this chapter because these are all options typically considered when major changes in leadership or the retirement of key partners occurs.

What About Mergers and Sales?

Securing the Future volumes 1 and 2 were written to provide guidance to professionals seeking to create options for internal succession management transfers. However, we know that some readers will have questions about mergers and sales, as well, so we are going to provide some high-level coverage of those types of transactions.

One question to begin this discussion is, What are some important issues or nuances that affect value? Our answer is *All of the things you have been putting off addressing and that you don't want to spend money implementing.* Firm owners kid themselves every day regarding the value they are building because of haphazard management practices. For example, what firms have been buying historically (or looking to acquire through mergers) are the client list and revenue stream of other firms; however, today, what firms are really looking for is a combination of people to do the work and the revenue stream, with revenue stream by itself diminishing somewhat in importance.

In the case of either a sale or merger, when owners retire or sell their practice or merge into a larger practice, the acquiring firm needs to not only retain the profitable clients but also find someone to do the work to make the acquisition of that practice viable. For these reasons, smaller practices are still occasionally earning seemingly higher sales prices today (more on that later) because integrating a few profitable clients using the existing staff of the buyer may be feasible. However, the bigger the firm, the more the acquirer shifts his or her focus toward the combination of the people, the revenue, and the profits simply because the buyer will need the additional capacity and funding to make the deal work.

In the end, the seller almost always gets paid only for clients the purchaser retains. The first thing the buyer does to maximize the value of his or her purchase and minimize the amount owed the seller is to run off any clients who (1) won't pay standard rates, (2) are one-off unique engagements, or (3) are problem clients, such as collection problems. Similarly, the equity interest in the new firm that the owner of a firm merging upstream will get will reflect client retention. So, all of those clients whom you (the seller) continue to service that would fall into this "marginal" client category are likely of no value for an exit strategy.

Typical Acquisitions of CPA Firms

Acquisition Multipliers

Most acquisition stories have a multiplier of revenue in common. Over the last 20 years, we have seen that multiplier range anywhere from 50 percent (.5) to about 225 percent (2.25). Today, revenue multipliers ranging from 85 cents on the dollar to $1 for each dollar of revenue are most often quoted as examples. Rarely today do we hear of numbers in excess of $1. However, as you will see in the example that follows, this benchmark can be very misleading.

Acquisition Purchasers

There have been several times in the history of our profession when firms would go on a buying frenzy (as they have recently), acquiring as many firms that met their criteria as they could. High volumes of activity can temporarily create a supply-and-demand anomaly that will drive up market prices, especially when the criteria for acquisition are loosely defined. We saw this phenomenon originate from the corporate marketplace, with mergors such as American Express and H&R Block (a *mergor* is defined in our book as either a firm that is acquiring another firm or the firm into which another one will be folded). In today's marketplace, these transactions are not coming from the big consolidators, but in many cases, from regional firms and large local firms looking to expand geographically or in terms of services, industries, or volume.

The more a firm has experience with mergers, the more constrained and conservative their approach to acquisition because of the many scars and financial losses they have incurred from sloppily managed mergers early on. Mergor firms have found that when diverse cultures collide, the result is often a terrible explosion that creates casualties for all sides. Firms have discovered that owner competencies, roles, responsibilities, and accountability can be extremely different from one firm to the next. Unfortunately, the idea that all owners can easily be reshaped was fabricated on the same logic as the process of herding cats. The philosophy that two firms will be far better off by uniting their superstars has over and over yielded friction and annulment as power struggles fragment the new firm. The misguided belief that all clients are good clients has led to the purchase and then the fairly immediate firing or loss of those clients as a result of issues of price sensitivity, profitability, or negligible opportunity for service expansion.

> The presumption that two well-run firms with strong processes and methodology will seamlessly combine has too often led to a loss in accountability, organizational chaos, and controversy over hierarchy, procedure, and policy. Together, this has generated the recognition and observance of a success factor critical to the merger and acquisition process. Once the mergor firm has found a synergistic target firm with seemingly compatible cultures, comparable personnel expectations, and a fair price, any transaction that takes place will come with the following caveat from the mergor firm: "Although we will listen to your ideas, and we are willing to consider your suggestions, there can only be one firm in charge. By agreeing to join us, you need to be clear that everyone in your organization will be forced to conform to our way of operating the firm."

Without clear communication on this important point, the entire organization will become confused by the politics and power struggles that begin to rip through the fabric of the institution. It is this reorganizational cost that has been the most damaging to firms that have sustained it. The most frequent response from CEOs and managing partners on this topic is, "It wasn't the money we spent that was so detrimental. What was most destructive was the internal chaos, the loss in organizational direction, and the time and resources required to not only unravel parts of the deal but remove the people who could not be salvaged." To take this a step further and demonstrate the experience of a typical (and far too common) acquisition or merger, we are sharing the following scenario:

> Facilitator: "So, how successful has your acquisition/merger strategy been?"

> Client: "It is working fine. We bought numerous small firms over the past 15 years and merged in a couple as well."

> Facilitator: "Could you summarize the most recent acquisition or merger?"

> Client: "Well, we bought a firm with an $800,000 book about five years ago from a partner that wanted to retire. He worked with us for about a year before he retired. We originally planned on him staying around for several years, but he was too disruptive, so we told him he didn't have to stay the entire period. We got a few good clients from the deal; several are still our clients. We got a great manager, and she is currently on our partner track, but most of the others didn't really fit in. The best news of all is we made our last payment on the deal about two years ago."

> Facilitator: "If I can summarize, what I am hearing is that you paid about $800,000 for a firm..."

> Client: "Stop. No, we didn't pay $800,000. We probably only paid $500,000 because we ran off a good number of his clients right at the beginning."

> Facilitator: "Okay, so you paid $500,000 for a partner to transition the work, which he did such a bad job of that you let him go early; it took you several years to get rid of a number of marginal employees; you have kept about $300,000 worth of clients, and you salvaged one manager that's on your partner track. Is that the story?"
>
> Client: "That about sums it up."

The point is that mergers and acquisitions, at best, come with a great deal of baggage. Most firms simply look at the price paid, but from our experience, the hidden cost is clear, as described in the preceding story. That real cost results from the chaos that occurs and management focus required to clean up a plethora of issues so that the firm can get back on track.

Acquisition Structures

The challenges inherent in the merger and acquisition experience have led firms to conduct much more complex and comprehensive investigations pertaining to the culture and operating processes before a deal is seriously considered. Let's take a simple example regarding client make-up alone. Years ago, a buying firm might have offered the seller a simple deal of a dollar for each dollar of gross revenues and closed the deal, with no look-back period or reduction for lost clients. Today, you might hear someone express a willingness to pay that same amount, but with caveats such as the following:

- We will only pay you $1 for each dollar in revenue for the clients that you transition to us and that we decide to keep.
- There would be a cap per client based on last year's billings. Should we bill the client more, that is our gain. Should we bill the client less, that is your loss.
- We will pay you 20 percent of the total due based on what we bill your client base each year, over five years, with that amount limited based on the per-client cap.

Although some brokers will tell you they make deals all the time for a fixed price upfront with no retainer caveats or look-back provisions, we don't see them. Most likely, our clients are just too savvy, but would you buy anything, either through an internal or external deal, where you pay the money up front, with the retiring partner having no consequences or accountability for what he or she is doing, has done, or has promised to do but does not deliver? We believe that these deals should be paid over a period of time (we like five years, but some deals are small enough that three or four years might make sense), based on the clients that the buyer decides to keep. This is a far more common current scenario than cash up front with no accountability.

Sometimes, when a mergor buys or merges with a firm, they are willing to pay a premium over market. Premiums are often used to motivate deals that might not come together otherwise or wouldn't come together in the timeframe that interests the mergor. For example, the acquisition target may have people with a specialty, skill, talent, or niche that the mergor really wants to build up; the mergee firm may be in a location the mergor has strategically targeted (with an acquisition or merger saving the mergor hundreds of thousands of dollars over opening an office from scratch); or the profitability of the firm being acquired could be much higher than normal.

Typically, most premiums are paid through one of the following methods:

- Offering more than $1 for each dollar of revenue.
- Placing the cap described earlier not on the client level of revenue, but on total revenue. This would allow the selling firm that has lost money due to dropped clients from the mergor firm to have a chance to make up some or all of it with growth in business from the clients they keep.

- Agreeing to a floor on the revenue number.
- Allowing the acquisition or mergee firm to share in any growth that occurs during the look-back or pay-out period. This may be a simple straight calculation, or it might be one that diminishes. For example, you might pay a firm dollar for dollar for the first $150,000 of growth, then 75 cents on the dollar for the next $150,000, and maybe 50 cents for anything above that for the duration of the pay-out period.

All of these, and many other variations, can occur. But, as we mentioned previously, too many people get fixated on the payment amount per dollar of revenue as the key, when in fact, it is the whole deal that matters. For example, buying a firm for $1 for each dollar of revenue retained and paying that out over five years could easily be a far better deal than being paid $1.25 for each dollar in revenue paid out over eight years. Being paid 75 cents for each dollar in revenue retained paid over four years with interest could be a much better deal than either of the other two described previously. So, our warning is that the deal, down payment, floor, ceiling, payment period, guarantees (rare), interest or not (the common option is without interest), payment per revenue retained, and much more all need to be considered together when looking at whether a deal is good or bad. Just because some other CPA firm is willing to make a stupid offer doesn't make it a good deal. Even if you lose a couple of deals because someone is outbidding you, each stupid deal the other firm makes will make them weaker. A fair deal is a good deal for both parties. If either side is looking to take advantage of the other, run, because it is hard enough to make smart deals work. You can rest assured that stupid deals never work; the firms that make them spend all of their energy just trying to work through and survive them.

One other caution: Most firms being acquired *don't* have exceptionally trained people, premium-level profits, or strong, well-known specialty niches. If they did, the firm's owners would most likely be selling to their internal people rather than through an external transfer, such as an acquisition or merger. Most partners that tell you they could sell a million dollars of work if they had the capacity can't because if they could, they would have hired the capacity. Sellers commonly oversell what they have to offer. If you believe someone can truly do extraordinary things, then tie those touted deliverables to future performance pay but not to the deal.

In today's market, after everything is said and done, if you sell your practice for the price of $1 for each dollar of revenue retained, this will still likely only net you considering retention over four or five years (as the seller) between 60 and 75 cents on the dollar unless your firm is exceptional enough to be granted some significant premium privileges (and most firms are not). However, almost all sellers think their firm deserves premium considerations.

This brings up a common point of confusion: We often hear that you will make more by selling your book or practice externally rather than internally. It might be that you have no confidence selling internally, so you discount the probability of ever being paid in full. Other than this assumption, we have not found external deals to be more lucrative than internal deals. Although the stated payment for revenues you are offered might be higher from an external buyer, we find the net that you will receive will be lower. On the rare occasion when we work with a firm that has created a retirement formula of something less than market, we push them to "make it right." This isn't because we don't want the junior partners to get a good deal. It's because when this is the case, 9 times out of 9.3, the senior partners will just sell or merge the firm so that they can receive a closer-to-market benefit package.

We believe that there is a number the junior partners are willing to pay in excess of market, and a number that senior partners are willing to take below market. We usually quote, for simplicity, the 20 rule. Junior partners might be willing to pay up to 20 percent more than a partner's share of the business is worth, and a partner might be willing to take up to 20 percent less than his or her share of the business is worth, but the closer you get to these extremes, the more you are asking for something bad to happen—for a split to occur, or a forced sale or merger, for example. When this condition exists, and unfortunately, it occurs far more often than it should, it is often about greed. Someone wanted more than he or she deserved for what he or she was offering, with a result that's worse for everyone.

Here is why we see internal purchases or retirement benefits as more lucrative than an external transaction. It is straightforward business logic. The internal transaction requires far fewer changes for the continuing or take-over parties. Change creates discomfort, and the absence of that discomfort usually drives a willingness to pay a little extra. Think of it this way: When junior partners buy out a senior partner, they are not being asked to change cultures, operating systems, technology, clients, and so on. When the senior partner retires, the junior partners have the luxury of continuing to work with the same clients and staff, doing almost exactly what they were doing before retirement. When someone buys or merges with a firm, clients are being asked to change firms, and partners and staff are being asked to adapt to a different culture, set of policies and processes, technology, and more. In other words, everything is changing for everyone. Therefore, logic demands that the external market, although potentially offering more for revenues, will likely end up paying less for the firm by the time the dust settles regarding client retention. As well, external sales typically cost more because they have an exceptional number of integration, organizational, and structural issues to deal with, which carry the high price tag of non-chargeable resources, downtime, relearning, acculturation, and much more. For these reasons, most of the time, our experience has been that internal sales ultimately end up delivering more dollars to the seller and cost less to the buyers.

The exception to this has come from sole practitioners or small practices of several hundred thousand dollars in annual revenue. Often, these deals are done for a variety of reasons, and upfront cash deals with no look-back provisions are more common. But in these situations, factors such as a staff member, access to a couple of clients, eliminating competition in the small market, or just the size of the transaction might be driving the justification to structure the deal simply and get it done. Think of a buyer of real estate who only has an interest in the land, not the house on the land, so the buyer doesn't care what the house inspection uncovers—the buyer is just planning on demolishing it anyway. So, a firm might buy a practice in a small rural town just to take out the low-end price competition so that there is less resistance to their own fee structure, rather than allowing someone to continue that firm with similar pricing practices. Or, because of the small size of the practice being considered, the purchasing firm just wants access to a couple key clients and doesn't want the seller around, so they offer $200,000 cash up front with no look-back provisions for a $300,000 practice, just to simplify and immediately wrap up the deal. There are a lot of examples like this, but don't confuse one of these strategic moves as a reflection of market price. They are more akin to a seller being in the right place at the right time for the buyer.

Acquisition Networks

Another marketplace mechanism, often a precursor to acquisition, is for small firms to band together through strategic alliances, networks of firms, or overhead- and office-sharing arrangements. Because it has become increasingly more difficult for sole proprietors and small firms to handle the vast array of work their clients are demanding, more and more small firms are coming together to assist each other. Although these arrangements run the gamut from simply sharing specific overhead while keeping the businesses totally separate, to combining the businesses but splitting profits on an EWYK basis, these arrangements are providing these small firms with advantages. Benefits include access to additional staff when needed, reductions in operating costs, quick access to peers to exchange ideas, and groups to whom they may sell their clients when the time comes. We not only believe that this option will continue to build momentum on its own, but it will exponentially explode when for-profit groups and CPA societies or associations put together localized networks seeded with agreements, talent-sharing policies, billing procedures, practice continuation agreements, and succession plans. Note that we believe these networks will flourish when they are built around quality SOPs supporting an EWYK model that allows the group to run smoothly within the administrative structure created.

Typical Mergers of CPA Firms

Merger Sellers and Purchasers

The primary driver for most merger transactions is the creation of an exit strategy for one or more of the senior owners of the mergee firm. Small firms are joining larger firms to ensure that their clients can continue to receive quality services while the owners are simultaneously being assured that their retirement benefits are financially secure. As you might imagine, the snag in these deals usually comes from answers to the following questions:

- How long do the senior owners have to work for the merged firm?
- What will be the owners' base salary, and how will their annual compensation be derived?
- What guarantees exist? Are there none? Is there a one- or two-year guaranteed salary?
- Most importantly, how is the retirement benefit to be calculated; what will it likely be, what conditions can reduce that benefit, and when are the owners eligible to start drawing it?

Merger Structures

Currently, the merger deals being executed involve minimal to no cash. They are more of a pooling of assets than anything else. Although the mergee firm might get to keep its cash in the bank (partially to pay the payables), typically the receivables, WIPs, and whatever fixed assets are considered valuable to the new firm form the basis of the new owners' capital accounts and ownership percentage (in other words, the mergee firm moves their balance sheet into the mergor firm, and ownership is granted for value contributed). If those amounts fall short of the mergor firm's minimums, then it is common to negotiate a timeframe for the new owners to bring their balances up to expectations.

The deal larger mergor firms typically make to mergee firms is "Join us, and

- we will put our name on your door."
- the partners—those of your owners whom we accept as partners—will be entitled to our retirement benefits package" (usually some multiple of salary, sometimes with some consumer price index adjustment).
- we will guarantee the partners' minimum compensation for a year or two at what you have been making."
- because you will be part of our bigger firm, you will be able to sell services to larger clients, which will give your office access to more profitable work. Although the partners are likely to share a little in the overall success of the firm, most of the compensation centers on office profitability."

Some (but very few) firms will kick in a little money up front to sweeten the deal, maybe as much as 15 percent. When they do this, expect something to offset the money on the back end. No one would pay a 15-percent premium without an offset somewhere else; otherwise, everyone would be selling or merging with the same firm. And when cash is on the table, the mergor firm wants to make sure it is not all going to the partners who are leaving. It should come as no surprise that the senior owners of the mergee firm are pushing for exactly the opposite.

Although it is far less common, some firms are looking at the acquisition and merger market from a multiple-of-profit perspective. Given that most businesses in the United States trade on this type of model, it is predictable that this approach will become more and more commonplace in our profession over time. Profitability is viewed in two key ways: total profits (excluding all partner payments, which would be consistent with the generic small business market model) or excess earnings of partners (the more corporate model). Depending on which one is used, the multiples will be different. We have heard of numbers being tossed around between two and eight times, with somewhere from three to five times being the target multiples for the excess-earnings variation.

Regardless of the pricing approach—whether it be offered as a percentage of net revenues, size of a book, or a multiple of profits—firm profitability, client mix, ease of assimilation, and staff talent levels and availability (a right-side-up pyramid with appropriate numbers of staff at every level) affect the "cents on the dollar" or "multiple" being contemplated as the price of the deal. For example, a recent deal for marginally profitable work with poor client mix, but a good staff mix, ended up at around 50 cents on the dollar for a firm with millions in revenues. Without the good staff mix, the deal would have been significantly south of 50 cents, or, most likely, not even a deal at all. Logically, the variables mentioned previously will have either a positive or negative effect on the adjustments that will be proposed.

Adjustments that are ordinarily considered to offset the various identified inequities, either pro or con, would be as follows:

- **Salary guarantees.** Minimum salary guarantees, typically at current levels, but could be higher or lower, as well.

- **Retirement formulas.** For owners who will be retiring soon, the mergor firm might establish a minimum annual salary and freeze the retirement amount so that these owners can focus their time on transitioning their clients. The reason for this is because some retirement formulas increase with firm growth. If the partner is only coming in long enough to transition clients, then the firm might freeze his or her benefits at the levels at which the firm is operating at the time of merger. If the mergor firm is trying to sweeten the pot, they could identify a minimum retirement benefit but also let them share in the success of the organization until the day they actually depart or sell their ownership.

- **Adjustment to the variables.** A number of retirement systems have both a years-of-service component and an age component, which affect the retirement calculation. Most firms will tinker with these variables, making either positive or negative adjustments, to reflect the exceptional or marginal characteristics of the target firm. For example, adding to the years of service, or to the years of age, or both, are examples of trying to reflect a premium value for the unique niche or profitability of the target firm being merged into a fixed retirement system. Or, these are also common sweetening adjustments to allow a senior partner or two in the mergee firm to have access to the mergor firm's retirement benefits a little earlier.

- **Ownership allocation.** Agreements in a number of mergers will freeze the gross income or profitability of the firm at the time of merger, whereas others will consider changes to revenues and profits for some period of time after the merger for ownership and benefit allocation purposes. For example, a firm might make negative adjustments against owners versus what would have been calculated on day one of the merger because of key clients lost during transition, especially when those clients were an impetus to the deal. Or, to satisfy a different situation, that same firm might allow the allocated revenue and profit numbers to upwardly adjust and be credited to the mergee firm's owners to reflect new services sold during a specific window of time. In other words, there is an ownership percentage calculated when the deal is consummated, but the deal might be set up from the onset to allow for adjustment of that percentage up or down based on the performance of the partners during a specific window of time.

- **Partner slots (the number of partners in the mergee firm that would be made partners in the mergor firm).** This is always an issue in any negotiation. It is common for some partners in the mergee firm to be brought over to the mergor firm as senior managers. This is because, in smaller firms, the criteria (statistically, economically, technically, competencies) to become a partner often are less formalized. As firms grow larger, the reverse is true. So, although it might be commonplace for a $2 million firm to have four partners, in larger firms, just on volume alone, only two partners could be justified (and, more likely, just one). Sometimes, added hurdles are inserted to make sure the mergee partners are a good fit for the mergor firm by only allowing a limited number of partners to come over as equity partners, with other partners in the mergee firm tagged as income partners or principals with specific performance criteria identified for them to meet before being admitted as an equity owner in the new firm.

No matter what adjustments are made at the time of merger, most of these arrangements, except for those affecting retirement, will quickly default to everyone operating within the mergor firm's operating procedures and processes. It is a bad practice to cut every partner a deal of their own. So, if the mergee firm owners are offered guaranteed minimum salaries, then all of those salaries are likely to be guaranteed for the same period of time. After that protected period, owners will have to earn their money based on whatever performance system is in place.

In years past, some firms made the terrible mistake of cutting special long-term compensation contracts not only with each merged firm, but with different owners within each firm. This backfired most of the time because rather than having a united owner group working to achieve the firm's strategy, the mergor firms ended up with multiple owner groups managing their own disconnected compensation strategies. Silos appeared everywhere, with the owners' personal interests in direct conflict with firm interests. Until these owners had their contracts renegotiated, were paid off, or retired, the mergor firm was trapped within its own expansion success. Firms learned very painfully that adjustments to compensation or retirement had to be made within one existing framework, or the mergor firm's theoretical step forward through merger could easily become a couple of steps backward.

A strategy we strongly recommend (and are often challenged for suggesting it by other consultants and some larger firms) with any merger is an opt-out agreement, so that either party can walk from the deal. This allows a new owner a window of time (often no more than a year, but we have worked with firms that set it at two years) to determine whether he or she can operate within the mergor firm's organization. If the owner cannot, he or she has the right to leave and take his or her clients, assuming all the pre-identified financial issues have been resolved. The same is true on the other side—the mergor may want the right to disconnect the mergee firm. This desire to annul the merger may be due to a conflict between owners of the two firms, personal differences, ethical perspectives, an unwillingness of the mergee firm partners to be held accountable to the mergor firm's processes, and so much more. Interestingly, in our experience, when this clause exists, most often the mergee and mergor firm waive their rights to this clause within the first seven to nine months because both parties know what they are getting and want to put the possibility of splitting up behind them.

There are two schools of thought regarding opt-out agreements. One is that you want to penalize whichever firm uses the opt-out escape clause because they have wasted the resources the other firm has put into integrating the two. This makes sense—integration, training, and indoctrination are time-consuming, expensive, and resource intensive (especially because the hardship is more often due to the consumption of scarce resources versus the cost of those resources). However, we prefer that there be no penalty; we don't want a financial penalty to be the reason a deal holds together. When a financial penalty becomes a strong influence on the break-up decision, the firm likely will be the beneficiary of inaction (meaning, people stay when they really want to leave). This will result in unnecessary and constant conflict; poor unity in the partner group; growth in passive-aggressive behavior; too much outside-of-meeting politicking; and an inability to accomplish as much as the firm should because of a lack of a unified strategy and structure. We like the fact that an opt-out agreement shifts attention away from penalty and toward the rules of the breakup.

If a merger is not working and doesn't look like it is ever going to work, why would you want to hold that together? This is dysfunction at its peak. For our clients that have joined large firms with no opt-out strategy when the merger didn't work out, the absence of an opt-out clause didn't stop the divorce; it just forced them to take a much more damaging strategy of suing their way out of the deal, and litigation is an option that causes financial and emotional damage to both sides. Opting out of a merger may happen 1 or 2 times in 10 based on our experience. But when this is the option chosen, to us, it makes much more sense to have an orderly breakup process that has been agreed to in advance, rather than involving the clients and staff in an ugly battle.

Merger Hybrid Strategy

You are likely to encounter a hybrid merger and acquisition strategy more and more frequently. Rather than buying or merging with an entire organization, firms are soliciting niche, industry, or specialized teams of people to join them. For instance, if a firm needs additional support for one of its niches or is interested in building a new service or industry specialization, it might find a small team within a competitive firm and make them an offer they can't refuse. Although these firms might pay a nice bounty to their new employees for a niche-specific group of clients to transition with them, many are more interested in acquiring the expertise and are happy to pay their new employees to rebuild the niche business from scratch. Who would have thought that a group of CPAs with no clients but a strong specialty expertise would be considered a good merger target? Logically, most firms have not put anything in place to address this possibility because the traditional thinking is that owner groups merge as a whole. So, buckle up and get ready; the stage is set for some very interesting deals in the decade to come.

By the way, it is during deals such as this that exceptional pricing can be found. It might be worth paying high signing bonuses and twice the market rates for client revenues to get access to a niche service group synergistic with the mergor firm. However, just as we discussed when we mentioned the small firm cash deal earlier, don't mistake a strategic buy/

merger with market price. When you consider the cost of recruiting, paying head hunters, advertising for specific skillsets, and perks and bonuses to move people from one city to the next, it could be significantly cheaper to carve out part of a local competitor's firm than build your own niche service group from the ground up.

We have included some templates that you may wish to review or use if you are going to pursue a merger or a sale.

Tools and Resources

Policies for Consideration

The following is sample wording for a couple of policies that might be helpful for creating more structure around some of the issues discussed in this chapter. As with all of our policy examples, please consult your legal counsel for what is appropriate for your firm.

The Succession Institute's Maximum Payout of Guaranteed Payments for Retired Partners Policy

The firm is not required in any year to pay more than 15 percent of the firm's net income for that year (this number is the accrual basis net income of the firm before subtracting partners' base salaries or partner incentives paid through the incentive compensation plan) to cover all the retired, deceased, or disabled partners' retirement payout obligations. If the total retirement obligations for all retired partners exceed 15 percent of net income as defined previously in any year, then the firm, in its sole discretion, can proportionally reduce each retired partner's payments for the following year so that the total equals 15 percent of the firm's net income based on the performance of the preceding year.

Any reduction in retirement pay to a retired partner for any year's retirement payout due to this ceiling will extend the benefit period until the full, original obligation to the partner is paid in full. Additionally, if a retired partner's retirement payout obligation is reduced in any year, then the firm will pay up to the maximum payout each year thereafter in order to attempt to catch up the retirement payout obligation in accordance with the original payment plan for the retirement benefit. Interest will be paid on any amounts withheld due to the ceiling articulated in this policy but not on the entire remaining balance.

The Succession Institute's Sale or Upstream Merger of the Entire Firm Policy

Effectuating a sale or upstream merger of the firm requires a vote of the equity interest equal to 66 2/3 percent and at least one of the following:[1]

- Payment in full of the present value of any outstanding retirement liabilities or other liabilities outstanding due to disabled or deceased partners
- Agreement to the sale or merger by those partners or retired partners and representatives of disabled and deceased partners who have outstanding retirement liabilities

Once the preceding conditions have been met, the remaining proceeds, if any, will be divided among the current partners at the time of the sale or merger according to their equity ownership interests at the time of the sale or merger.

Definition of Upstream Merger

The firm's definition of an *upstream merger* will be a transaction in which the existing partners of the firm lose controlling interest in the combined entity.

The following are examples of common issues that arise when partners retire and how to divest those partners from buildings and other companies the firm operates. We included a couple of different examples for your review not to set an example of an appropriate buyout, but to share the idea that the firm needs to be specific about how value will be determined, when it will be determined, when the sale will occur, how it will be paid, and so on. As with all of our policy examples, please consult your legal counsel for what is appropriate for your firm.

---

[1] These conditions are more common for small firms than for large firms, which will normally just articulate the voting requirement.

The Succession Institute's Purchase Price of Other Companies Policy

The purchase price for the other companies' ownership interests shall be as follows:

Firm-Owned Building

Only equity owners in the firm can be owners in the firm's building. All equity owners in the firm will have an ownership interest in the firm's building equal to their ownership in the firm (some firms sell every equity owner an equal interest so that adjustments to ownership never have to change until sold).

When a partner retires or reaches mandatory date of sale of ownership, he or she will sell his or her interest in the building at the end of the calendar year in which he or she retired. The purchase price will be set based on the appraisal process that follows. Within 30 days of the calendar year-end of the year the partner retires, if the firm and the retiring partner can agree to a qualified and registered real estate appraiser, then they will sign a document prior to the appraisal that they have both agreed to live by the results of the appraisal for determining the value of the building. If the firm and the retiring partner cannot agree, each will hire his or her own qualified and registered real estate appraiser. The appraisals are to be completed on, or prior to, 30 days after the calendar year-end. Any appraisals not completed within this timeframe will be void for consideration unless both parties agree otherwise. For those appraisals completed within the required timeframe, the firm and the partner will review. If the firm and the partner can agree to a value for the building within 60 days of the calendar year-end for the year in which the partner retired, then their agreement will set the value of the building. If the firm and the retired partner cannot agree to a value within this 60-day period, then the value will be set by an arbitrator. The firm and the retired partner have 30 days to agree to an arbitrator and if they cannot, then the arbitrator, Joe Lawyer, will be hired on the 30th day to set the value of the building. Once the value has been determined, the retired partner will be bought out by the firm, and his or her ownership in the building will be sold or distributed to other partners in the firm.

Affiliated Company A

The equity owners in the CPA firm have a majority interest in Affiliated Company A. That majority interest is spread to all the equity owners in the CPA firm representing their same proportional share. Only equity owners in the firm can be part of this majority ownership in Affiliated Company A. Minority interests in Affiliated Company A can be sold to non-partners of the CPA Firm.

When a partner retires or reaches mandatory date of sale of ownership, he or she will sell his or her interest in Affiliated Company A at the end of the calendar year in which he or she retired. The purchase price will be set based on the following formula:

> 4 times EBITA (earnings before interest, taxes, depreciation, and amortization) determined by the company financial statement, less any compensation or management fees paid to the CPA firm, times the ownership interest of the retired partner in Affiliated Company A.

The amount due the retiring partner for his or her interest in Affiliated Company A will be determined within 90 days of the end of the year in which he or she retired, with his or her first annual payment due the next calendar year-end. The retired partner will be paid for his or her share in Affiliated Company A over a three-year period without interest in annual installments.

Wholly Owned Company B

The equity owners in the CPA firm have the same ownership interest in the Wholly Owned Company B. Only equity owners in the firm can be an owner in Wholly Owned Company B.

When a partner retires or reaches mandatory date of sale of ownership, he or she will sell his or her interest in Wholly Owned Company B at the end of the calendar year in which he or she retired. The purchase price will be set based on the following formula:

> Net revenues for the two previous years (starting with the year the partner is retiring and the revenues for the year before that) are averaged. The average of net revenues is multiplied by 65 cents on the dollar to establish the total value of Wholly Owned Company B. The equity ownership of the retiring partner is multiplied by value of Wholly Owned Company B to determine the amount the retiring partner is to be paid for his or her interest in Wholly Owned Company B.

The amount due the retiring partner for his or her interest in Wholly Owned Company B will be determined within 90 days of the end of the year in which he or she retired, with his or her first annual payment due the next calendar year-end. The retired partner will be paid for his or her share in Wholly Owned Company B over a 5-year period with interest in annual installments.

The following group of tools are included for your consideration and review when buying or selling a firm or merging your firm.

The Succession Institute's Using the Transfer of an Accounting Practice Checklist

We've created the following checklist to provide you with a tool to help you sort through your options for firms that may be likely candidates to buy or merge in your practice. The checklist is designed around 10 key areas that we've found can make the difference between successful transfers and dismal failures. These areas are as follows:

1. Cultural compatibility, in general
2. Compatibility of owners
3. Strategic perspective
4. Compatibility of client base and service offerings
5. Compatibility of performance management and pay systems
6. Compatibility of firm ownership and governance models
7. Compatibility of businesses, processes, and practices
8. Compatibility of succession management processes
9. Overall stability of the acquiring firm
10. Other factors

The checklist is organized with columns for an exit planning strategy: sale, merge upstream, buy or merge in, and transfer within seamlessly. Keep in mind that, for the most part, these are subjective factors that you must consider. There's no one right answer here and no multiple choices. The idea is for you to use this as a mental model to help you decide which path to pursue. Then, if you decide to transfer the practice to another firm, it will assist you in finding a compatible practice on your way out, thereby putting a little more security in the mix for your ultimate buyout. This checklist doesn't take the place of traditional, quantitative due diligence procedures. It should probably be completed first before you waste time going through minutiae for deals that don't make sense for you.

You can print off a copy of the checklist and use it to help score (relatively speaking) the desirability of candidates who might be buying you out or merging you in or whom you might be merging in or buying out, as well.

The Succession Institute's Transfer of an Accounting Practice Checklist

Factors	Sale	Merge Upstream	Buy or Merge In	Transfer Within Seamlessly
"How we do things around here."				
Core values in action.				
General styles and style differences between and among owners.				
Collegiality among owner group, such as how they talk to, with, and about one another.				
Nature, level, and types of conflicts within owner group, if known.				
Ages of owners and how well spread over next two decades.				
Gap in book size between owners, differences in leverage, and general approach to business and life.				
Existence of firm's long-term direction, strategy, or vision shared by all owners.				
Use of strategy to drive budgeting, operations, and behaviors of owners.				
Compatibility of owners' strategies.				
Industries served.				
Nature of clients served.				
Service offerings provided to clients.				
Service policies and practices.				
Charge rates and fee structure.				
Geographic locations and differences among locations.				

(continued)

Factors	Sale	Merge Upstream	Buy or Merge In	Transfer Within Seamlessly
Performance metrics in use by owners.				
Articulated compensation system used by owners.				
Owner fringe and benefit policies, such as insurance, cars, clubs, dues, CPE, vacations, and so on.				
Leadership development practices for junior partners and managers.				
Staff performance metrics used.				
Staff ages, backgrounds, pay, and benefits.				
Other than pay and benefits, staff policies for CPE, CPA exam, flex time, child care, civic involvement, and so on.				
Staff evaluations, such as nature and frequency, including career-pathing.				
Formal or informal requirements for admission as a partner.				
Spread of current equity ownership among partners.				
Governance model used, such as committee, managing partner with committee, managing partner, unclear, and so on.				
Decision-making processes, such as consensus, majority vote, managing partner, and so on.				
Standard operating procedures in place for decision making, conflict resolution, voting, partners' duties, and so on.				
Roles and responsibilities defined for partners and staff.				
Existence of one signed owners' agreement.				

Factors	Sale	Merge Upstream	Buy or Merge In	Transfer Within Seamlessly
Types and quality of communication within the firm, such as formal and informal.				
Formal or informal business development processes in place.				
Billing and collection practices.				
Standardized administrative processes in place, such as internal accounting and timekeeping, working paper preparation, review, filing, paperless or other, and so on.				
Amount of leverage, such as partner to staff time.				
Firm staffing structure, such as pyramid, inverted pyramid, or other.				
Extent of functional specialization and niches.				
Formal or informal succession management plan and implementation being done to achieve it.				
Expected retirements within the next five years, specifically who, how much equity and cost to firm, as well as amount funded, if any.				
Written documentation stating exactly when senior partners will be retiring and their expected payout under current policies.				
Likelihood acquirer will itself be merged upstream or sold.				
Investment in people.				
Investment in technology.				
Appropriate leadership in place.				
Absence of critical, unresolved issues among owners.				
How will we undo this, or how can we undo this, if it is not working?				

The Succession Institute's Sample Practice Summary for a Firm That Is Being Sold

	1/1/20YY – 7/31/20YY	20XX	
Audit	40	140	
Compilation	80	160	
Consulting*	80	185	High-level summary of services billed. This could also be boken down to show gross and net billed by service category
Review	130	120	
Tax – C corp	50	50	
Tax – Fiduciary & other	10	15	
Tax – Individual	125	145	
Tax – Partnership/LLC	70	70	
Tax – S corp	100	90	
	685	975	
Write-downs	(100)	(120)	
Net billed	585	855	

Audit and review includes amounts for contractor book of business:

	Annual Estimate	
Heavy underground contractor audit & taxes	40 (incl 401(k) audit)	
Specialty subcontractor review & taxes	15	
Specialty subcontractor review & taxes	15	
Specialty subcontractor comp & taxes	30	This summary shows total fees for some major client groups. These totals include taxes and assurance services, so they don't total to above categories
Homebuilder taxes	5	
Heavy underground contractor audit & taxes	50	
Specialty subcontractor review & taxes	15	
Homebuilder/comml contractor review/taxes	15	
Paving contractor review & taxes	15	
	200	
Medical group review and taxes & misc.	80 (incl 401(k) audit)	
	280	

Tax and comp includes various other businesses, e.g., MD's

	Annual Estimate
Industrial/auto parts – wholesale/retail corp	15
Surgeon corp and 1040 + P/sharing acctg	15
Surgeon corp and 1040 + real estate + farm	15
Surgeon + farm	15
Surgeon + related real estate & other entities	25
Private placement R&D LLC tax + audit prep	25
MD 1040's	10
Med practice LLC + 1040	10
Chiropracter	5
	135

The Succession Institute's Sample Mutual Confidentiality Agreement

DISCLAIMER: This publication is distributed with the understanding that the contributing authors and editors, and the publisher, are not rendering legal, accounting, or other professional services in this publication. If legal advice or other expert assistance is required, the services of a competent professional should be sought.

Note: This exhibit is illustrative only. It does not conform to the legal requirement of any particular state. Practitioners who think this material would be useful in their own agreements are advised to consult legal counsel.

THE AGREEMENT made as of the _____ day of _____, 20XX, by and between <u>ABC</u>, a [*professional service corporation, a partnership, or sole proprietor*], of [*city and state*] (hereinafter referred to as ABC), and <u>XYZ</u>, a [*professional service corporation, partnership, or sole proprietor*], of [*city and state*] (hereinafter referred to as XYZ).

WHEREAS, ABC is presently operating an accounting practice being served from an office in [*city and state*]; and

WHEREAS, XYZ is presently operating an accounting practice being served from an office in [*city and state*]; and

WHEREAS, ABC desires to explore the transfer to XYZ the right to service the clients served by ABC from its [*city and state*] office; and

WHEREAS, in the course of exploring such an agreement ABC and XYZ may need to provide access to, non-public, proprietary information and materials concerning the operations of each other, including but not limited to, information about its business practices, management, partnership agreements, finances, marketing or strategic plans, contractual arrangements; staff compensation and billing rates, client fees and profitability; and

WHEREAS, both parties regard it essential to their business purposes to guard against the use of this information by the other party in the course of any future contact with the staff or clients of the other;

NOW, THEREFORE, in consideration of the mutual promises herein made and the considerations herein expressed, the parties hereto mutually covenant and agree as follows:

1. *Treatment of Confidential Information.* Neither party shall use the confidential information of the other party nor circulate it within its own firm except for the extent necessary for analysis of the feasibility of the potential acquisition of ABC.

2. *Return of Confidential Information.* Should the acquisition of ABC by XYZ not occur, both parties agree to return all confidential information to the other party without retaining any of the information in any form.

3. *Survival of Agreement.* This agreement shall survive the termination of termination of discussions between the parties.

4. *Amendments.* This agreement may not be amended except in a writing duly executed by both parties.

5. *Governing law.* This agreement shall be governed by and construed in accordance with the laws of [*state*] and with applicable federal laws and regulations.

6. *Severability.* In the event that any portion of this agreement is found to be void, illegal or unenforceable, the validity or enforceability of any other portion shall not be affected.

IN WITNESS WHEREOF, the parties hereto have executed this Agreement the day and year first above written.

From the AICPA *Management of an Accounting Practice Handbook*

The Succession Institute's Press Release Sample

For Release: December 15, 2014

Contacts:

Joe Doaks: 512-555-0000, joed@www.xyzgroup.com

Jane Doe: 213-555-1111, janed@www.xyzgroup.com

San Antonio Firm Merges With Austin Accounting Firm

San Antonio, Texas (December 15, 2014): The San Antonio accounting firm ABC CPAs, LLC, today announced its upcoming merger with XYZ CPAs, LLC, an Austin-based accounting firm. Effective January 1, 2015, the new firm will be known as XYZ Group, LLC (www.xyzgroup.com).

"This strategic merger provides us with tremendous opportunities to broaden our professional services and geographic reach," said Joe Doaks, managing member of ABC CPAs, LLC, adding, "We are excited about being associated with a firm that has the stature and reputation of XYZ."

"This merger will bring benefits to the clients and employees of both firms," said Jane Doe, managing member of XYZ Group, LLC. "Our clients will have access to increased levels of service and expertise, and our firms will have additional opportunities for growth and expansion. By building on both firms' strengths and reputations as CPAs, business advisers, and management consultants, we will be able to continue to attract the most talented professionals in the industry."

Established in 1963, ABC CPAs, LLC, is recognized for its management consulting expertise, as well as its industry specializations in construction, manufacturing, and professional service firms. Mr. Doaks is nationally recognized for his consulting work in strategy, organizational infrastructure, performance measurement, and organizational development.

Founded in 1969, XYZ CPAs, LLC, has been providing professional services to large and small businesses throughout the central Texas area for nearly 50 years. The firm was recently recognized as the top accounting firm in Austin and is highly regarded for its business auditing, accounting, tax, and management advisory services, as well as individual tax planning and preparation. "The combination of talents between our two firms will bring a wealth of new offerings to our service menu—offerings that many of our clients have been asking for," said Jane Doe.

The Succession Institute's Client Letter From the Mergee

(*Date*)

Dear (*Client*):

I am writing this to share some important news with you. My firm (ABC CPAs, LLC) is merging with the Austin firm of XYZ CPAs, LLC. This is an exciting and strategic move for us!

I very carefully selected XYZ CPAs, LLC, as the right choice for our merger because it is a highly regarded firm with a wonderful reputation for taking great care of its clients. Through this merger, we will not only be able to continue to provide the quality of services you have come to expect, but we can expand our offerings to include some of the many services you have requested over the years. In addition, by building on the strengths of both firms as CPAs, business advisers, and management consultants, we will be able to continue our ability to attract the most talented professionals in the industry.

XYZ CPAs, LLC, is recognized as Austin's top accounting firm for its management consulting expertise, as well as audit, accounting, and tax services. The firm also has extensive experience serving clients in construction, manufacturing, wholesale, retail, nonprofit, and service industries, such as professional practices.

The new firm will be known as XYZ Group, LLC. The merger becomes effective on January 1, 2015. Please take a moment and look at our new website to read about some of the superb talent available to you (www.xyzgroup.com).

I look forward to talking with you about this soon. In the meantime, please don't hesitate to contact me if there is anything we can do for you, if you have questions about the merger, or if you would like some additional information.

Sincerely,

ABC CPAs, LLC, Partner

The Succession Institute's Client Letter From the Mergor

(*Date*)

Dear (*Client*):

We are writing this to share some important news with you. Our firm (XYZ CPAs, LLC) is merging with the San Antonio firm of ABC CPAs, LLC. We chose to merge this firm into ours because of the special talent and services it offers, which would be valuable to many of our clients.

We very carefully selected ABC CPAs, LLC as the right choice for merger because they are a highly regarded firm with a wonderful reputation for taking great care of its clients. Through this merger, we will not only be able to continue to provide the quality of services you have come to expect, but we also can expand our offerings to include some of the many services you have requested over the years. In addition, by building on the strengths of both firms as CPAs, business advisers, and management consultants, we will be able to continue our ability to attract the most talented professionals in the industry.

Due to its management consulting expertise and industry specialization in construction, manufacturing, and professional practices, the firm brings a wealth of new offerings to our menu. The new firm will be known as XYZ Group, LLC. The merger becomes effective on January 1, 2015. Please take a moment and look at our new website to read about some of the superb talent available to you (www.xyzgroup.com).

The management of our firm will remain the same post-merger, so you can continue to expect the same levels of service, core values, care, and pricing to which you are accustomed. We look forward to talking with you about this soon. In the meantime, please don't hesitate to contact me if there is anything we can do for you, if you have questions about the merger, or if you would like some additional information.

Sincerely,

XYZ CPAs, LLC, Managing Partner

The Succession Institute's Sample Letter Notifying Client of Change in Firms

(*Date*)

Dear (*Client*):

I've decided to retire from the practice of accounting and spend more time with my spouse, doing some of the things we've dreamed about for years—traveling, spending more time on the trout stream, and spending a lot more time with our grandchildren.

Once I decided to retire, my attention immediately shifted to you! You are important to me, both as a friend and a client. Therefore, I wanted to find and recommend a new accountant who (1) I respect, (2) will take great care of you, and (3) has a similar service philosophy. After interviewing firms for the past couple months, I am pleased to recommend XYZ Company as a firm ready and anxious to work with you.

The managing partner of XYZ Company, Jane Doe, and I started out together in the profession of public accounting more than 30 years ago. She has been running her own firm since 1989. She and her young, energetic partners and 15 staff are an impressive group. They are known for their expertise in the _____ industry and serve clients in that industry throughout the state of _____.

My staff accountants, Jackson, Mitzi, Alice, and Leonard, have accepted full-time positions with XYZ Company, and they look forward to continuing to serve you through the new firm. As you may know, they did quite a bit of the work on your account and are familiar with your situation. I will still be around for a while on a part-time basis to ensure that you are well taken care of.

I would consider it a personal favor to me if you would allow me the opportunity to arrange a time to introduce you to a partner from XYZ Company within the next couple weeks. I will be calling you soon to discuss this change and answer any questions you might have.

[*Name*], I really appreciate the opportunity to have worked with you all these years, and I will definitely miss that as we go forward. Thanks for everything!

Sincerely yours,

Selling CPA

The Succession Institute's Sample Letter Notifying Client of Change in Firms (Not Seeking Appointments or Meetings With a New CPA Firm)

> *DISCLAIMER: This publication is distributed with the understanding that the contributing authors and editors, and the publisher, are not rendering legal, accounting, or other professional services in this publication. If legal advice or other expert assistance is required, the services of a competent professional should be sought.*

(*Date*)

Dear (*Client*):

I've decided to retire from the practice of accounting and spend more time with my spouse, doing some of the things we've dreamed about for years—traveling, spending more time on the trout stream, and spending a lot more time with our grandchildren.

Once I decided to retire, my attention immediately shifted to you! You are important to me, both as a friend and a client. Therefore, I wanted to find and recommend a new accountant who (1) I respect, (2) will take great care of you, and (3) has a similar service philosophy. After interviewing firms for the past couple months, I am pleased to recommend XYZ Company as a firm ready and anxious to work with you.

The managing partner of XYZ Company, Jane Doe, and I started out together in the profession of public accounting more than 30 years ago. She has been running her own firm since 1989. She and her young, energetic partners and 15 staff are an impressive group. They are known for their expertise in the _____ industry and serve clients in that industry throughout the state of _____.

My staff accountants, Jackson, Mitzi, Alice, and Leonard, have accepted full-time positions with XYZ Company, and they look forward to continuing to serve you through the new firm. As you may know, they did quite a bit of the work on your account and are familiar with your situation. I will still be around for a while on a part-time basis to ensure that you are well taken care of.

Jane's office will be in touch with you shortly. I would consider it a personal favor to me if you would allow us the chance to show you why this firm is the right firm to take care of you. Please call me with any questions or if you are uncomfortable in any way with the new organization.

I really appreciate the opportunity to have worked with you all these years, and I will definitely miss that as we go forward. Thanks for everything!

Sincerely yours,

Selling CPA

The Succession Institute's Steps to Consider When Selling Your Practice

Suggested Activities for Retiring CPA	Comments	Target Date	Completion Date
• Identify likely candidates to buy your practice based on factors identified in the Transfer of an Accounting Practice checklist.			
• Contact potential buyers and discuss the potential sale of your firm briefly and conceptually with them in the following manner: – Initial contact—Call managing partner or CEO of likely prospects. – Conduct subsequent discussion if interest exists after initial contact.			
• For prospective buyers interested in pursuing discussions: – Prepare a nondisclosure agreement for prospective buyers to sign. – Obtain a signed nondisclosure agreement from prospective buyers. – Provide prospective buyers with a high-level summary of practice statistics, such as the performance metrics we covered in the previous chapter.			
• If further discussions are warranted at this point, provide the potential buyer with more detailed information on client groupings and your personnel.			
• Continue discussions through to closure in the following manner: – If discussions lead to no deal, consider adding another prospect to your list. – If discussions lead to signs of a deal, prepare a preliminary draft of the business terms (letter agreement) and provide it to the prospect. – Discuss and negotiate letter agreement with the prospect. – Send draft letter agreement to legal counsel to convert into a contract for sale.			

Suggested Activities for Retiring CPA	Comments	Target Date	Completion Date
• Stay focused on keeping this matter confidential so that it doesn't get out to your staff or into the community until you're ready to announce a deal.			

• Announce the deal to your employees, clients, and referral sources in the following manner:
  – Discuss the deal with employees as a group.
  – Follow up group discussion with individual discussions with each employee to re-recruit them.
  – Let buyer know when you've completed the preceding steps.
  – Call key clients to let them know what's happening.
  – Follow up with letters and e-mails to key clients.
• Send letters and e-mails to the rest of your clients.			

• Be available to help with transitioning the practice and the clients to the new firm in the following manner:
  – Contact key clients to set up meetings with them, the new CPA firm representative, and you.
  – Meet with key clients and the new CPA firm representative.
  – Go over specific likes, dislikes, and nuances of each key client with the new CPA firm owner.
  – Be available to talk with the new CPA firm about clients' files and activities.
  – Be available to clients for their calls with complaints, but stay out of the new firm's relationship with them unless the clients contact you.
  – Make yourself unavailable and selectively incompetent when clients try to engage you in providing technical advice. Either refer them back to the new firm or set up a call between you, the client, and the new firm representative, and set the new firm representative up to shine when discussing the client situation.			

Additional Learning Resources

As you know from the materials at the end of the first chapter, additional self-study CPE courses are available for your review. Many of them are all-video courses developed from our streaming video webcasts, and others were created from the various books we have written. These courses can be found at www.successioninstitute.com/PMRC.

Remember to take advantage of your discount by entering the word "succession" into the coupon code field.

Here are some courses we recommend that could provide you some additional insight into maximum payout, purchase price of other companies, and the merger and sale marketplace.

- The Succession Management Landscape (all-video)
- Building Your Firm's Succession Plan—Part 2 (all-video)
- Pulling It All Together With a Partner/Shareholder Agreement (all-video)
- Making Your Way Through the Merger/Sale Maze (mostly text)

Building Your Firm's Robust Succession Plan

We are now back to the succession planning development phase. As we have covered before, once you complete this last section of each chapter, by the time you finish the book, you will have written down foundational ideas to review with your partners. Once you pull together these final sections, you will have identified your recommendations about how to handle each succession planning area (or, at a minimum, questions the partner group needs to answer), and you will have a document that can be presented for discussion, modification, and eventual approval that will guide the changes in policy, agreements, governance, and culture your firm will undertake to implement this succession plan over the next few years.

Now that you have thought more about setting up policies for maximum payout, purchase price of other companies, and the merger and sale marketplace, respond to the following questions to articulate your thinking about this topic:

Describe the maximum payout strategy you recommend to ensure that you don't put the firm at risk of falling apart or splitting up because of an onerous debt repayment schedule for the remaining partners.

_____

_____

_____

_____

_____

_____

_____

_____

_____

_____

What method are you suggesting (percentage of net income before partner pay, gross revenue, and so on) and why?

_____

_____

_____

_____

What percentage limit are you recommending and why?

_____

_____

_____

_____

Describe how the process works once the percentage ceiling has been hit. How do you propose handling any underpayments to retired partners? How do you propose making them whole for delaying their retirement benefits?

_____

_____

_____

_____

_____

_____

_____

_____

_____

List any companies, buildings, or separate assets that your firm should purchase from a retiring partner.

1. _____

2. _____

3. _____

For each company, describe when the retired partner will be bought out, how the retiring partner's value in that asset will be determined, under what terms will it be repaid, and so on.

1. _____

_____

_____

_____

2. _____

_____

_____

3. _____

_____

_____

_____

Describe your thoughts about the appropriateness of sales or mergers for your firm. Consider this same section from chapter 2, volume 2, when you shared your ideas regarding firm strategy. Based on your thoughts that follow, consider updating your strategy pages in chapter 2, volume 2, if appropriate.

_____

_____

_____

_____

_____

_____

_____

_____

_____

Chapter 15: Creating a Partner Accountability and Compensation Plan

Key Themes from *Securing the Future, Volume 1: Building Your Firm's Succession Plan*, Chapter 15

- Accountability: It should apply to everyone
  - Setting clear expectations to create accountability
  - Commitment to results
  - Delegating versus "dumping"
  - Revisiting the notion of accountability
- Accountability for partners
  - Accountability requires action and commitment
  - Accountability and performance variability
  - Objective performance criteria
  - Subjective performance criteria
  - Establishing the accountability process
  - Benefits of implementing the accountability process
  - Who is in charge
  - Performance pay for the managing partner's allocation

Accountability in CPA firms is one of those areas that often fits into the old adage, "When all is said and done, usually more is said than done." It doesn't have to be that way, though. Chapter 15, volume 1, describes the benefits and reasons for the process and provides a high-level overview of the process.

In this chapter, we'll provide you with some concrete action steps and examples to which your firm can adapt in order to create or improve accountability at your firm. We begin with an outline of key steps to consider in your process, and then we add in some samples to give you an idea of what it might look like in practice. Keep in mind that any partner goal-setting process needs to take into account your firm's strategy as well as partners' strengths and weaknesses.

The Managing Partner Goal-Setting Process— Detailed Steps and Samples

Strategy: First, the firm needs to identify a vision. That vision, based on the market conditions and the specific situation within the firm, might be strategic (long-term focus, such as three years or so) or tactical (12- to 18-month focus). Regardless, the partner group needs to decide where the firm needs to be going in order to drill down to the next level. Notice that we clearly said the *partner group* needs to determine strategy—not the managing partner. Although the managing partner can come to the strategic planning meeting with research, ideas, and even a draft of a plan, it is up to the partner group to determine the firm's direction. A managing partner who is setting direction is an example of someone wielding too much power in that position. If the managing partner is also the majority shareholder or owner in the firm, then as managing partner, although he or she alone shouldn't be permitted to determine the firm's strategy, he or she can do it. So, situations like these complicate best practice discussions because in these cases, one person is filling two roles (what should be accomplished through the attainment of a majority vote of the partners versus reasonable managing partner powers and duties). Unfortunately, the result is often excessive power being extended to the managing partner role, which we have seen continue long after the managing partner has lost voting control.

Objectives: The next step is to break down the firm's strategies into specific objectives for departments, committees or task forces, partners, and so on. This is the managing partner's job: to operationalize the firm's strategy. It is important, based on this last broad statement, to digress a bit here.

The managing partner does not dictate where to go, but he or she needs to identify the logical steps to get there as well as how to utilize the various resources of the firm to make it happen. The controls the partner group has over the managing partner are the firm's budget, processes, policies, and strategy. The partner group decides where to go, the powers and constraints for the managing partner to operate within, and the goals the managing partner will be held accountable to achieve. Then, the managing partner determines how to get there, operating within the boundaries established by the partner group. As you can see, there should be a nice separation of duties there, with some checks and balances. If the managing partner is deemed to be exercising greater autonomy than expected, then the partner group should create policy or process changes to generate additional boundaries (rather than stepping in and making decisions, the partner group should put a framework in place for the managing partner to operate within). To be clear, anytime the partner group steps in to manage the day-to-day operations, they are, in effect, taking over the managing partner function, which no longer allows them to hold the managing partner accountable. The hierarchy is simple. The managing partner is accountable to the entire partner group (or board). Each individual partner is accountable to the managing partner.

Let's continue our dive into the managing partner's act of operationalizing the strategy within the policies, process, and budget set forth by the partner group. To keep this simple, and because it can get very complex extremely fast, let's say that the firm has three strategies the partner group has mandated:

1. For every partner to spend quality time with his or her top clients on a routine basis.
2. To close the competency gaps between partners and managers by better developing the firm's managers.
3. To generate greater leverage for each partner so that they can manage more work and increase the bottom line.

These are examples of very common goals set by firms today.

So, where does the managing partner go from here?

Guidance Phase: Continuing to keep our example simple, the managing partner would create goals for each partner in each of these three areas. Because all partners are different, not only in their aptitudes and attitudes but also due to their specific job duties, current book of clients they manage, current skills of the people they work with, and so on, the actual goals for each partner will differ. While the goals of the firm are the same for everyone, how they are operationalized can differ dramatically from partner to partner.

We suggest that a managing partner's first step should be to create a document that paints the strategies for change with a broad brush. We then suggest some customized ideas that the managing partner believes can help each partner play his or her part in achieving the firm's strategic plan. We call this first round *guidance*. We want the managing partner to point each partner in the best direction for them to focus. For example, regarding the goal of improving partner leverage, the managing partner might provide guidance to a partner who has poor delegation skills, such as, "I would like for you, over the next seven months, to push down the responsibility of managing $200,000 of your current workload to our managers, John and Becky. Please put together a plan for how this can be accomplished, clients you plan on transitioning, timeframes for the transition, and how you suggest that I monitor this to make sure it happens."

This instruction might be followed with, "As this change is being made, estimate how much of your time will be freed up as well as how you would like to use that excess time to either fulfill this goal or help you better accomplish one of your other two goals." During the guidance phase, we are guiding the partner to where the managing partner would like to see change but still giving the partner the ability to develop a plan that is comfortable to him or her. This allows the partner to build expectations around efforts already being made but possibly being overlooked.

Consider this same goal now for a different partner who is already highly leveraged but with a number of marginal clients. The managing partner's guidance might be totally different, such as "Identify $120,000 of the least profitable and least desirable work you manage and put together a plan for what you can do to change the overall profitability of this work. This could include raising fees, turning over client management of some clients to others, firing clients, developing missing skills needed to do the work economically, and so on." This instruction might be followed by, "Please put together your plan to approach this, covering when I can expect the process to be complete and how you suggest I monitor this to make sure it is done." So, clearly, we have the same firm strategy, but when applied to each individual, the direction is customized to the particular strengths or weaknesses of each partner.

Suggestion Phase: Following the guidance phase is the partner's suggested approach, or the suggestion phase. During this phase, the partner responds to the broad direction of the managing partner and puts together his or her recommended detailed approach for accomplishing that directive while simultaneously suggesting metrics to be held accountable to, as well as identifying monitoring steps to ensure that the managing partner is kept abreast of the partner's actual performance.

Discussion Phase: The next round is the discussion phase. During this stage, the partner will sit with the managing partner and defend why his or her suggestions from the suggestion phase are reasonable, comprehensive, fair, and in line with firm strategy. Often during this phase, because of the open dialogue, the managing partner gains new insight into the problems or issues as well as a better understanding of the effort being requested.

Directive Phase: The final phase is the directive phase. This is when the managing partner, at his or her sole discretion, locks in a partner's goals, their relative priority to each other (among the several goals identified for each partner), and the allocation of performance incentives towards each of those goals.

Remember, the first cut at the partner goals is based on the firm's strategic plan. When we set goals for the managing partner to implement the strategic plan and hold him or her accountable for achieving those identified objectives, know that those same expectations will then be broken down and cascaded to the partners, and ultimately, to staff.

An Example of the Process

Following is an example of this process with more detail to show how it might look in actual practice. Let's assume that one of the goals of a partner is to increase the most trusted business adviser activity for his or her top clients. The initial goal sheet for this one particular goal from the managing partner might look like this:

Guidance

Most Trusted Business Adviser	Value of Incentive: 30%

Partner Expectations

a) Continuously updating his or her understanding of key client's current and future priorities and the personal and business needs of its management

b) Develops relationships with "A" and high "B" key clients and referral sources of the firm that go beyond the services rendered

c) Maintains regular contact with key clients

d) Finds opportunity to assist the client outside of the partner's specific competency areas

Actions Identified to Obtain or Improve Attributes or Achieve Expectations

1. Schedule quarterly meeting with "A" clients and semiannual meetings with high "B" clients. Prepare a list or schedule to review during your meetings with the managing partner.

2. During those meetings, update your understanding of these clients and look for ways to develop relationships with clients that go beyond the service we render.

3. Look for cross-selling opportunities, introduction to other firm personnel, and opportunities to refer other professionals from your network. During your meetings with the managing partner, review the context of some of those meetings.

Most Trusted Business Adviser	Value of Incentive: 30%

4. Some of the information that would indicate that your understanding of the A and B clients is expanding beyond merely attest and tax would be by having an understanding and knowledge of the following:

   a) Revenue goals of clients for 20XX

   b) Strategic initiatives for each client for the next years

   c) Tactical priorities for each client for the next 18 months

   d) Opportunities clients are hoping to be able to leverage

   e) Product or service offering changes

Note to partner from managing partner: *The preceding items are for your consideration. Please review the expectation, and then look through the actions identified. The preceding actions are ideas. Please consider how you think you should best approach the objective of improving as your clients' most trusted business adviser and list an approach with which you are comfortable to achieve this objective.*

The first round was initiated by the managing partner with the information delivered previously. In some cases, the managing partner might simply suggest that the partner create an action plan and metrics based on 360° assessments for this competency area, such as those provided by the Succession Institute Performance Assessment™ (SIPA™). Also note here that we are only focusing on one goal to keep this simple. In a normal situation, several goals would be identified during this process, and they would total up to 100 percent of the managing partner incentive offering. In this case, the managing partner has suggested that this one goal should represent 30 percent of this partner's incentive.

Next, it is time for the partner to respond, which triggers the suggestion round.

Suggestion

Most Trusted Business Adviser	Value of Incentive: 35%

Partner Attributes or Expectations

   a) Continuously updating his or her understanding of key clients' current and future priorities and the personal and business needs of their management

   b) Develops relationships with "A" and high "B" key clients and referral sources of the firm that go beyond the services rendered

   c) Maintains regular contact with key clients

   d) Finds opportunity to assist the client outside of the partner's specific competency areas

Actions Identified to Obtain or Improve Attributes or Achieve Expectations

1. I will deliver a list of my "A" and high "B" clients and referral sources to you (the managing partner). That list will identify the people in those companies that I plan on contacting.

(continued)

Most Trusted Business Adviser	Value of Incentive: 35%
2. I will create a calendar identifying the month I plan on visiting each of my "A" clients. I intend to see each of them during tax season, and I will schedule three other visits during the year on the calendar.	
3. I will create a calendar identifying the month I plan on visiting each of my high "B" clients. I intend to see each of them during tax season, and I will schedule one other visit during the year on the calendar.	
4. I will sit with you and do a high-level review of the visits I made as well as review my plan for the near-term visits.	
5. After I have met with one of my identified "A" or high "B" clients, I will update our salesforce.com customer relationship management system with the information I gathered during my meeting with my clients.	
6. I will keep a running ledger of new work scheduled by each of the clients I visit.	
Note to managing partner: *I am suggesting increasing this goal from 30 percent to 35 percent because of the time this process will take and the benefit I think it will provide to the firm.*	

After the managing partner receives the updated goals from the partner, the managing partner should review them and verify whether they are reasonable and in line with the work effort expected from the other partners (this does not mean that each goal should have a comparable work effort from partner to partner but, rather, that the overall goals for each partner would require a similar work effort to complete them).

The discussion phase could happen through an iteration of notes on the goal sheets, but normally, the best approach is for the partner and the managing partner to sit down, go over them, and have a discussion about them.

There is an important overarching theme that occurs in all of the many discussions we have facilitated between partners and the managing partner. That theme is for the managing partner to ask, regarding every action item outlined for a goal, "What can we do to make sure I catch you doing this?"

In other words, the intent of the goal process is for the partner to know clearly what is expected, and then to do it, and even exceed performance expectations. The best way to accomplish this is to build in specific monitoring activities, date expectations, meetings, performance metrics, or any other techniques that ensure the partner can regularly and efficiently communicate his or her progress and accomplishment.

Let's take what came out of the suggestion phase and look at some notes the managing partner would likely write and use for his or her discussion of those ideas with the partner).

For the sake of simplicity, let's just focus on the actions section for now:

Discussion

Most Trusted Business Adviser	Value of Incentive: 35%

Actions Identified to Obtain or Improve Attributes or Achieve Expectations

1. I will deliver a list of my "A" and high "B" clients and referral sources to you (the managing partner). That list will identify the people in those companies that I plan on contacting.

   Note from the managing partner: *By when will you complete this?*

2. I will create a calendar identifying the month I plan on visiting each of my "A" clients. I intend to see each of them during tax season, and I will schedule three other visits during the year on the calendar.

   Note from the managing partner: *By when will you complete this? Additionally, I would like to know the nature and circumstances of the meeting, such as whether it was a lunch meeting, a visit at the client's workplace, and so on.*

3. I will create a calendar identifying the month I plan on visiting each of my high "B" clients. I intend to see each of them during tax season, and I will schedule one other visit during the year on the calendar.

   Note from the managing partner: *By when will you complete this? Additionally, I would like to know the nature and circumstances of the meeting, such as whether it was a lunch meeting, a visit at the client's workplace, and so on.*

4. I will sit with you and do a high-level review of the visits I made as well as review my plan for the near-term visits.

   Note from the managing partner: *How often will we sit down and meet? Who is responsible for setting these meetings? What does the phrase "near-term visits" mean?*

5. After I have met with one of my identified "A" or high "B" clients, I will update our salesforce.com customer relationship management system with the information I gathered during my meeting with my clients.

   Note from the managing partner: *When will you update our customer relationship management system (the day after the meetings or at another time)? What level of information will you commit to updating in the system?*

6. I will also keep a running ledger of new work scheduled by each of the clients I visit.

   Note from the managing partner: *I think this is a great idea. When will we review this ledger (will you just forward it to me monthly, or will we sit down and discuss it at some interval)? In addition, new work scheduled is only one of the benefits these visits are likely to accrue to our firm. I want to make sure you get full credit for the effort you are putting in. How about keeping track of substantial price increases or change orders for the annuity work we perform, new work scheduled, or new clients referred to you by these clients?*

   Note to managing partner: *I am suggesting increasing this goal from 30 percent to 35 percent because of the time this process will take and the benefit I think it will provide to the firm.*

   Note from the managing partner: *Based on what you have described previously, I don't have a problem agreeing to this effort being raised to 35 percent.*

The partner revises his or her discussion actions in response to the managing partner's feedback.

Discussion Response

Most Trusted Business Adviser	Value of Incentive: 35%

Actions Identified to Obtain or Improve Attributes or Achieve Expectations

1. Before January 31st, I will deliver a list of my "A" and high "B" clients and referral sources to you (the managing partner). That list will identify the people in those companies that I plan on contacting.

2. Before January 31st, I will create a calendar identifying the month I plan on visiting each of my "A" clients. I intend to see each of them during tax season, and I will schedule three other visits during the year on the calendar (which I will identify as a breakfast meeting, lunch meeting, dinner meeting, entertainment outing, or on-site company visit).

3. Before January 31st, I will create a calendar identifying the month I plan on visiting each of my high "B" clients. I intend to see each of them during tax season, and I will schedule one other visit during the year on the calendar (which I will identify as a breakfast meeting, lunch meeting, dinner meeting, entertainment outing, or on-site company visit).

4. Quarterly, at a meeting you schedule, I will sit with you and do a high-level review of the visits I made during that quarter as well as review my plan for the upcoming quarter.

5. My objective is that by the end of each week during a week when I have a meeting with one of my identified "A" or high "B" clients (but I want to be held accountable for a two-week compliance period), I will update our salesforce.com customer relationship management system with the information I gathered during my meeting with my clients. I will include in that update that client's expected revenues for the coming year, what we are currently doing for them, scheduled work we have in the backlog, services I think they need over the next 18 months, and the client's current priorities during that same 18 month timeframe. Four times a year, at your discretion, you should check the customer relationship management system after an appointment you know I have made to verify whether I am updating the system on a timely basis.

6. I will also keep a running ledger of new business referred by each of these clients, new work scheduled for each of these clients, price increases of more than 4 percent or $1,000 (whichever is more) for existing recurring work for each of these clients, and change orders for existing work for each of these clients and report that to you during our quarterly meetings scheduled per preceding item 4.

In this case, because the partner addressed each of the issues very well, the managing partner simply would send back the goal sheet as approved. The directive phase of this simply involves communicating back to the partner what is expected. Had the partner left something out or not specified a way for the managing partner to catch the partner achieving each action of his or her goals, that information would have been included in the final version sent to the partner.

The important point to make here is that the managing partner should be setting goals that are based on the normal expectations of a partner. The goals, as mentioned earlier in this document, shouldn't be established assuming exceptional performance. When exceptional performance is achieved, some reward calculated at something greater than 100 percent for that goal incentive should be given.

Conclusion of the Goal Process—Monitoring

Evaluation of performance and goal achievement is something done that should be performed multiple times during the year. Unfortunately, many CPAs tend to think of management as a waste of time and evaluations as purely an HR requirement created by the government to protect employees to the disadvantage of the organization. Well, that is one way to look at it, but we think it's the wrong way. We think that the higher you rise in your firm's organizational chart, the more time you need to dedicate to the development of others with thoughtful and constructive feedback. So, this is not something you should be doing for five minutes every few months, but a normal, recurring part of every work week. That is, you should be thinking about and monitoring those who report to you as well as monitoring your own progress and checking in with your boss routinely.

Although it is normal protocol to monitor those who report to you, why would we suggest that you monitor yourself as well? Because it is your job, as management, to provide appropriate feedback and coaching to your people, and it is your job as a direct report to keep your boss informed about progress, resource requirements, and problems as you tackle your own work assignments.

If we approach this phase from an HR perspective, many partners will default to giving one appraisal per year (or one formal feedback session), and that simply is not enough. It could be enough to have one formal appraisal or feedback session as long as there are several informal feedback sessions (clearly set up for that purpose) in the interim. For higher level personnel, the importance of making sure they are focusing on the priorities of the organization and working toward the organization's goals is critical. The absurd thing is that in most companies, the lower the hierarchical level of the employee, the more often feedback is given, but at the higher levels in the organization, the more we find people talking about expectations but never actually holding anyone accountable to their commitments or actions.

The theory behind this is simple. When you are a lower level employee, you don't know anything, so we need to regularly tell you how you are falling short of expectations so you will try harder. Higher level people have already proved themselves; we just need to get out of their way. In our opinion, this is misguided thinking (and common thinking from an EWYK mindset). For example, partners should be the best at knowing what is expected of them, making commitments to the firm, and being expected to perform based on those expectations and commitments. Partners should be the role models to every other employee, but we all know that is not the case. Partners regularly violate various operational policies by claiming some "client service" exceptions. They teach other employees that the following message is acceptable: Policies and procedures are for everyone else to follow. I will follow them as long as it suits me, but as soon as I don't like a policy, I will simply ignore it and do things my way. This is appropriate because when you get to be a partner with my level of accomplishment, my judgment about what is appropriate supersedes what we have agreed to follow as a firm. Although we all know that at times I violate policy because it is just inconvenient for me to follow it, and although my violation of policy can make it extra difficult for staff to support me, because of my position, I have earned that right to place the firm and its employees secondary to my personal preferences.

Wow… when you read that, it sounds pretty ugly, doesn't it? Well, if your firm is like most, when you watch the behavior of a number of your partners, doesn't this statement actually match up pretty well? It is why accountability continues year after year to be a top issue that firms need to address.

If we can get our top performers and key people acting as a group, supporting the firm, then getting everyone else at each layer down in the organizational chart to respond accordingly gets much easier. However, most firms focus on making the lowest levels accountable first when the fact is that the higher level people in the firm keep complicating the system. Every leadership and management book will have some statement saying that the top people in any organization need to "walk the walk" before they talk they talk. That is all accountability is—walking the talk, setting the example that you want others to follow.

Therefore, it should not be surprising that we believe that the managing partner should be conducting frequent, informal feedback sessions on how he or she feels each partner is performing. This might be every month, every other month, five or six scheduled times a year dropping out the busiest of deadline months, or whatever schedule works for your firm (once a quarter should be the minimum, adjusting the timing for busy seasons). But to be clear, this isn't about an HR function. It's about aligning the most powerful and talented assets you have in your business.

Tips for Providing Performance Feedback

Once you decide on the schedule of these meetings, publish the schedule early so people can make appointments around them. Consider the following tips, based on what we've seen in practice:

- Focus on the goals everyone agreed to that were established at the beginning of the year.
- Make sure the managing partner is prepared for the meeting. If the managing partner just wants to use this forum to remind everyone that they work for him or her, then fire this managing partner.
- The managing partner needs to have reviewed evidence and talked with people, if appropriate, reviewed logs or other monitoring devices, and made an effort to observe the areas of focus in the goals. This takes time. This is not something the managing partner should be doing the morning of the feedback session. If the managing partner does not want to make the continual effort to understand how his or her partners are performing as part of this feedback process, then find a managing partner who does.
- We feel it is best if the managing partner starts the process off by asking the partner being evaluated how he or she thinks they have performed against the listed goals.
- We believe it is important for the managing partner to also understand what other forces or factors have been unusually occupying the partner's time outside of those goals.
- Based on the advance preparation done by the managing partner, the assessment of the partner being evaluated, and any additional, unusual factors that have surfaced through this conversation, the managing partner should provide feedback on his or her assessment of goal attainment at that time.

A lot of people get off track at this point. There are several key issues to keep in mind once the managing partner starts to share his or her feedback. Some important points that immediately come to mind are as follows:

- Tell the truth. If you don't know something, say it. If something is simply hearsay, introduce it as such and ask for commentary. Realize that as managing partner, your opinion is not fact; it's just your opinion. Identify assumptions within your feedback as assumptions.

- You don't have to find something to criticize. It is common management protocol to think that all employees need to improve, so management should always give someone something to work on to be better. Don't confuse performance management commentary with the conversation you might have with someone about where you see them in a few years. The latter is about personal aspiration, and although the conversation is important, it has nothing to do with performance. Performance is only about what we expect from an employee now and how we believe an employee is performing against those expectations now!

- If someone has not performed up to expectation, simply, clearly, and concisely state your opinion regarding their performance, and if appropriate, what you are basing that conclusion on. Once you are done sharing that fact, stop talking. The most common mistake managing partners make is to keep talking and trying to justify himself or herself. Additional information either weakens the conclusion or causes interjections of new hearsay and assumptions, which put into question the validity of the initial position.

- Don't make a big deal about someone falling short on a specific goal. The reason you have feedback sessions is to help people see where they are falling short so they have time to correct it. This is not a final assessment; it is an interim feedback session. Use it as such.

- A very common misuse of power in the goal-setting process is that managing partners believe this is their time to try to fix every little idiosyncrasy or irritating habit of each partner. This process is not about perfection because if it was, no one could live up to being the managing partner, or any other partner, for that matter. It is about focusing the attention of the partner group on the strategic issues of the firm and how those strategic issues get layered into the various partner goals. Don't bring up or harp on insignificant issues. It doesn't matter that a partner's little habits bother you unless they are truly affecting that person's ability to perform their job. These issues are low priority and should stay out of the feedback sessions. If you can't help yourself and try to micromanage every little thing, then it is time for a new managing partner to be appointed.

- Rate each goal independently. Consider what you know, consider what you have heard from the partner, consider the evidence in front of you, consider what you have observed, consider the time of year (meaning if we are only halfway through the year, performing half of expectation would be 100 percent, not 50 percent), and make a judgment. In the end, this process is full of judgment no matter how many objective monitoring tools we include.

- Rate using a scale from 0 percent to infinity, not 0 to 100 percent. In reality, you will probably never give someone less than 25 percent (as it is hard to perform at a zero level, but on rare occasions, people can surprise you), and rarely greater than 300 percent to 400 percent. The high numbers are possible in that you might have a goal for a partner to bring in $75,000 of new work, and instead, the partner brings in $300,000. Obviously, just a straight calculation of this would be 400 percent, if that was the method you decided to use.

- Multiply your rating of each goal by its value (the amount of the bonus allocated to that goal). Add all the goal calculations together to estimate what the bonus might be if it had to be determined today.

By going through all of this, you can help your partners know what is expected, but more important, how they are doing. It gives you a chance to clarify the importance of certain high profile behavior, either good or bad. It gives you the opportunity to point out to someone the areas where they are doing very well and gives them some guidance early enough to adjust what they're doing in areas where they are falling short.

Make no mistake about it, this is a lot of work, but the reward will very likely show up quickly in the bottom line because you are getting the most powerful and talented people to focus on what is best for the firm. The managing partner's job in this process is to help the partners, provide them resources when needed, remind them of what is expected, and provide them feedback regarding their performance.

As the managing partner, you are not your partners' babysitter. If a partner is falling short on something, it is his or her responsibility to take care of it, assuming he or she has done that work before and have a successful track record doing it. If he or she needs additional resources to reach the objectives, it needs to be clear that each partner has a responsibility to come to you for help and assistance. That doesn't take away the managing partner's requirement to monitor and provide a higher level of oversight for any activities for which a partner has little experience handling. In some cases, you may need to provide more direction to help a partner get over a hump. In the end, though, firms need good managing partners; they don't need managing parents.

Tools and Resources

The Succession Institute's Steps Normally Required to Establish or Strengthen Partner Accountability Checklist

Action	By Whom	By When
The partner group establishes or updates the firm strategy or vision and strategic initiatives needed to attain the vision (one initiative should be to create or refine a partner compensation framework that will support the vision).		
The managing partner or task force, including the managing partner, prepares a draft of the new partner compensation framework, which will identify the following key factors: • Allocation of compensation to incentive pay (in the beginning, this usually is set at a fairly conservative level, such as 15 percent to 20 percent of total compensation) • General performance goals all partners are expected to achieve • Establishment of managing partner's authority to negotiate incentive goals with each partner, based on the firm's strategy and the partner's needs and strengths • Incentive goals for the managing partner, based on overall firm success and firm strategy • How and when increases or decreases in base pay will be determined and approved		
The partner group reviews, modifies, if necessary, and approves the new compensation framework.		
The firm, under the leadership of the managing partner or his or her designee, conducts 360° assessments of partner competency to establish baseline performance levels and identify competency strengths and weaknesses.		
Managing partner* reviews each partner's individual 360° assessment report and identifies the top two or three areas he or she can focus on this coming year.		
Managing partner* works individually with each partner to establish mutually agreed action plans, goals, metrics, and incentive pay opportunities.**		
Implement compensation plan and monitor results with both the managing partner* and each individual partner receiving feedback about the partner's progress.		
Managing partner* meets periodically throughout the year with each partner to review implementation status of action plans and resulting performance outcomes.		

* In larger firms, group or department leads would be involved in this process, as well.
** This step is iterative in nature and will require two or more sessions between the managing partner or department lead and the line partner.

The Succession Institute's Sample Managing Partner Goal Worksheet

Area Covered by This Plan:	Value of Incentive:	%
Partner Expectations (see 360° assessment report for details to use) *a)* *b)* *c)* *d)*		
Actions Identified to Obtain or Improve Attributes or Achieve Expectations 1. 2. 3. 4.		
Notes to partner from managing partner:		

Additional Learning Resources

As you know from the materials at the end of the first chapter, additional self-study CPE courses are available for your review. Many of them are all-video courses developed from our streaming video webcasts, and others were created from the various books we have written. These courses can be found at www.successioninstitute.com/PMRC.

Remember to take advantage of your discount by entering the word "succession" into the coupon code field.

Here are some courses we recommend that could provide you some additional insight into partner goal setting and accountability.

- Implementing Roles, Responsibilities and a Competency Framework in Your Firm (all-video)
- Implementing the Partner Goal Process: Step-by-Step Instructions (all-video)
- How to Build a Partner Compensation System that Supports Accountability (all-video)
- Dynamic Leadership™ Part 1 (all-video)
- Dynamic Leadership™ Part 2 (all-video)
- Dynamic Leadership™ Part 3 (all-video)

Building Your Firm's Robust Succession Plan

We are now back to the succession planning development phase. As we have covered before, once you complete this last section of each chapter, by the time you finish the book, you will have written down foundational ideas to review with your partners. Once you pull together these final sections, you will have identified your recommendations about how to handle each succession planning area (or, at a minimum, questions the partner group needs to answer), and you will have a document that can be presented for discussion, modification, and eventual approval that will guide the changes in policy, agreements, governance, and culture your firm will undertake to implement this succession plan over the next few years.

Now that you have thought more about partner accountability and goal setting, respond to the following questions to articulate your thinking about this topic:

Is partner accountability an issue in this firm? If so, describe how.

_____

_____

_____

_____

Does your firm hold partners accountable to achieving the firm's strategic plan? If so, describe how.

_____

_____

_____

_____

Does your firm articulate individualized goals for each partner to achieve based on the current strategic plan? If so, describe the process.

_____

_____

_____

_____

_____

_____

_____

Does your firm's current managing partner position have the authority and responsibility to hold partners accountable to specific goals? If so, itemize the specific duties, authority, and responsibilities that support this.

_____

_____

_____

_____

_____

_____

_____

_____

_____

Does your firm want to create goals tailored to all partners to maximize their strengths; improve their critical weaknesses; hold them accountable for fulfilling the role they serve as partners; and reward or sanction them based on their performance against those goals, expectations, and role?

_____

_____

_____

_____

Based on what you have read in chapter 15 of volumes 1 and 2, describe the partner accountability system you want to recommend to the partner group. Include specific detailed changes you want the new accountability system to address or improve that you believe are being poorly handled in the current system.

_____

_____

_____

_____

_____

_____

_____

_____

_____

Chapter 16: Addressing Death and Disability in Your Buy-Sell and Retirement Policies

Key Themes from *Securing the Future, Volume 1: Building Your Firm's Succession Plan*, Chapter 16

- Policies dealing with the death of a partner
- Policies dealing with disability
- Policies dealing with partial disability

At the end of the day, the purpose of a good succession plan and buy-sell agreement is to protect the partners and the firm. It needs to be fair for both sides of any transaction, but when everyone is grieving the loss of a friend and partner, it's often difficult to maintain that level of objectivity. That's why we suggest addressing these difficult issues far in advance of a potential death or disability.

Included in the "Tools and Resources" section are some sample terms you might want to have your attorney consider when drafting your agreements for your firm.

Tools and Resources

The following sample policies are being presented to give you a starting point for thinking about how you want to approach partner death, partial disability, and full disability within your firm. The percentages that firms use to discount the retirement benefit are all over the board. Almost all firms start off the discussion regarding these policies with the idea of not discounting at all, but we feel it is our job to remind the partner group that during these times of chaos and crisis, the firm does not do well. The partners are negatively affected by the plight of their unfortunate partners, and productivity and profits wane. In the end, it is our position that we need to set up these policies with the idea that the firm needs to survive to not only compensate the disabled partners or deceased partner's estate, but be in a position to sustain the organization for the remaining partners and employees. Although it is important to be generous and supportive, it is also important to be prudent in determining what these benefits should be. With that said, it is up to each firm, directed by its core values, to determine how these events should be dealt with and at what valuation.

The following are a number of variations. As you will see from the death policy, there is no distinction regarding tenure or vesting when applying the discount. Some firms choose this alternative for all of these policies. Alternately, some firms choose to show different discount amounts depending on tenure or vesting (as shown in the disability policies), and sometimes they simply name exceptions that will receive a different amount (usually a higher percentage amount) due to their specific circumstances (often founding owners or people close to retirement when these policies are created). As for discounts, they typically range from 50 percent to 15 percent and everywhere in between.

Finally, you will notice some additional language in the partial disability policy, some of which is added to the full disability policy. It is the language that allows the firm to declare partners partially or fully disabled. Many firms have experienced partners who were either partially or fully disabled and would not declare or file for their disability benefits. They would simply expect the firm to continue to pay them as a working partner on an extended vacation. For this reason, firms have added language to address this. As well, as we discussed in chapter 16, volume 1, because it is very difficult for a firm to handle a partner coming in and out of disability over a long period of time (meaning client assignment, short-term project management, long-term succession and capacity management, and so on), which is unfortunately more common than you would expect due to diseases like cancer, the firm needs to formalize a clear way for it to move on. The partial disability policy does this by allowing the firm to declare that the partially disabled partner will become fully disabled when he or she is out for any 12 of 24 months and retire that partner. This allows the firm to start paying that partner retirement benefits, but more important, to start making long-term plans regarding partner replacement, client management, necessary skill development, and so much more. With this in mind, here is some sample language our firms have used to start their thinking on these topics. As always, when it comes to policies, please consult your legal counsel about what is appropriate for your firm.

The Succession Institute's Sample Terms for a Policy Addressing Partner Death or Disability

Shareholder Leaving Due to Death

Upon the death of the partner, the deceased partner will be deemed fully vested and entitled to the retirement benefit as if the partner was retiring on the mandatory date of sale of his or her ownership, with the following caveat. The deceased partner's retirement benefit will then be discounted by a factor of 35 percent. The 35-percent discount to firm value is automatically assessed to compensate the firm for likely lost clients and additional resources and costs required to manage and maintain the work, client relationships, and referral source relationships of the deceased partner.

The previously calculated amount will be paid over a 10-year period without interest.

If the firm is the beneficiary of life insurance coverage, the proceeds will be used to pay off the present value of any amount owed to the shareholder for his or her interest in the firm, with excess insurance proceeds retained by the firm.

Shareholder Leaving Due to Total Disability

Upon total disability of a shareholder, the firm will be obligated to purchase, and the shareholder will be obligated to sell, the equity interest of the shareholder as provided in this policy. Upon total disability of a shareholder, prior to attaining the minimum partial vesting level of the vesting requirements, the value of the equity interest of the totally disabled shareholder will be determined as if the shareholder was fully vested and retiring at the mandatory date of sale of ownership, with that fully vested amount being discounted by 40 percent and paid out over 10 years at no interest. The 40-percent discount to firm value is automatically assessed to compensate the firm for likely lost clients and additional resources and costs required to manage and maintain the work, client relationships, and referral source relationships of the totally disabled shareholder.

Upon total disability of a shareholder who meets the minimum partial vesting level of the vesting requirements, the value of the equity interest of the totally disabled shareholder will be determined as if the shareholder was fully vested and retiring at the mandatory date of sale of ownership, with that fully vested amount being discounted by 20 percent and paid out over 10 years at no interest. The 20-percent discount to firm value is automatically assessed to compensate the firm for likely lost clients and additional resources and costs required to manage and maintain the work, client relationships, and referral source relationships of the totally disabled shareholder.

For purposes of the preceding payment schedule, the payments will be reduced by the amount of disability insurance proceeds received directly by the disabled shareholder from any policies for which the firm pays policy premiums.

Definition of *Total Disability*

The firm's definition of *total disability* will be the then current definition of the insurance carrier of the firm's disability policy. If no policy is in place, then the definition in the AICPA's Disability Insurance Program will be used, with the caveat that the definition is based on the shareholder's ability to perform his or her current responsibilities and duties.

Shareholder Partially Disabled

If a shareholder becomes partially disabled, either physically or mentally, and cannot work for a period of time, during that period, the shareholder is not entitled to any bonuses.

However, the firm will pay the shareholder in accordance with the following schedule during this period:

1. First three (3) months of disability—full base salary
2. Second three (3) months of disability—seventy-five percent (75%) of full base salary
3. Thereafter—no payments

The full-time return to practice in the firm at any time during the 12 months after the disability occurs will restore the disabled shareholder to full compensation and benefits, commencing with the first month following this resumption of active shareholder responsibilities.

If the shareholder has been disabled for the 12 consecutive months after the date of disability, then (i) the shareholder will be required to voluntarily withdraw from the firm, and (ii) the firm will be obligated to purchase, and the shareholder will be obligated to sell, the equity interest of the shareholder as follows:

- If the shareholder has been partially disabled for the 12 consecutive months after the date of disability and prior to his or her attaining the minimum partial vesting level of the vesting requirements, the value of the equity interest of the partially disabled shareholder will be determined as if the shareholder was fully vested and retiring at the mandatory date of sale of ownership, with that fully vested amount being discounted by 30 percent and paid out over 10 years at no interest. The 30-percent discount to the firm value is automatically assessed to compensate the firm for likely lost clients and additional resources and costs required to manage and maintain the work, client relationships, and referral source relationships of the totally disabled shareholder.

- Upon the partial disability of a shareholder who meets the minimum partial vesting level of minimum vesting requirements, the value of the equity interest of the partially disabled shareholder will be determined as if the shareholder was fully vested and retiring at the mandatory date of sale of ownership, with that fully vested amount being discounted by 15 percent and paid out over 10 years at no interest. The 15-percent discount to firm value is automatically assessed to compensate the firm for likely lost clients and additional resources and costs required to manage and maintain the work, client relationships, and referral source relationships of the partially disabled shareholder.

If a shareholder (i) becomes partially disabled but returns to work for a minimum of 30 consecutive full business days performing his or her full responsibilities and duties with the firm during the initial 12-month period and (ii) is not able to perform his or her normal work responsibilities and duties during any rolling 12 out of a 24-month work period from the date of disability forward, then the voluntary withdrawal or termination requirement will be triggered based on the shareholder being partially disabled.

Any shareholder who suffers a disability is required to file for disability under the firm's disability insurance immediately, if so covered. If a shareholder with disability insurance refuses to file for disability within 30 days of the date the shareholder became disabled, for the purposes of this policy, the firm can declare at any time after that period that the shareholder is partially disabled as of a specific date with a 66 2/3 percent vote of the equity interest. For the sake of this policy, the voting interest of the person being considered for partial disability is removed from the calculation.

At this point, the declared partially disabled shareholder can go before a medical doctor of the firm's choice for a professional opinion. The doctor will be asked to give his or her professional opinion based on the firm's definition of *partial disability*. The doctor's opinion will either ratify the firm's declaration of partial disability for the purposes of this policy or rescind that declaration.

<u>Definition of *Partial Disability*</u>

The firm's definition of *partial disability* will be the then current definition of the insurance carrier of the firm's disability policy. If no policy is in place, then the AICPA's Disability Insurance Program will be used, with the caveat that the definition is based on the shareholder's ability to perform his or her current responsibilities and duties.

Additional Learning Resources

As you know from the materials at the end of the first chapter, additional self-study CPE courses are available for your review. Many of them are all-video courses developed from our streaming video webcasts, and others were created from the various books we have written. These courses can be found at www.successioninstitute.com/PMRC.

Remember to take advantage of your discount by entering the word "succession" into the coupon code field.

Here are some courses we recommend that could provide you some additional insight into your death, partial disability, and full disability policies:

- Building Your Firm's Succession Plan—Part 2 (all-video)
- Pulling It All Together with a Partner/Shareholder Agreement (all-video)

Building Your Firm's Robust Succession Plan

We are now back to the succession planning development phase. As we have covered before, once you complete this last section of each chapter, by the time you finish the book, you will have written down foundational ideas to review with your partners. Once you pull together these final sections, you will have identified your recommendations about how to handle each succession planning area (or, at a minimum, questions the partner group needs to answer), and you will have a document that can be presented for discussion, modification, and eventual approval that will guide the changes in policy, agreements, governance, and culture your firm will undertake to implement this succession plan over the next few years.

Now that you have thought more about how you might want to handle partner death, partial disability, and full disability, respond to the following questions to articulate your thinking about this topic.

Describe what you want to recommend regarding your firm's policy pertaining to benefits and ownership repurchase for the death of a partner. Include how you would determine those benefits, what will affect the value, the terms and conditions for payment, and if any discounts will apply.

_____

_____

_____

_____

_____

_____

Describe what you want to recommend as your firm's policy pertaining to benefits, retirement benefits, and ownership repurchase, if applicable, when a partner becomes partially disabled. Include how you would determine those benefits, what will affect the value, the terms and conditions for payment, and if any discounts will apply. As well, for partial disability, what level of absenteeism will trigger full disability or ownership repurchase?

_____

_____

_____

_____

_____

_____

_____

_____

_____

Describe what you want to recommend as your firm's policy pertaining to benefits, retirement benefits, and ownership repurchase when a partner becomes fully disabled. Include when ownership repurchase will be triggered, how you would determine the applicable benefits, what will affect the value, the terms and conditions for payment, and if any discounts will apply.

_____

_____

_____

_____

_____

_____

_____

_____

_____

Chapter 17: Conclusion

After having read through this book and its companion text, *Securing the Future, Volume 1: Building Your Firm's Succession Plan*, thinking through the questions, and filling out the forms at the end of each chapter, you are well on your way to creating a robust succession plan for your firm. The purpose of these two books was to guide you through the issues that we have found critical to long-term sustainability of CPA firms, as well as to introduce you to best practices in each of the areas we covered. It is now time to take the materials you've created from this process and run those ideas by your partner group to generate buy-in and, where necessary, build the support to revise your partner agreements so these changes can actually take place.

As noted at the end of each chapter in this book, there are specific video courses identified which you can view, or have your partners review, if you feel you need greater detail regarding an area that is likely to be controversial. Be sure that key partners in the process also review this volume's companion text, *Securing the Future, Volume 1: Building Your Firm's Succession Plan*. It was developed to provide a perspective on why changes should be considered, while this book was created to help you think through the specific changes that the succession implementation team should be recommending. With this said, we'd like to leave you with a few concluding thoughts that might make your journey more pleasant along the way and perhaps even shorten the route for you.

It's About Choices

Ultimately, life is about choices. One choice today will create a chain of events that will create or eliminate certain future choices. If your owner group chooses to operate with the day-to-day individual autonomy characteristic of a firm that is predominantly "Eat What You Kill" in nature, then your choices for succession planning, retirement, and buyout terms should reflect that business model. There's nothing wrong with the "Eat What You Kill" business model—make the most of it if that's your choice. Just don't expect your owner group to commit to a buyout or retirement benefit that applies to a firm operating under a strong "Building a Village" business model if you want to continue with the "Eat What You Kill" autonomy. You can't have it both ways. Make your decisions and move on, implementing retirement plans that make sense for your business model.

It's About Success, Not Perfection

Our profession has attracted a somewhat higher percentage of people with strong concerns for doing things right, following the rules, and so on than exists in the natural population. Those traits make for excellent professionals within the context of the technical demands facing the profession and its clients; however, technically focused CPAs often get caught up in trying to do everything just right. These motivational needs can easily get in the way of major change management initiatives, resulting in the desire to do more analysis, obtain more information, and spend more time planning, which are displayed as a general disposition toward procrastination rather than taking action.

In the world of managerial leadership, no one should be looking for accuracy with multiple decimal places of precision. In fact, there often are multiple ways of doing something that will get you where you need to be within the broad constraints of best practices and your particular facts and circumstances. There is no room for perfectionism as you begin to implement your succession plan. Do something. Take action. Constantly evaluate your progress, and then modify your next action based on the results you've found. You may need to change direction a bit from time to time, but that's the way life works, and it certainly is the way change management and business evolution works. As is often said in the publishing world, "Don't get it right, get it written." That same intent works just as well here. When it comes to making your firm better, faster, and stronger, it's about success, not perfection. This motto embodies a simple process of taking action, evaluating, and responding.

Things Change

Over time, your business model may move in one direction or another—either toward or away from the "Building a Village" business model. Other significant changes may occur within your practice that affect the retirement provision as well. As is the case with your clients for whom you provide succession and business continuation assistance, your firm's buyout, deferred compensation, and retirement provisions will need to be reviewed and possibly updated from time to time. In our opinion, an overriding concern should be whether what you have is fair—fair to the firm and fair to retiring partners. As the market place changes and as your operations change, you should always be re-evaluating your provisions for fairness. There is no answer you can come up with today that will always stand the test of time. The changes you are making now are no more a negative reflection on where you have been than the changes you will make in years to come. At the foundation of this discussion is a simple concept: Your success has created your current need for change, and your continued success will require more need for change in the future. As we have mentioned throughout both volumes, "what got you 'here' won't get you 'there'."

Enjoy the Journey

Change can be disconcerting at times, but it doesn't have to be. Keep the collective vision you and your partners have for the future of your firm in front of you. Continually remind yourselves of how good it will be as you make the changes necessary to move toward that vision. Monitor the outcomes of your actions as well as your actions taken, and make sure that you all recognize the positive movement that occurs, no matter how large or how small the movement is at any particular time. Your destiny—your firm's destiny—await you! Thank you for allowing us to play some small part in your wonderfully successful journey!